A Cultural Citizen of the World
Sigmund Freud's Knowledge and Use of British and American Writings

LEGENDA

LEGENDA, founded in 1995 by the European Humanities Research Centre of the University of Oxford, is now a joint imprint of the Modern Humanities Research Association and Maney Publishing. Titles range from medieval texts to contemporary cinema and form a widely comparative view of the modern humanities, including works on Arabic, Catalan, English, French, German, Greek, Italian, Portuguese, Russian, Spanish, and Yiddish literature. An Editorial Board of distinguished academic specialists works in collaboration with leading scholarly bodies such as the Society for French Studies and the British Comparative Literature Association.

MHRA

The Modern Humanities Research Association (MHRA) encourages and promotes advanced study and research in the field of the modern humanities, especially modern European languages and literature, including English, and also cinema. It also aims to break down the barriers between scholars working in different disciplines and to maintain the unity of humanistic scholarship in the face of increasing specialization. The Association fulfils this purpose primarily through the publication of journals, bibliographies, monographs and other aids to research.

Maney Publishing

Maney Publishing is one of the few remaining independent British academic publishers. Founded in 1900 the company has offices both in the UK, in Leeds and London, and in North America, in Boston. Since 1945 Maney Publishing has worked closely with learned societies, their editors, authors, and members, in publishing academic books and journals to the highest traditional standards of materials and production.

S S Prawer
2008

A Cultural Citizen of the World

Sigmund Freud's Knowledge and Use of British and American Writings

❖

S. S. Prawer

LEGENDA

Modern Humanities Research Association and Maney Publishing
2009

Published by the
Modern Humanities Research Association and Maney Publishing
1 Carlton House Terrace
London SW1Y 5AF
United Kingdom

LEGENDA is an imprint of the
Modern Humanities Research Association and Maney Publishing

Maney Publishing is the trading name of W. S. Maney & Son Ltd,
whose registered office is at Suite 1C, Joseph's Well, Hanover Walk, Leeds LS3 1AB

ISBN 978-1-906540-42-5

First published 2009

Printed in Great Britain

Cover: 875 Design

Copy-Editor: Nigel Hope

CONTENTS

Vergessen wir auch nicht, daß jeder Kulturweltbürger sich einen besonderen 'Parnaß' und eine 'Schule von Athen' geschaffen hatte . . . Keiner von diesen Großen war ihm darum fremd erschienen, weil er in einer anderen Sprache geredet hatte . . .

('Zeitgemäßes über Krieg und Tod', 1915)

This book is gratefully dedicated to

THE DIRECTOR AND STAFF OF THE LONDON FREUD MUSEUM

Benevolent Keepers of the Flame

ACKNOWLEDGEMENTS

This book is based on the German editions of Freud's works and letters listed in the Select Bibliography. Translations, unless otherwise indicated, are my own. I have also gratefully drawn on the Comprehensive Catalogue of Freud's library by J. Keith Davies and Gerhardt Fichtner, and on transcriptions of passages Freud marked in books he owned, made for me by Mr Davies. Michael Molnar, the Director of the London Freud Museum, kindly gave me access to a few relevant passages from the as yet unpublished correspondence between Freud and his fiancée (and later wife) Martha Bernays. Professor Ritchie Robertson, Professor Gerhard Fichtner, and Lady Susan Budd have generously shared their knowledge and understanding of Freud's writings and personality with me, and I have had valuable help in tracing books and editions from Helen Powell and a number of Oxford librarians — notably Tessa Shaw of The Queen's College and Jill Hughes of the Taylorian Institution. I am grateful to Christine Nelson, who computerized my untidy typescript; to Nigel Hope, who copy-edited the book; to Emily Troscianko, who compiled the index; and to Graham Nelson, the managing editor of Legenda, who nursed the book towards its publication with exemplary care and patience.

My Select Bibliography supplies a key to abbreviations used throughout the book, and lists all primary sources; but from the vast array of books on Freud it selects only those few which have proved of immediate relevance to my limited subject. I hope that my listing of such books will be taken as acknowledgement of the debt I owe to their authors. My greatest debt, however, is owed to wide-ranging discussions with colleagues who include T. J. Reed, Christopher Collard and the late George Caird — and beyond that to the Provost and Fellows of The Queen's College, Oxford, who have generously supported my somewhat eccentric research over the many years I have been privileged to live and work among them.

S.S.P., April 2009

INTRODUCTION

The Moravian family into which Sigmund Freud was born grew an English branch when Emanuel and Philipp Freud, sons of his father's previous marriage, emigrated to Manchester, where they established lucrative businesses. They did not, however, lose touch with their father and his second family, which in its turn moved permanently to Vienna. Emanuel had two daughters slightly younger than Sigmund, and the families thought that he might marry one of these and settle into the family business in England. Sigmund was an Anglophile from the first. Using a medical metaphor he wrote to his friend Eduard Silberstein on 6 August 1873 that he was in danger of catching 'the English disease' ('die englische Krankheit'): 'I read English history, write English letters, declaim English verses, listen to descriptions of England, yearn to attract English eyes'.[1] Alongside Goethe, Heine, the Book of Job, Herodotus, Ovid, and Cervantes, the same letter alludes to Robert Burns's 'My heart's in the Highlands' — suggesting that his declamation of 'English' verses may have included some of the Scottish ones Ferdinand Freiligrath had made familiar in German translation. His one regret, he told Silberstein, was that nothing had so far come of his plans to visit England. Two years later, however, he had his wish: he crossed the Channel, stayed with his Manchester family, made excursions to St Anne's on Sea, decided against marriage and the wool trade, but thought that 'despite rain, drunkenness and conservatism' England was more pleasant to live in than Austria-Hungary.[2] He had been delighted to find that one of his Manchester nephews bore the first name Samuel, which Dickens had bestowed on both Mr Pickwick and his man Sam Weller. The English books, however, which most inspired him at this time were not novels or collections of poetry, but works by scientists who wrote in a style accessible to the common reader: Darwin, John Tyndall, Thomas Huxley, Charles Lyell, and Norman Lockyer. In the years that followed he acquired representative books by such writers, which became a permanent part of his library; they helped to wean him away from a heavily specialized scientific and philosophical style, reinforcing lessons he had already absorbed from Lessing and Heine. They also helped to hone his command of the English language, which enabled him to treat, or address lectures to, Britons and Americans who sought him out in quest of help or instruction.

Freud's Anglophilia never abated, despite disagreements with the direction psychoanalysis took when Melanie Klein settled in England and opposed the more orthodox Freudian positions on child-analysis propagated by his daughter Anna. It contrasted with his irrational dislike of the United States, although that country bestowed on him the first of the few public honours that ever came his way when, in 1909, he gave a prestigious series of lectures on his work at Clark University in Massachusetts and had an honorary degree conferred on him. He met senior American psychologists, including the aged William James and G. Stanley Hall, the President of Clark University; but though he mentions such figures with respect in his published work, none of them had any discernible influence on his thinking, nor did they mitigate his dislike of their country.

The year before his American visit Freud had travelled to England for the second time, and conceived far happier impressions of the country and its people. He relished especially his first experience of London, but was also pleased with visits to Manchester, Blackpool, Southport, and St Anne's.[3] He even liked the food! He was also grateful for the fees paid by English and American patients who found their way to his consulting room after the First World War, when the Austrian currency fell through the floor. The hard currency with which they met his charges saved him and his family from the sort of middle-class poverty depicted by G. W. Pabst in *The Joyless Street* — a film set in Freud's Vienna. And when Hitler annexed Austria and Freud's very life was threatened, he not only found refuge in England alongside his immediate family, but also saw the centre of the psychoanalytic movement shift from Vienna, Berlin, and Prague to London and ultimately — what will have pleased him less — New York.

The English experience resonates in Freud's American lecture series in a particularly characteristic way. Attempting to explain, to his mixed audience, what he meant by 'Erinnerungsymbole' (mnemonic symbols), he drew on his encounter with London landmarks whose history he had taken care to learn. In the very first lecture he mentioned Charing Cross, explaining that it was a replica of one of the stone crosses set up, in 1291, by Edward I to mark a resting place of the funeral cortège of his Queen Eleanor as it wound its way towards Westminster Abbey; and the massive Doric column known simply as 'the Monument', which commemorated the Great Fire of London in 1666. Structures of this kind served Freud as metaphors, illustrating in the physical world what he meant by such statements as 'hysterical patients suffer from reminiscences'. His English reminiscences, ranging from Parliamentary debates about Irish Home Rule to Madame Tussaud's waxworks, are scattered throughout his writings.[4]

The English and American writers whose presence in Freud's works and published correspondence the present book seeks to trace are not only poets, dramatist, and novelists, but also philosophers like Bacon, Locke, and Hume, armchair anthropologists like Sir James Frazer, archaeologists like A. H. Layard and Arthur Evans, economists like Adam Smith and Thomas Malthus, and historians of religion like William Robertson Smith. The many natural scientists, however, whose writings Freud studied in the course of his life, are here represented only by Charles Darwin, English and American psychologists and psychoanalysts by Ernest Jones, and sexologists by Henry Havelock Ellis. Overrepresentation of the imaginative writings subsumed in German by the term *Dichter* should not induce us to forget that Freud always hoped that a physiological basis could one day be give to psychoanalysis by neuroscientists and investigators of the different regions of the brain, and that he thought of psychoanalysis as a *science* subject to the kind of 'grammar' Karl Pearson had tried to provide. He owned the 1911 edition of Pearson's *Grammar of Science* and underlined operative words in such sentences as:

> to know requires exertion, and it is intellectually easiest to shirk effort altogether by accepting phrases *which cloak the unknown in the indefinable* (p. ix)
>
> the scientific man has above all to *strive at self-elimination* in his judgments, to provide an argument which is as true for each individual mind as for his own (p. 6)

The importance of other passages in the same book Freud highlighted with his more usual lines at the sides of key phrases, again italicized in the transcription below:

> Because the glitter of the great metaphysical systems becomes as dross when tried by this touchstone, *we are compelled to classify them as interesting works of the imagination, and not as solid contributions to human knowledge.* (p. 25)
>
> *Nobody believes now that science explains anything; we all look upon it as a shorthand description, as economy of thought.* (p. v)
>
> *The 'universality' of natural law, the 'absolute validity' of the scientific method, depends on the resemblance between the perceptive and reflective faculties of one human mind and those of a second . . .* (p. 101)
>
> *Science for the past is a description, for the future a belief; it is not, and has never been, an explanation . . .* (p. 113)

(Transcriptions made by J. Keith Davies, Chief Librarian of the London Freud Museum.)

Freud learnt this lesson well. He told Marie Bonaparte: 'Only the real, rare, true scientific minds can endure doubt, which is attached to all our knowledge. [. . .] Mental events seem immeasurable and probably always will be so'.[5] And he wrote to Stefan Zweig on 17 November 1937: 'Doubt is insoluble from scientific enquiry, and I am sure no-one has been able to extract more than just a tiny fragment of the truth'.[6]

He also believed, with Karl Pearson, that 'there is no short cut to truth, no way to gain knowledge except through the gateway of scientific method', and resisted all attempts to classify psychoanalysis as an art rather than a science, or to see its founder as more of a poet than a scientist. At the same time he discovered in works of imaginative literature anticipations of his own findings, and responded to them with psychoanalytic concern. What must never be forgotten however, is that though he believed that his analyses and the theories he built upon them had widened and deepened human knowledge and understanding, no-one knew better than Freud how small a fragment of truth could be seized by any individual thinker at any period of human history. True to that belief Freud often stressed that he approached literature as a psychologist, and that he was not competent to judge aesthetic qualities. One cannot read far into his writings, however, without perceiving how fine a stylist he was himself; how directly and sensitively he responded to a wide variety of works; and in how many ways he related what he read to his own life and concerns. What this meant in practice the following pages will seek to demonstrate through a specific example: the knowledge Freud acquired of British and American writing within the limits of taste formed early in his life, and the use he made of this knowledge in his published works, letters, and journals.

Notes to the Introduction

1. *Jugendbriefe*, p. 40. A key to abbreviations used throughout this book will be found in the Select Bibliography.
2. 9 September 1875, *Jugendbriefe*, p. 143.
3. See *Reisebriefe*, p. 240–61.
4. *GW* VIII, 11–12, *GW* VI, 75, 102, 137.
5. *Jones*, II, 466.
6. *Freud/St. Zweig*, p. 213.

CHAPTER 1

❖

Shakespearean Autobiography

On 13 September 1908, while visiting London, Freud walked into the National Portrait Gallery and lingered before what there passed for a portrait of Shakespeare. 'Not an English face', he confided to a manuscript now usefully edited by Michael Molnar;[1] and he reminded himself that he had once heard the dramatist's name derived from the French 'Jean Pierre'. 'A typical head', he continued,[2] like those of Homer, Socrates, and some distinguished philologists and archaeologists Freud had met in Vienna. Shakespeare, then, belonged to a world wider than his native country; a universal genius, whose work had woven itself into Freud's life ever since he had been given or lent his first copy of the plays when he was just eight years old. Scholars such as Ritchie Robertson and Graham Frankland have left English-speaking readers in no doubt about the solace, refreshment, and inspiration Freud found in imaginative literature; and what the present chapter seeks to do is to trace some of the ways in which Freud continually used Shakespeare to reveal something of his own most pressing concerns.

Freud's first copy of Shakespeare was presumably that classic translation by August Wilhelm Schlegel, Ludwig Tieck, and their circle which he would continue quoting throughout his life; but he soon grew to understand, love, and quote the English original too. When, as a teenager, he fell in inarticulate love with a young woman called Gisela Fluss, he drew on his knowledge of *Hamlet* to convey his inhibitions. Why could he not converse naturally with this 'half native, half educated' girl? In a letter to his friend Eduard Silberstein he attributed this unaccustomed backwardness to his 'insensate Hamletdom' — 'mein unsinniges Hamlettum'.[3] He clearly expected his friend to recall that Hamlet accuses himself of being 'sicklied o'er with the pale cast of thought', and 'thinking too precisely on th'event'. Freud's 'Hamletdom', however, leads him further than this; for soon afterwards he launches into a paean to Gisela's mother, whose standard of cultural awareness and all-round capability he contrasts with those of his own beloved mother to the latter's detriment. That places him between two women, an older and a younger, a virgin and a mother, as Hamlet stands between Ophelia and Gertrude, whose sexuality repels and fascinates him. This passage from the young girl to the mother-figure we shall meet again later; it is part of a syndrome to which Otto Rank referred when, during his stay in America, he dared to criticize his master's over-emphasis on relations with the father, assuring his audiences: 'on ze contrary — ze mozzer'.

We can now follow the young Freud into Vienna University, where, two weeks later, he found himself having to work through some dry-as-dust textbooks when he would much rather have been reading Goethe or Carlyle. He expressed his frustration by recalling the exasperated 'Words, words, words' with which Hamlet answers Polonius's question — 'What do you read, my lord?' — but Freud characteristically caps it with a variant of his own. Words, after all, have meanings; but what he has to read resolves itself in his mind into the lowest common denominator of print: mere paper.[4] He feels cabined, cribbed, confined by his studies, at which he was very good but which he was constantly striving to widen out; and this leads to another *Hamlet* quotation, introduced into a letter in which Freud asks Silberstein to tell him something about the Austrian variant of such socialist ideas as he had recently encountered in the writings of John Stuart Mill. There is room for improvement, he contends in his letter of 7 March 1875; for 'a good deal is rotten in this prison called earth'.[5] Here Freud asks his friend to understand his feeling of constriction by recalling two of Hamlet's sayings at once. 'Something is rotten in the state of Denmark' merges with Hamlet's complaint of the 'bad dreams' which make him feel first Denmark and then the whole world a prison with 'many confines, wards and dungeons'.

Such melancholy feelings did not prevent the younger Freud from making solid contributions to animal and human studies: the histology of the nervous system of fish, the presence or absence of gonads in eels, the study of aphasia and infantile paralysis, and the anaesthetic properties of cocaine. As early galley-proofs began to arrive on his desk, he saw in his mind's eye a successions of works he would publish; a vision he compared, humorously, with Macbeth's terror at a succession of kings not sprung from his own loins stretching out 'to the crack of doom'.[6] Here the Shakespearean context, which will later engage Freud with torturing seriousness, is part of a joke, pointing to a sense of humour which he shared with his friends and which he liked to gloss with Corporal Nym's catchphrase in *Henry the Fifth*: 'That's the humour of it'.[7] Freud is mistaken in the speaker, attributing the saying to Pistol rather than Nym, but we may presume him to have been familiar with that doctrine of 'humours' governing different temperaments for which he would find, in later years, equivalences in his theory of drives, psychic energies, and Lamarckian inheritances.

Pistol was much in Freud's mind because of his 'speaking' name — a name with which Falstaff plays as Freud's contemporaries were all too apt to play with the meaning of the name 'Freud'. In *The Psychopathology of Everyday Life* he would remember how, in the second part of *King Henry the Fourth*, Falstaff orders Pistol off with the punning 'Discharge yourself of our company, Pistol'. Freud quotes this in Schlegel's congenial translation: 'Drück dich aus unserer Gesellschaft ab, Pistol'. He might be amused by that; but when analogous games were played with his own name, he was as irritated as Goethe had been when Herder had tried to play the same game with the name 'Goethe'.[8]

Freud was notoriously deaf to music that was not made rationally accessible through the addition of words and dramatic action, as in Mozart's operas. He found in Shakespeare, however, words and scenes that pointed to possibilities of experience closed to Freud himself. Thinking of the opening of *Twelfth Night* and the final act of *The Merchant of Venice*, he wrote to Silberstein on 20 August

1873 that Shakespeare felt music to be 'the key to the heart' — 'der Schlüssel zum Herzen'.[9] Here, we might think, literature served to supplement or enlarge Freud's experience. It would seem, however, as though he encountered Shakespeare mainly as a reader; the only performance of his plays he described in some detail is an *Othello* starring the Italian tragedian Ernesto Rossi; and Freud's account of it, in a letter to Silberstein dated 2 August 1873, makes wicked fun of actors and audience alike.[10] This will not, however, impede Freud's readiness, in a later essay entitled 'Some Character Types Encountered in Psychoanalytical Practice',[11] to comment favourably on Shakespeare's stagecraft.

Nine years after the last-quoted letters to Silberstein Freud found a woman who held the keys to his heart more surely than Gisela Fluss and her mother: Martha Bernays, whom he would eventually marry. His letters to her, both light and grave, mingle professions of love with schoolmasterly instruction; and those I have been able to see, with the kind help of Michael Molnar, enlist four of Shakespeare's plays in preparing Freud's bride for her eventual married state.

The first of these is *Twelfth Night*. Freud assumes the voice of Feste, the saddest of Shakespeare's clowns before *King Lear*, distancing it still further by introducing it with a sentence in archaizing German which declares *Twelfth Night* to be the work of an English poet who has written many merry and sad plays and acted in them himself: 'Gedenkt, was ein engelländischer Dichter, so viel lustige and schmerzliche Stücke erfunden und selbst in ihnen agiert hat, Wilhelm Shakespeare, singt'. The distancing continues when he quotes Feste's song in its original English — a song that speaks of love in an uncertain world, caught in the onrush of time:

What is love? 'tis not hereafter;
Present mirth hath present laughter;
What's to come is still unsure.
In delay there lies no plenty,
Then come kiss me, sweet and twenty,
Youth's a stuff will not endure.

Fearing that Martha's English might not come up to his own, he counselled her to consult *Der Dreikönigsabend oder Was ihr wollt* — Schlegel's version of *Twelfth Night, or What You Will*. In this letter we can watch Freud distancing his own emotions while asking his fiancée to share his cultural enthusiasms.

The second Shakespeare play Freud enlists in the task of wooing and educating his future wife is *Much Ado about Nothing*: and unlike his playful enlistment of *Twelfth Night*, Freud's use of this piece is designed to prepare Martha for the prose as well as the poetry of married life. 'I am', he writes to her on 13 July 1882, 'your fiancé for every day, not just for Sundays and Feast-days — the kind Beatrice wanted to have; and you will surely love me a little even on bad days'.[12] The reference here is, of course, to the scene in the second act in which the Prince of Aragon asks Beatrice: 'Will you have *me*, lady?' and receives the answer: 'No, my lord, unless I might have another for working days; your Grace is too costly to wear every day'.

The third of these plays is, not unexpectedly, *Hamlet*. Martha had been raised in an orthodox Jewish household, and Freud now needed to prepare her for a household, and a life, in which a sensible and life-affirming Judaism would be professed, but religious customs would be outlawed. There would be no lighting of Sabbath candles, no Passover Seder, no Yom Kippur fasts. A recent acquaintance, Freud reports, had reminded him of the approach of Tisha b'Av, a day of mourning for the destruction of the Jerusalem Temple in 586 BCE — a day commonly reserved for fasting and prayer, and not a day to be pleasurably passed in the company of one's fiancée. Freud applied to his own and Martha's case Hamlet's words about the tears shed by the First Player when his recitation reaches the fate of Priam's wife during the sack of Troy: 'What's Hecuba to him, or he to Hecuba | That he should weep for her?' 'What's Hecuba to me', Freud writes on 23 July 1882. 'Why should we mourn because a faulty dating reminds us that around this time Jerusalem was destroyed? Jerusalem *is* destroyed, and dear Martha and I are alive and happy'.[13]

The fourth and (as far as I know) last play Freud enlists in these letters to his bride is *King Lear.* When Martha has a throat infection her indistinct speech reminds him of the Shakespearean character whose 'voice was ever soft, gentle and low — an excellent thing in a woman'. 'Mein Cordelia-Marthchen', he writes on 13 July 1883; and he explains that when he spoke to Josef Breuer about the 'sweet Cordelia' to whom he was engaged, Breuer confessed that he called his wife by the same Shakespearean name.[14] Later Freud will speak of Cordelia, and her relation to her father, in an essay that connects the three caskets in *The Merchant of Venice* with the three daughters in *King Lear.*[15] That both Freud and Breuer should have called their future and present *wives* by the name of Lear's *daughter* suggests something of their patriarchal attitude to the women whose task it was to run their households and bear their children.

The most important correspondence of Freud's life — important, that is, for the shape of his future career — is that with Wilhelm Fliess, which spans the transition from the medical and neurological researcher to the physician and codifier of Psychoanalysis, and ultimately from the private man to the ever controversial public figure. Freud begins, as before, by giving Shakespeare the task of conveying his frustration — that of a man engaged on medical treatment and physiological research who would much rather delve into what he conceived to be the secrets of the human heart and soul. 'My heart', he quotes in the wake of Mark Antony, 'is in the coffin here with Caesar', changing Antony's 'there' to 'here' in order to indicate his feeling of constriction here and now, along with a sense of being buried in the past instead of striking out into the future.[16] What shape his future investigations would take is suggested by a reference to *A Midsummer Night's Dream* in a manuscript Freud sent to Fliess some time in 1897, which deals with the vagaries of the sexual drive. 'Titania', Freud writes, 'who refuses her love to her legitimate husband Oberon, is forced to bestow it instead on the phantastic ass Bottom'.[17] 'The phantastic ass Bottom', 'dem Phantasieesel Zettel', brings beautifully together the phantasy of Titania, whom magic had forced to think an ass a more suitable mate than her husband Oberon; that of Bottom, the most imaginative of the mechanicals, who will characterize his experiences in the enchanted wood as 'Bottom's dream, because it hath no bottom'; and, of course, that of Shakespeare, who conceived these characters and gave them a life of their own. That leads over to Freud's reflections on poetic inspiration, for which he thinks he has found an apt phrase in

Theseus's speech on lunatics, lovers, and poets in the last act of *A Midsummer Night's Dream*: 'So Shakespeare is proved right when he juxtaposes imaginative literature with delusion: 'fine frenzy'.[18] Freud had sufficient self-knowledge to realize that theorizing about literature was not his strong point; but he loved and revered great writing, and found that Sophocles, Shakespeare, Goethe, Cervantes, and other imaginative writers portrayed in their works much that psychoanalysis tried to tease out in its own more laborious fashion.

The letters to Fliess also harbour the first version of Freud's theory that Hamlet, who shows himself perfectly capable of swift action, cannot 'sweep to his revenge' for his father's murder because the murderer has done what Hamlet himself secretly desired. This involves a split type figure: a good father, old Hamlet, who is safely dead and cannot therefore bed the mother, and a bad father, Claudius, the mother's sexually active new husband, on whom the guilt for killing the good father can be safely shifted. *The Interpretation of Dreams,* into whose argument this notion is integrated,[19] makes no secret of its autobiographical background: Freud's own ambivalent attitude to his father and mother, and his need to have a cherished friend and a hated enemy at the same time — contrary roles that could be, and sometimes were, filled by the same person. As for the contrast between the actual parricide and incest portrayed in Sophocles' *Oedipus Tyrannus* and the mere desires Freud diagnoses in Hamlet: these connect themselves, in his mind, with the greater incidence of repression and denial in later societies, including his own, and the increased virulence of the inner 'censor' who seeks to prevent material from the unconscious reaching consciousness. The pros and cons of Freud's view of *Hamlet* have been admirably set out in a lecture by David Bevington entitled 'Hamlet's Two Fathers', delivered before the British Academy in 2007 and reprinted in that Academy's *Proceedings* in 2008; but in our context we must not forget that Freud finds other plays besides *Hamlet* anticipating and confirming findings gained through introspection or the analysis of patients. He covertly proclaims his atheism by converting Prince Hal's epitaph on the supposedly dead Falstaff from 'Thou owest God a death' to 'Thou owest Nature a death'. That is in Part I of *King Henry the Fourth*, of course; but he also finds 'psychic displacement' in *Othello*, wishful thinking in *Romeo and Juliet*, sexual revulsion in *Timon of Athens*, and an image for social bluff when the lion is asked to reveal himself as Snug the Joiner in *A Midsummer Night's Dream*. Freud even finds occasion to connect a gift of flowers to an unnamed lady to the scene in *King Henry the Sixth* in which the feud between York and Lancaster finds expression in the choice of white or red roses, leaving it to his readers to draw conclusions about the war of the sexes from this horrendous analogy. All these observations are to be found in what Freud would always regard as his most important pioneering work: *The Interpretation of Dreams*.[20]

In later years Freud projected the ambivalences that had fuelled *The Interpretation of Dreams* into world history. This happens most prominently in *Totem and Taboo,* first published in 1913, which finds a secular equivalent for the religious notion of Original Sin by positing a primal slaying: that of a father by a band of sons.[21] That, Freud believed, had its repercussions in the psychic make-up of subsequent generations, including that into which he himself had been born. The feelings of guilt fostered by the supposed primal parricide, Freud argues in *Totem and Taboo* and elsewhere, fed into superstitious fears of malevolent spirits — particularly fears of the slain — haunting primitive societies. These, he thought, lead a shadow-life among us; Shakespeare brought them onto the stage in key scenes of *Hamlet*, *Macbeth*, and *Richard the Third*. *Totem and Taboo* also uses Claudius's vain attempt to purge his guilt through prayer — 'My words fly up, my thoughts remain below' — to argue that a prayer must prove ineffective if there is no conviction or real remorse behind it, while Ariel's deceitful song about a drowned father in *The Tempest*:

> Those are pearls that were his eyes,
> Nothing of him that doth fade
> But doth suffer a sea-change
> Into something rich and strange.

becomes for Freud an attempt to soften the sense of inherited guilt and those parricidal death-wishes he diagnosed in himself, his patients, and Shakespeare's plays.[22]

Freud sought reflections of Shakespeare's own psyche in his plays, believing that the problems of Hamlet were related to the deaths of Shakespeare's father and his son (significantly named Hamnet), and that the sexual hang-ups revealed in speeches by Hamlet, Lear, and Timon of Athens, Freud conjectured, spoke of similar feelings in the dramatist himself at the period of composition. When he became convinced, by Thomas Looney's *'Shakespeare' Identified* (1921), that the real author of the plays was Edward de Vere, Earl of Oxford, he looked for events in the Earl's life which might offer similar parallels, and went to the *Sonnets* to confirm his conjectures. Believing that the fair youth addressed in them could be identified with Henry Wriothesley, Earl of Southampton, he speculated, in a letter to Arnold Zweig dated 22 June 1936[23] how unlikely it was that a jobbing actor would address a patron in this way, and that the opening of the sixteen-line poem that concludes the section devoted to the 'fair youth',[24] where the poet indicates that on ceremonial occasions he had borne the canopy over the Sovereign, again indicated a nobleman rather than a lowly commoner:

> Were't aught to me I bore the canopy
> With my extern the outward honouring . . .

This tracing of the author in his work supplements Freud's analysis of the characters Shakespeare created, the plays as psychologically self-sufficient entities, and their effects on particular readers — on Sigmund Freud, who even took them into his dreams, and on the patients, with whom he discussed literary works that they had read and that might have influenced their conscious and unconscious lives.

As Freud began to spread his message in lectures and publications he became increasingly conscious of the need to carry audiences and readers along with him. For this he sought and found rhetorical aids in Hamlet, using quotations his contemporaries were more likely to recognize than references to *King Henry the Sixth*. To show his awareness of the obviousness of some of his contentions, he liked to quote Horatio's 'There needs no ghost, my Lord, to tell us this'; but he soon shows that he uses such sayings as a springboard into the less obvious. For such forays into remoter regions Freud prepares his audiences with another of those quotations of which Hamlet is proverbially full: 'There are more things in heaven and earth, Horatio, than are dreamt of in your philosophy'. By quoting this in German, Freud is able to introduce three variants. Schlegel renders 'philosophy' as 'Schulweisheit' — an academic wisdom, academic philosophy, a subject of which Freud was ever suspicious. That leads to a second variant: Lichtenberg's sceptical addition to Hamlet's remark, which warns us that 'there is much in philosophy — *Schulweisheit* — that's to be found neither in heaven nor on earth'; something that exists only in the philosopher's head. The third variant occurs when Freud substitutes *our* philosophy — 'unsere Schulweisheit' — for Hamlet's 'your', suggesting a bafflement Freud shares with the common reader but not necessarily with imaginative writers, 'Dichter', who 'can draw on sources not yet opened up to science'.[25]

If, as inevitably happened, Freud's readers or listeners found some of his arguments overly strange, he liked to remind them of another of Hamlet's injunctions to Horatio: 'And therefore, as a stranger, give it welcome'.[26] Readers are also warned, however, that the enterprise on which Freud is engaged cannot be undertaken by just anybody. To make this clear, Freud quotes Hamlet's rebuke to Rosencrantz and Guildenstern, who sought to pluck out his mystery when they could not even elicit music from a simple recorder: ''sblood, do you think I am easier to be played on than a pipe? . . . Call me what instrument you will, though you fret me, you cannot play me'.[27] As for the method to be employed when trying to fathom the mysteries of the human mind, here Freud can call on the old statesman Polonius, who advises Reynaldo to find out 'directions' by 'indirections', using a 'bait of falsehood' to 'catch a carp of truth'. For 'falsehood', Freud substitutes 'error'; even an erroneous diagnosis of the cause of a patient's problems may lead to a useful correction and a more accurate aetiology later.[28]

The metaphor of the carp of truth caught with a bait of error connects itself with another favourite parallel Freud discovered in Shakespeare — this time in Part I of *King Henry the Fourth* rather than *Hamlet*. 'What, upon compulsion?', Falstaff exclaims, when asked to give reasons for his gross and palpable lies; 'if reasons were as plentiful as blackberries, I would give no man a reason upon compulsion'. Yes, Freud implies, ignoring the situation in which Falstaff, driven into a corner, employs this famous comparison; yes, reasons *are* as plentiful as blackberries; but they may be specious, and may, unbeknownst to those of us who advance them, be directed by influences from below our daylight consciousness.[29] What we come up against here is, of course, the central insight Freud's self-analysis brought him: that our consciousness is a façade, that we need depth analysis of dreams, involuntary associations, parapraxes, and a host of other clues to find out what is really going on in our minds.

Shakespeare served Freud as an Arnoldian touchstone with which to 'place' other writers, from Hebbel to Dostoevsky, and as occasion for exercises in comparative literary criticism: like his comparison of Falstaff, who is conscious of, and plays on, the comic effect his appearance and prevarication have on his entourage, with Don Quixote, who cannot recognize the comedy his chivalrous actions and sentiments bring into a world governed by different codes. Shakespeare's characters also, however, provided him with a valued means of characterizing his enemies and — on occasions — his followers. A critic who had argued that it was dangerous to drag the contents of the unconscious into the light of day is made to speak with the voice of Dogberry, the stupid constable of *Much Ado about Nothing*, who instructs the watchmen under his charge: 'If you meet a thief, you may suspect him, by virtue of your office, to be no true man; and for such a kind of man, the less you meddle or make with him, why the more is for your honesty'.[30] Or again: an opponent, who used some of the terms of Psychoanalysis to devalue the Freudian enterprise itself, is lent the voice of Caliban, who articulates his hostility to Prospero by saying: 'You gave me language, and my profit on't is I know how to curse'.[31] As for Freud's followers: there is Isidor Sadger, whose notoriously long-winded articles Freud glosses, in one of his letters to Jung, with Hamlet's response to Polonius's complaint about the length of the First Player's recitation: 'It shall to the barber, with your beard'. Even the faithful Ernest Jones, whom Freud found 'a very interesting and valuable human being', inspired in Freud a feeling that he called 'an almost racial estrangement'. 'He is a fanatic and eats too little', Freud writes to Jung on 3 May 1908: 'Caesar says "let me have men about me that are fat" . . . He almost reminds me of the lean Cassius'.[32]

Shakespeare's *Julius Caesar* also enables Freud to convey something of the rhythms of his thoughts: his fondness for polar opposites and for ironical speech. Antony's oration after Caesar's death provides a welcome instance of the kind of irony which says one thing — the assassins are all 'honourable men' — while implying its opposite. Since his schooldays, however, when he had recited the part of Brutus while a slightly older nephew, with whom he had a love-hate relationship, had enacted Caesar, Freud had inclined towards Brutus rather than his victim and his adversaries; and he found in Shakespeare's rendering of Brutus's oration over Caesar's body a more accurate reflection of ambivalences, antitheses, and reversals characteristic of his own way of thinking: 'As Caesar loved me, I weep for him; as he was fortunate, I rejoice at it; as he was valiant, I honour him; but as he was ambitious, I slew him'. Freud first quotes this in *The Interpretation of Dreams*, remembering that he had identified with Brutus in one of his dreams. He quotes it again later, to characterize the feelings of one of his patients, the Rat Man, towards his father; but as so often, Freud found his own feelings reflected in his patients, and both anticipated in Shakespeare's plays.[33]

Among the many traits Freud recognized in his own psychic make-up after the self-analysis that preceded and accompanied the composition of *The Interpretation of Dreams* are ambition and avidity for honours: 'mein Ehrgeiz'. For this he thought he had found an adequate image in Part II of *Henry the Fourth*, where Shakespeare shows Prince Hal unable to resist trying on the crown by the bedside of his dying father. Hal's protest, that he only did this because he thought his father already dead, is countered by the king with words that had a special resonance for Freud: 'The wish was father, Harry, to that thought'.[34] Among the 'honours' he craved were the professorship that was so long withheld from him, and later the Nobel Prize which never came his way. He did achieve fame in his lifetime, and knew that it would outlast him; but his very success brought constant attacks that were scornful, or indignant, or (more often) both. The nature of these attacks lends force to Freud's diagnosis of the appeal of Falstaff, whose humour arises, in Freud's view, from the resilience of an ego that knows its own faults and physical defects, but also knows, deep down, that he has to humour and placate someone more powerful than himself who is able to cast him off whenever it suits him. Applying his Helmholtz-inspired theory of conservation and balance of psychic energy Freud argues that the enjoyment Falstaff's auditors on and off the stage find in Falstaff's antics and rogueries is due to a saving of affective energies that they would have had to expend on scorn and indignation had Falstaff been differently presented. Scorn and indignation — 'Verachtung und Entrüstung' — the very energies called into play by attacks on Freud himself.[35]

It is one of the many ironies in Freud's life that among the most gifted followers he found in his later years was a group of women that included Anna, his youngest daughter, whom he analysed and encouraged, with excellent results, to become a psychoanalyst in her own right. And as Freud confessed to Sándor Ferenczi it was Anna who inspired his essay on the choice of caskets in *The Merchant of Venice*, which Freud linked with choice between three daughters in *King Lear*, and beyond that with similar choices in mythology and fairytale. The personal background to all this is a double one. In *The Interpretation of Dreams* Freud had reported a dream of three women, one of whom was his mother, which he connected with the three Fates, with nourishment, and with death; and by the time he wrote his essay he had, of course, himself become the father of three daughters, the youngest of whom assumed ever greater importance in his life. The essay links the leaden casket, whose 'plainness' moves Bassanio 'more than eloquence', with Lear's youngest daughter, Cordelia, who cannot heave [her] heart into [her] mouth'; and it interprets the image of Lear carrying the dead Cordelia in his arms as a dreamlike inversion of the dead carried to some beyond by a valkyrie or some other messenger of death, or borne to their rest by Mother Earth herself. As the tokens of death multiplied in this essay the image of the daughter is once again succeeded by that of the mother. Freud describes

> [. . .] the three forms that the image of the mother assumes in a man's life: the mother herself, the beloved bride he chooses in the mother's likeness, and Mother Earth who receives him at the last.[36]

In this passage from daughter to mother can we not perceive again a pattern set by his early infatuation with an older and a younger member of the Fluss family, and hear once again the voice of Otto Rank, emboldened by his American distance from his mentor to question Freud's excessive stress on relations with the father: 'On ze contrary — ze mozzer'?[37]

It would be tedious to go on listing the many other instances in which Shakespeare is given the task of conveying Freud's own thoughts. We might just recall how Hamlet's 'Thus conscience does make cowards of us all' is used to convey the notion, central to *Civilization and its Discontents*, that we pay for advances in civilization with a loss of happiness through the heightening of our sense of inherited guilt;[38] and how an essay first published in 1922 cites two lines of Desdemona's 'Willow' song to show her using Barbara to condone infidelities Desdemona in her own person vehemently rejects:

> I call'd my love false love, and what said he then?
> (Sing willow, willow, willow)
> If I court moe women you'll couch with moe men.[39]

One set of references, however, is worth looking at in a little more detail because it shows the way Freud applied, in his dealings with Shakespeare's characters, the important insight self-analysis and clinical practice had confirmed: that human beings could never be taken at face value. Take Polonius, 'the rash intruding fool' and garrulous babbler on whom Hamlet unleashes all his scorn before he kills him in mistake for the king. Freud recognizes how much wisdom — of a worldly sort — resides in this apparently so ridiculous old man. We have already seen Freud's approval of Polonius's method of finding directions by indirections and using a 'bait of falsehood' to catch a 'carp of truth'. He caps this by showing that paradoxically we owe to this 'Schwätzer', this blatherskite, the succinct and correct formulation: 'brevity is the soul of wit' — an observation Freud couples, in *The Joke and its Relation to the Unconscious*, with that of Rosaline in *Love's Labour's Lost*: 'A jest's prosperity lies in the ear | Of him that hears it, never in the tongue | Of him that makes it'. And though Polonius is mistaken in attributing what he takes to be Hamlet's genuine madness to thwarted love for Ophelia, he does point towards the sexual component of Hamlet's problem, and rightly discerns the 'method' in the prince's 'madness'. Polonius's 'Though this be a madness, yet there's method in't' serves Freud, in a letter to Jung, to justify his own faith in the way apparently eccentric numerical calculations could predict the course of a person's life, including the probable date of his death.[40]

Freud's essay on the Three Caskets was first published in 1913, on the eve of the First World War. Its comforting vision of death in the arms of Mother Earth was succeeded by a much sterner one under the impact of the carnage and savagery of that war, the death of Freud's daughter Sophie in the influenza epidemic which followed it, the impoverishment of Austrians as their currency collapsed, the increase of political anti-Semitism in Austria as in Germany, and not least the first of those operations for cancer of the jaw which made life such a physical torture for Freud from the mid-1920s onwards. All these darkened his horizons. He now came to envisage a death-drive, a drive towards dissolution and destruction turned inward as well as outward, joining Eros, or the libido, in mutual antagonism or temporary adjustment. For these darker views too Freud sought and found objective correlatives in Shakespeare's plays. He came to adopt as his own a saying of Hamlet's he had earlier treated as a sign of the prince's neurosis: 'Treat every man after his desert, and who shall 'scape whipping'; he compared the German people's enchantment by the braying Hitler with Titania's love for a transmogrified ass; and he greeted the clash of parties in the Austria of the 1930s with Mercutio's dying curse: 'A plague on both your houses!'.[41] Just before his enforced flight from Vienna he wrote to his half-brother Alexander: 'The rest — you will understand me — is silence'.[42] What Alexander Freud would understand was that Gestapo surveillance made written communication perilous; but for the aged Freud, who had seen his published work consigned to the flames, his institutions shut down or forcibly 'Aryanized', his house searched and his daughter arrested, and menace to his very life, seek exile abroad, leaving his sisters as hostages among their enemies — for such a man Hamlet's dying words had a resonance that make other words inadequate. As another eminent quondam resident of Vienna has so memorably said: 'Whereof one cannot speak, thereof one must be silent'.

Hamlet is not the only Shakespearean character in which Freud invested much of his self-knowledge. There are at least three others in whose analysis, in Freud's writings, carried autobiographical revelations: Richard the Third and the two Macbeths.

Richard made a brief appearance in *Totem and Taboo*, where Freud termed the ghosts of Richard's victims that terrify him before the final battles his 'hallucinations' — though they also, of course, address more comforting words to Richmond in the opposing camp. Freud's most elaborate and telling account, however, of the fascination Shakespeare's presentation of Richard has held for generations of actors and audiences occurs in a paper entitled 'Some Character Types Encountered in Psychoanalytic Practice', first published in 1915.[43] Here Richard is introduced as 'eine von dem grössten Dichter geschaffene Gestalt' — a figure created by the *greatest* imaginative writer, who knew how to leave room for his audience's reflections on what is implied as well as what is said. Freud quotes part of the opening monologue in which Richard dwells on his physical imperfections, and proclaims that since he cannot play the lover, he is determined to be a villain. This frivolous motive, Freud comments, would prevent any kind of audience sympathy with Richard did it not cover something many readers and listeners knew by introspection: that one is justified in thinking oneself an exception, and therefore not bound by everyday morality, if one feels oneself disadvantaged by Nature in ways that lift one out of the common crowd and its prescriptive codes.

At this point we should remember that Freud had what Joseph Conrad called a 'secret sharer' — a possible alter ego that bore the typically Austro-Germanic name 'Oberhuber'. 'Be assured', Freud wrote to Karl Abraham on 23 July 1908, 'if my name were Oberhuber my innovations would have found, despite all, far less resistance'.[44] With that in mind, let us listen to Freud's account of how Shakespeare ensures audience sympathy with the boldness, dexterity, and cynical humour with which, in the early part of the play, Richard makes his way towards the coveted throne. 'We feel', Freud writes in 'Some Character Types Encountered in Psychoanalytic Practice',

> that we ourselves could be like Richard — in small measure we already are like him. We all believe that we have cause to be angry with Nature, and with our destiny, because our heredity and infancy have caused us to fall short. We all demand compensation for early injuries to our narcissism, our self-love. Why has Nature not given us Baldur's blond locks, or Siegfried's strength, or the noble features of an aristocrat'? Why were we born into a bourgeois household instead of a royal palace? We could be just as good at being beautiful and noble as those whom we now envy because they are just that.[45]

Can't one just hear the personal note in all this parody? This yearning for Germanic gods and heroes, presumed blond, like Baldur and Siegfried, is surely related to Freud's distaste for the Jews from Eastern Europe, the *Ostjuden* among whom his parents were born, his speculations about a remoter ancestry in what he thought the more respectable German Rhineland, and his description of himself as a 'Mediterranean Man' as opposed to the 'Celt' Ernest Jones and the 'Germanic' Jung.[46] As for the 'family romance' that transports the bourgeois daydreamer into the aristocracy — should not that remind us of Freud's attempt, prompted by Thomas Looney, to make us believe that a presumably ill-educated petty-bourgeois jobbing actor like Shakespeare could not have had the knowledge and experience attested by his plays, and that these, like the Sonnets, must have been written by an aristocrat who used Shakespeare's name as a front? It also reminds us, of course, of the efforts of Freud's last years to prove his hero Moses not an Israelite foundling, but a high-born Egyptian.[47] And is it not strange that whenever Freud, in his letters and published works, speaks of *The Merchant of Venice*, the view is directed to Portia, Bassanio, and Belmont; if he ever so much as mentions Shylock, I must have missed the reference. The obvious contrast here is with Heine, who had undertaken to write on Shakespeare's female characters, but felt he could not deal with Portia, Nerissa, and that thieving turncoat Jessica, without a long and impressive disquisition on what he thought the wrongs suffered by Shylock.

And so to *Macbeth*, a play Freud had worried at ever since, in a very early essay, he had described Lady Macbeth's compulsive handwashing as an attempt to make up by physical purity for the moral purity whose loss she regretted.[48]

In *The Interpretation of Dreams* Macbeth is placed in the same family constellation as Hamlet: as that play dealt with the relation of a son to his parents, Macbeth broached the complementary theme of childlessness, which had a special significance for the philoprogenitive and family-conscious Freud. Such childlessness (the 'babe' to whom Lady Macbeth remembers having 'given suck' has, presumably, died) takes on a wider meaning when Macbeth laments his 'fruitless crown', 'no son of mine succeeding'. Freud connects this with the problem of succession experienced by Elizabeth I, who had to contemplate that her successor to the English crown would be the son of Mary, Queen of Scots, the guest in her country, for whose death she bore the ultimate responsibility. By signing the death-warrant Elizabeth killed Mary as surely as Macbeth killed Duncan.[49] This, in its turn, linked up with Freud's worries over his own succession in the psychoanalytic movement, especially after the revolt, as he saw it, of his designated crown prince, C. G. Jung.

When Otto Rank overstressed, as Freud saw it, the 'trauma of birth' in the generation of anxiety, Freud believed he had found a counter-example in Macduff, whose anxiety, if any, must have had some other, possibly inherited, cause — though I would have thought that being 'untimely ripped' from the mother's womb, with primitive surgical instruments, would have been likely to cause traumata even more surely than the usual rite of passage. But for Freud the play raised weightier problems than that. Did not Lady Macbeth prove that one could be 'Wrecked by Success' as easily as by failure?[50] Did not the witches, with their uncertain promises, resemble that spectre of 'metapsychology' which lured Freud away from the psychoanalyst's couch onto uncertain theorizing territory?[51] And could not the bisexuality Fliess had taught Freud to recognize in himself as well as others help to explain why Macbeth and his Lady seemed to exchange character halfway through the play? Were they not really two sides of one character — another split-type figure, in fact?[52]

Freud never found the answers he sought; and in order to stop the play churning around in his mind, mingling with life-stuff all the way, he 'handed it over', as he put it, to Ernest Jones, who had done so well with *Hamlet* — only to find that he could not let go. 'Da sind dunkle Mächte im Spiel', he wrote to Ferenczi.[53] Dark powers are at work, not only in the play but in the mind of the man who could not leave off puzzling over it. And this sense of dark forces at work is not confined to Freud's dealings with *Macbeth*. We have already found him drawn to plays with supernatural apparitions — *Hamlet, Macbeth, Julius Caesar, Richard the Third* — eager to present their uncanny aspect as the characters' hallucinations, or Shakespeare's poetic licence to draw on superseded beliefs. But Freud's work is full of references to demons of a more terrifying kind: demons seen at work in the Parisian populace (and later, of course, in Nazified Austria); legions of evil spirits let loose against psychoanalysts by a hostile society, or possessing rebellious disciples like Otto Rank: 'An evil demon makes you say that this psychoanalytic movement is a fiction, and puts in your mouth the very words of the enemy'. And it was demons that Freud thought he had himself summoned from the depths and was forced to fight:

> He who, like myself, awakens most evil demons that have slumbered, imperfectly controlled, in the human breast, and sets himself to fight them [Freud writes as his analysis of 'Dora' comes to its disastrous end] must be prepared not to emerge unscathed from this wrestling.[54]

In that last quotation we could watch Freud wrestling with demons as Jacob wrestled with the angel. This is the man who declares early in his essay on 'The Uncanny' that he is himself insensitive to the feelings denoted by this term, but goes on to relate two classic encounters with the Uncanny in his own life: meeting a *Doppelgänger* when he sees an apparition he instantly dislikes coming towards him, only to realize that he had been seeing his own reflection in a glass door; and suffering an uncanny *Wiederholungszwang*, compulsion to repeat, when he found himself in a street of ill-fame, tried to find his way out, and was led back to the same spot time after time.[55] Might one not feel that this, like the numerological and other superstitions Freud was prone to, is the reverse side of that programmatic atheism with which Freud displaced the religion of his forefathers? As Novalis, whose novel *Heinrich von Ofterdingen* Freud had quoted with approval, has so memorably said: 'Wo keine Götter sind, walten Gespenster' — where there are no gods, ghosts will hold sway.

What is to me the most moving passage in Freud's dealings with Shakespeare — especially if one recalls the physical martyrdom of his later years — may be found in a letter to Oskar Pfister dated 6 March 1910. 'What would one do', Freud writes,' on a day or at a time when thoughts fail and words refuse to come? One cannot but tremble at this possibility'. And the self-styled 'godless Jew' who had called on Shakespeare's Claudius to witness the futility of prayer when there is no conviction behind it, now confesses to the Protestant pastor who had become a cherished friend and eager disciple, that he, Freud, did very secretly address a wish to the Fate to which he submitted himself: 'No sickness, please, no paralysis of the ability to work caused by bodily ills'. And Freud ends this plea to whatever powers there be by recalling the words of Macbeth when the Weird Sisters' prophecies are coming true in an unexpectedly disastrous sense and his enemies are moving in for the kill:

> Blow wind, come wrack —
> At least we'll die with harness on our back.[55]

Notes to Chapter 1

1. *Reisebriefe*, p. 250.
2. *Reisebriefe*, p. 255.
3. 4 September 1872, *Jugendbriefe*, p. 22.
4. 13 August 1874, *Jugendbriefe*, p. 59.
5. *Jugendbriefe*, p. 1III.
6. Letter to Wilhelm Knoepfmacher, 6 August 1870, *Briefe*, p. 14.
7. 17 September 1874, *Jugendbriefe*, p. 74.
8. *The Interpretation of Dreams*, *GW* II/III, 213.
9. *Jugendbriefe*, p. 50.
10. *Jugendbriefe*, p. 36.
11. *GW* X, 3779f.
12. Unpublished letter transcribed by Michael Molnar.
13. *Briefe* ,p. 29.
14. 13 July 1883, *Briefe*, p. 47–48.
15. *The Motif of Choice between Three Caskets* — *GW* X, 24ff.
16. 27 April 1894, *Freud/Fliess*, p. 129.
17. Manuskript N, *Freud/Fliess*, p. 268.
18. Manuskript N, *Freud/Fliess*, p. 268.
19. *GW* II/III, 271–73.
20. *GW* II/III, 211, 183, 272, 465, 217.
21. *GW* IX, passim.
22. *Totem and Taboo*, *GW* IX, 186–87, 49, 104.
23. *Freud/A. Zweig*, p. 142.
24. Sonnets 125.
25. *The Interpretation of Dreams*, *GW* II/III, 181, 271; *Delusions and Dreams in Jensen's 'Gradiva'*, *GW* VII, 23. For Lichtenberg, see *The Joke and its Relation to the Unconscious*, *GW* VI, 77.
26. Theodor Reik, *From Forty Years with Freud* (London, 1942), p. 21.
27. 'On Psychotherapy', GW V, 18–19.
28. 'Constructions in Analysis', *GW* XVI, 488–89.
29. 'Towards a History of the Psychoanalytic Movement', *GW* X, 68; 'Timely Thoughts on War and Death', *GW* X, 339.
30. 'Analysis of the Phobia of a Five-Year-Old Boy', *GW* VII, 375.
31. *Jones*, III, 154.
32. *Freud/Jung*, pp. 312, 161.
33. *The Interpretation of Dreams*, *GW* II/III, 427; *The Joke and its Relation to the Unconscious*, *GW* VI, 78; 'Remarks on a Case of Compulsion Neurosis', *GW* VII, 404.
34. *The Interpretation of Dreams*, *GW* II/III, 488.
35. *The Joke and its Relation to the Unconscious*, *GW* VI, 264.
36. *The Interpretation of Dreams*, *GW* II/III, 210; 'The Motif of the Choice between Three Caskets', GW X, 24f.
37. *Gay*, 477.
38. *GW* 108–09, 111.
39. 'On some Neurotic Mechanisms of Jealousy, Paranoia and Homosexuality', *GW* XIII, 197.

40. *The Joke and its Relation to the Unconscious*, *GW* VI, 10, 162; 16 April 1909, *Freud/Jung*, p. 242.
41. 'Mourning and Melancholy', GW X, 432; letter to Arnold Zweig, 31 May 1936, in *Briefe*, p. 445); Reik, *From Forty Years with Freud*, p. 29; letter to Ernst Freud, 19 April 1938, in *Briefe*, p. 434.
42. 19 April 1938, *Briefe*, p. 458.
43. *GW* X, 367f.
44. *Freud/Abraham*, p. 57.
45. *GW* X, 369.
46. 'Selbstdarstellung', *GW* XIV, 34; letter of 18 July 1908, *Freud/Jung*, p. 183.
47. *The Man Moses and the Monotheistic Religion*, *GW* XVI, 103f.
48. 'Obsession and Phobias', *GW* I, 350.
49. *GW* II/III, 272–73; letter to Lytton Strachey, 25 December 1928, *Briefe*, p. 400; 'Some Character Types. . .', *GW* X, 375.
50. Some Character Types. . .', *GW* X, 373–75.
51. 'Finite and Infinite Analysis', GW XVI, 69.
52. Some Character Types. . .', *GW* X, 379–80.
53. 17 July 1914; quoted by Ilse Grubrich-Simitis, *Zurück zu Freuds Texten* (Frankfurt a.M., 1993), p. 154.
54. Letter to Martha Bernays, 3 December 1885, *Briefe*, p. 192; *Introductory Lectures on* Psychoanalysis, GW XI, 8; letter to Otto Rank, 27 August 1924, quoted in Ronald Clark's *Freud. The Man and the Cause*, p. 455; *Fragment of an Analysis of Hysteria*, *GW* V, 272.
55. 'The Uncanny', *GW* XII, 230, 262–63, 249.
56. *Freud/Pfister*, pp. 33, 64.

CHAPTER 2

Demolished Idols and Satanic Spokesmen

Freud's attempts to link the sequence of Shakespeare's plays to events in the dramatist's own life — particularly the deaths of his father and young son suggestively called Hamnet — depended heavily on a book on Shakespeare by the Danish critic Georg Brandes (1847–1931), whose German version was published in 1896. What *The Interpretation of Dreams* sees as signs of Shakespeare's increasing revulsion from sexuality, from *Hamlet* to *Timon of Athens*,[1] relies heavily on Brandes's chronology; and Brandes's account of the deaths of Shakespeare's father and young son enters materially into Freud's determination to use Shakespeare's plays to look into 'the deepest impulses in the creative poet's soul'. But he also issues a warning:

> Just as all neurotic symptoms, and even dreams, can be interpreted in multiple ways, and indeed demand such interpretation if one wants to understand them, so every genuine poetic creation will have more than one motive and will have sprung from more than one prompting in the poet's soul.[2]

Brandes's book alerted Freud to the work of Shakespeare's immediate predecessors and contemporaries. This had some curious consequences. Freud was haunted for years by a phrase that mirrored his own response to the helplessness of the newborn: 'O inch of nature!' He attributed it to Shakespeare, but never managed to track it to its source. Years after Freud's death Norman Holland, in his perennially useful book *Psychoanalysis and Shakespeare*, traced the phrase, via Brandes, to one of the sources of Shakespeare's *Pericles*: George Wilkins's *The Painful Adventures of Pericles Prince of Tyre*.

Preoccupation with Shakespeare led Freud to a study of his sources. His appetite for these was whetted by Brandes's book, and he sought to satisfy it further by purchasing authoritative collections by Rudolf Fischer and Alois Brandl. Published in 1914 and 1922 respectively, these brought together texts Shakespeare might have used in the composition of *Romeo and Juliet* and *King Lear*; Freud had them on his shelves in Vienna, and thought sufficiently highly of them to transfer them to his London house when he emigrated to England in 1938.

Before he made these purchases Freud had already been able to savour some characteristic Elizabethan prose when Ernest Jones had sent him extracts from a work first published in 1594. This was *The Terrors of the Night, or, A Discourse of Apparitions* by Thomas Nashe (1567–1601). Freud was sufficiently impressed to pass these enclosures on to the editors of the *Zentralblatt für Psychoanalyse* as examples of psychologically significant anticipations of psychoanalytic studies of dream and nightmare. The editors wrote back to say that they could not include such difficult texts, with their sixteenth-century spellings, in a foreign language, but would be glad to consider including a translation. Freud was too busy to provide this, and the matter was dropped.[3] Eighteen years later, however, Jones tried again, and sent Freud the same extracts; no response by Freud has been preserved, but Jones made sure he saw them by including both in his book *On the Nightmare*, published by the Hogarth Press in 1931, a copy of which went to Freud in the month of its first appearance in print:

> When Night in her rustie dungeon hath imprisoned our ey-sight, and that we are shut seperatly in our chambers from resort, the divell keepeth his audit in our sin-guilty consciences, no sense but surrenders to our memorie a true bill of parcels of his detestable impietis. The table of our hart is turned to an index of iniquities, and all our thoughts are nothing but texts to condemn us. The rest we take in our beds is such another kinde of rest as the weerie traveller taketh in the coole soft grasse in summer, who thinking there to lye at ease, and refresh his tyred limmes, layeth his fainting head unawares on a loathsome neast of snakes [. . .] Therefore are the terrors of the night more than of the day, because the sinnes of the night surmount the sinnes of the day.[4]

Jones adds a Freudian footnote to this passage: 'Psychoanalytical readers will observe the interesting Oedipus symbolism here'.[5] The second extract Jones thinks particularly likely to engage Freud's interest also figures prominently in *On the Nightmare*:

> It will bee demaunded why the likenes of ones father or mother, or kinsfolks, he (the devil) oftentimes presents himselfe unto us? No other reason can bee guiven of it but this, that in those shapes which hee supposeth most familiar to us, and that wee are inclined to with a naturall kind of love, we will sooner hearken to him than otherwise.[6]

Jones hardly needed to point out how such passages as this confirmed Freud's frequently made observation that imaginative writers had seen centuries ago what he attempted to codify in *The Interpretation of Dreams* and its successors.

A collection of essays by Georg Brandes entitled *Miniaturen*, published in Berlin in 1912, led Freud to marginalia Gabriel Harvey (*c.*1550–1631) had written into some of the books he owned, which had been collected and edited by A. B. Grosart in 1884–85. May of these referred to contemporary writers, including Spenser, Sidney, and Shakespeare. From these Brandes had extracted some dates which, Freud reports with some consternation in a letter to Ernest Jones dated 24 January 1921, made it highly likely that *Hamlet* was written at least two years before the death of Shakespeare's father — the event which, in Freud's view, had triggered the composition of that play. Jones sought to reassure him, in a letter of 3 February 1921, that Freud's theory could still be defended, and Freud never allowed his discovery of Harvey's marginalia to alter the dating on which so much of his conception of how Shakespeare came to write *Hamlet* depended. Here as elsewhere he fell victim to that biographical fallacy which held that an author's work must necessarily reflect the circumstances and tenor of his life at the time of writing.[7]

★ ★ ★

Shakespeare's history plays, and what Brandes's narrative of the dramatist's life and times could tell him, aroused Freud's interest in early British history. They pointed him to the *Chronicles of England, Scotland and Wales* by Raphael Holinshed (*c.*1520–*c.*1580), which enabled him to examine some of the ways in which Shakespeare modified his sources for his own dramatic purposes. He was particularly interested in changes Shakespeare made in Holinshed's account of the reign of Macbeth, and found two of them especially telling. The first of these was Shakespeare's psychologically profound elaboration of the character of Lady Macbeth, who is only briefly mentioned by Holinshed as an ambitious wife eager to see her husband become king and herself queen. The other modification concerned time-scale — the change from the slow evolution and degeneration of Macbeth over ten or more years in the Chronicle to the dramatically far more effective rapidity of the same events in the play. Freud recognized the justification for this, but found that it gave Shakespeare less scope for developing the tragedy of childlessness which linked the concerns of Macbeth with those of Elizabeth I.

The interest in British history that led Freud to Holinshed induced him also to acquire and study Thomas Babington Macaulay's *History of England* (1849–55); and not surprisingly he became fascinated particularly by the story of the Tudor dynasty and its relation to Shakespeare's plays and fortunes. In *The Interpretation of Dreams* Freud recalls a schoolfriend who seemed to have modelled himself, in later life, on Henry VIII — presumably because of his marital adventures.[8] Far more often, however, Freud delved into the history of Elizabeth I, whose relations with the Earl of Essex and, especially, with Mary Queen of Scots opened up intriguing psychological speculations — almost invariably in a Shakespearean rather than a Schillerian context. In 'Some Character Types encountered in Psychoanalytic Practice', for instance, and in a letter to Lytton Strachey to be considered again later, Freud seeks to show that when the question of succession is raised in *Macbeth*, Shakespeare had the problems of Queen Elizabeth in mind, who had remained without issue and had found herself forced to accept as her most likely successor the son of a queen who had been a guest in her country, as Duncan had been in Macbeth's castle, and for whose death she had been responsible, even though, unlike Macbeth, she had not personally wielded the instrument that cut off the life that stood in her way.

In *Totem and Taboo* Queen Elizabeth turns up again, in a non-Shakespearean context this time. She is introduced as testing the fabled efficacy of the royal touch in healing scrofula, 'the King's evil'. It had not been renamed 'the Queen's evil'; but despite this Elizabeth was, Freud reports, 'prepared as little as any of her successors to waive this royal prerogative'. Having mentioned her successors, Freud warms to his subject:

> Charles I is said to have cured a hundred sick persons at a stroke in 1633. Under his licentious son Charles II, after the great English Revolution had been overcome, these royal cures of scrofula had their mightiest flowering.[9]

This touches on another of Freud's favourite subjects in British history: the 'great English revolution', which precipitated one of Freud's cultural heroes to British leadership. He is, of course, Oliver Cromwell who, amongst his other feats, had facilitated the readmission of the Jews into the England from which they had been barred since medieval times. Freud put his seal on his devotion to Cromwell by naming his second son Oliver in Cromwell's honour. He took little interest in English monarchs after that, glancing briefly at what he thought the corruption at the court of Charles II. He sought out the portrait of William III in the London Portrait Gallery, judging him, on the strength of his physiognomy, to have been 'clever and perverse'.[10]

★ ★ ★

The most interesting context, however, into which Freud introduced Shakespeare when discussing men and women who affected the fate of nations, is an American one: the 'psychological study' of President Woodrow Wilson in which Freud agreed to collaborate with William C. Bullitt. Freud never sanctioned the publication of this grossly biased study, in which his anti-American prejudices combined with Bullitt's personal grudges. When it was ultimately published in London in 1967, Freud had long been dead and Bullitt had sole command of the text. How much of it Freud would have approved is impossible to say — only a few scraps of his autograph have survived. There is, however, one exception: a short Introduction credited to Freud alone.[11] Here Freud sets his American subject into a triple literary context, uniting great writers from three European language communities: Goethe, Cervantes, and — of course — Shakespeare.

Wilson, Freud argues, was a weak and neurotic man who allowed the good intentions expressed in his 'Fourteen Points' to be swamped and swept away by less well-intentioned men at the Versailles Congress that dictated such excessively hard terms to the defeated enemy. He thus became, in Freud's eyes, the polar opposite of Mephisto, who declares himself, in Goethe's *Faust*, a part of the power that desires evil but creates good:

> Ein Teil von jener Kraft,
> Die stets das Böse will und stets das Gute schafft.

At this point Freud stops in his tracks. Is he not letting his anti-religious bias, which links Wilson with the German Emperor Wilhelm II as leaders who thought themselves appointed and inspired by God, his resentment at the terms imposed on Germany and Austria after the First World War, and his anti-American prejudices, run away with his judgement? This leads him to the introduction of another, far more sympathetic literary figure, to whom he might liken Wilson: 'A measure of sympathy developed; but sympathy of a special sort mixed with pity, such as one feels when reading Cervantes for his hero, the naïve cavalier of La Mancha'.[12] Wilson was self-deluded like Don Quixote, but faced with a far more daunting task than Cervantes's lovable hero: a task affecting the fate of nations for which his temperament was unsuited. 'When one compares the strength of the man to the greatness of the task he had taken upon himself, this pity was so great that it conquered every other emotion'.

This gives Freud his signal for a psychoanalytic explanation of the weakness and neuroses he detects in Wilson's character — involving the theory of a 'quantitative mechanism' affecting 'the elementary material of psychic phenomena' which he had evolved in sympathy with nineteenth-century physics:

> The relative strength of any one of the many instincts which supply the psychic energy, the especial depth of one of those identifications upon which ordinarily the character is constructed, an exceptionally strong reaction-formation against which an impulse must be repressed — such quantitative factors decide the final form of a personality, stamp upon it a certain individuality and direct its activity into a certain channel.[13]

Freud now calls on Shakespeare to provide a counter-image:

> in his description of the dead Brutus, Shakespeare's Mark Antony says:
>
> The elements
> So mixed in him that nature might stand up
> And say to all the world: 'This was a man!'
>
> As a footnote to these words of the poet we are tempted to declare that the elements of the psychic constitution are always the same. What changes in the mixture is the quantitative proportion of the elements and, we must add, their location in different fields of the psychic life and their attachment to different objects.[14]

Wilson's early development had ensured, in Freud's eyes, that he was not as fortunate in 'the quantitative proportion of the elements and [. . .] their location in different fields of the psychic life' as Shakespeare's Brutus: he therefore deserved pity rather than the scorn which the rest of the book, whose final text was not under Freud's control, heaps on him.

I said earlier that when Freud speaks of *The Merchant of Venice*, Shylock never enters the picture. Shylock does, however, intrude unexpectedly into the final chapter of the prejudiced and one-sided portion of the book which contrasts strikingly with Freud's more balanced Introduction. He does so, strangely enough, in the guise of David Lloyd George:

> The British Prime Minister, who wished to turn the 'hell peace' into a 'heaven peace', was unwilling to abandon one molecule of the British pound of flesh. Thus the tragedy of the Peace Conference was lightened in its last days by the comic though somewhat nauseating spectacle of the little Welsh Shylock, his pound of flesh safely in his pocket, preaching unselfishness — for others.

This is so unlike anything Freud says of British statesmen past and present, and so counter to his favourable image of Britain, that I feel safe in assigning this passage to the pen of Bullitt alone.

My scrutiny of Freud's Introduction to the worst book ever associated with his name should help to redress the inevitably skewed perspective that results from a focus on Freud's knowledge and use of Anglophone authors. We must see his literary references as part of a network of allusions and quotations that range over many language communities — far more, in fact, than even our brief glance at the German and Spanish as well as the English inhabitants of his cultural world could suggest.

* * *

The contemporary of Shakespeare who influenced Freud's thinking most profoundly was the great demolisher of the Idols of the Tribe, the Marketplace and the Theatre: Francis Bacon, Lord Verulam (1561–1626). He had no truck with the theory that Bacon also wrote the plays of Shakespeare — no genius could be as universal as that! — and first mentions Bacon in a letter to Eduard Silberstein dated 2 August 1873, alongside Descartes, as essential reading for anyone seriously interested in philosophy.[15] Four years later he found his admiration confirmed and strengthened by Macaulay's essay on Bacon, which placed his ideas and their expression into the context of his life and times in a way Freud deemed 'the most perfect possible'.[16]

In Freud's published writing Bacon appears in two guises. The first is that of a pioneer of empirical research — and what Freud calls 'research without presuppositions' (*voraussetzunglose Forschung*) in his essay on 'A Childhood Reminiscence by Leonardo da Vinci'.[17] The second, obviously related to the first, makes him a forerunner of Sir James Frazer: Bacon is cited in *Totem and Taboo* as an ethnologically important recorder of beliefs he did not necessarily make his own, such ss that which ascribes to a sword that has inflicted a wound the power to heal that wound.[18]

The Freud Museum in London preserves three relevant items from Freud's library: one in English (*The Works of Lord Bacon, Moral and Historical*, 1877); one in Latin (*Novum Organum*, 1779); and one in German. The German volume, a translation of the Latin one under the title *Franz Bacons Neues Organ der Wissenschaften*, translated and introduced by Anton Theobald Brück in 1830, Freud had acquired from the patient he called Cäcilie M., whose real name was Anna von Lieven. In this last volume Freud marked several passages in Brück's Introduction: one of these called Bacon 'a thought of light in Mankind's head' ('ein Lichtgedanke im Kopfe der Menschheit') — a rather florid way of making him a precursor of the Age of Enlightenment or *Aufklärung*. Other passages Freud marked in this Introduction commend Bacon's 'athletic art of strengthening the powers of reason'; pronounce his understanding of the natural world superior to that of other philosophic luminaries; stress the psychological truths conveyed by the Greek myth of Narcissus; and declare Bacon a worthy contemporary and compatriot of the greatest psychologist and poet — who, of course, is Shakespeare. In the *Novum Organum* itself Freud's marginal markings draw attention to Bacon's belief that something not yet achieved needs an as yet unexamined method to make it happen; stress the role of accident and empirical groping in human inventiveness; assert that when one wins popular approval one must at once examine where one has gone *wrong*; and suggest that in the history of science alchemists fill the role of the dying man who tells his sons to dig for a treasure hidden in his vineyards — they found no gold, but the digging improved their crops.

The volume of Macaulay's essays that contained the piece on Bacon which Freud praised highly has not been preserved among his books; but he will have assented to passages that lauded Bacon as 'the great apostle of experimental philosophy'; as one who was able to 'pile high' because he 'dug deep', coupling 'attention, sagacity and judgement' with common sense; and one who exposed the 'Idols' that produced errors of judgement. That Macaulay thought it worthwhile to mention that Bacon took an interest in the way our daytime activities affect our dreams can only have increased Freud's respect for Bacon's insights.

But how empirical were Freud's methods? Much of his dream interpretation seemed arbitrary to intelligent patients from the 'Wolf Man' to Hilda Doolittle — they complained that he rode roughshod over their objections. In Karin Obholzer's *The Wolf Man Sixty Years Later, Conversations with Freud's Controversial Patient* Sergei Pankejeff tells his interviewer that even his famous cognomen was an unjustified invention: the dream he related to Freud was of white *dogs*, not wolves! 'The Dog Man' would not have had the same resonance as 'The Wolf Man', and Freud would not have been able to build the same folklore edifice over his analysis. We learn that Freud tried to redirect his patient's self-perception by telling him that though he could not now remember the events Freud's interpretation placed at the root of his illness, memory of them would return, with liberating and healing effect — but it never in fact surfaced. Failure to accept Freud's Oedipal analyses was brushed aside; only Freud's version counted. Such refusal to take his patients' objections into serious consideration hardly qualified as Baconian empiricism! Had Freud lived in Bacon's time, the latter could have added 'the Idols of the Analyst's Couch' to his famous four. This is just one of several instances in which Freud deviated from paths he believed, or claimed, he was following — including some he had set himself.

Macaulay's praise of Bacon's literary style was reinforced, in Freud's experience, by Ernest Jones, who drew his attention to Bacon's *Essays* — in particular to a characteristic sentence whose sentiments and expression chimed in so well with Freud's own: 'We know diseases of stoppings and suffocations as the most dangerous in the body; it is not much otherwise in the mind'.[19] This contribution to the 'theory of anxiety', Jones added, showed a degree of psychological insight that Baconians might be able to quote in support of Bacon's authorship of the plays ascribed to Shakespeare — which, of course, neither Freud nor Jones believed.[20] Freud's letter to Martha Bernays, dated 22 January 1883, disposed of Baconianism by arguing how unlikely it was that so disparate a body of work had been produced by one and the same person. Such a prodigy would have had to possess 'the most powerful brain the world has ever produced'.[21] Freud told Lytton Strachey on 25 December 1928 that he had 'always ridiculed the Baconian hypothesis', but went on to say that he found merit in Thomas Looney's equally unlikely proposition that Shakespeare was a front for Edward de Vere, the seventeenth Earl of Oxford.[22]

Late in life Freud acquired an edition of *The Anatomy of Melancholy* by Robert Burton (1577–1640), published by the Tudor Publishing Company of New York in 1938. This was, of course, a subject of great interest to Freud, whose essay 'Mourning and Melancholia' is one of the classics of the subject.[23] By the time Burton's book came into his hands, however, he was already mortally ill; he never commented on it, and his copy, still to be seen in the London Freud Museum, shows no sign of prolonged use.

* * *

The young Freud's most intense literary experience of post-Shakespearean English poetry was his encounter with Milton's *Paradise Lost.* A letter to Martha Bernays, dated 28 August 1883, calls Milton 'an even greater poet than Goethe' — high praise indeed from a man whole lifelong reverence for Goethe's writings was matched only by his equal reverence for Shakespeare's. In his letter Freud condensed lines 183–89 into one half-line as a prelude to lines 190–91 of Satan's speech to the infernal assembly:

> [Let us consult]
> What reinforcement we may gain from hope,
> If not, what resolution from despair.

He applies these lines to his own feelings, and Martha's, about their long absences from each other without immediate hope of being joined in the marriage they both desired; but he clearly relished their sonorous sound and their powerfully antithetical style, calling them 'the most sublime expression' of a state of mind analogous to Freud's own.[24]

Thirteen years later, answering a questionnaire from the publisher Hugo Heller, Freud listed *Paradise Lost* among his favourite books; but in a lifetime of writing crammed with quotations and near-quotations from Shakespeare and Goethe, no other quotation from Milton turned up in his work. The Freud Museum, however, has preserved Freud's two-volume copy of *Milton's Poetical Works*, edited by George Gilfillan in 1853, in which Freud's marginal marking draws attention to some lines from Mammon's speech in *Paradise Lost*, Book II:

> Our greatness will appear
> Then most conspicuous, when great things of small,
> Useful of hurtful, prosperous of adverse
> We can create, and in what place so e're
> Thrive under evil, and work ease out of pain
> Through labour and endurance.

The antithetical construction of this passage appealed to Freud, whose own way of thinking ran to antitheses which needed to be dialectically resolved; and working 'ease out of pain | Through labour and endurance' was something Freud, who said that he worked best when at least slightly unwell, knew from his own experience. He also, of course, sought to 'work ease out of pain' in his psychological practice.

Freud's edition of Milton's works included some biographical details; he learnt about Milton's work for Cromwell's commonwealth, and recalled Milton's visit to Galileo's house in Florence when he paid his own tribute to that great scientific pioneer by visiting the tower in which Galileo had conducted his experiments.[25] Milton thus took his place in that pantheon of superheroes which included not only Goethe and Shakespeare, but also Galileo and Cromwell.

The question that now has to be faced is: how much beyond Books I and II did Freud ever read this 'favourite book' of his? This must remain speculation; but two features of his thinking receive memorable treatment in the later books of *Paradise*

Lost. The first of these is Milton's take on the nature and place of women. Book IV reflects, in lines 296–99, on God's creation of Adam and Eve:

> Not equal, as their sex not equal seemed;
> For contemplation he and valour formed,
> For softness she and sweet attractive grace,
> He for God only, she for God in him [. . .];

and if he had penetrated as far as Book X, he would have seen Adam's angry reflection that this female 'novelty on earth' constituted a 'fair defect of Nature'. Milton's reference to God could have been dealt with as Freud did with Prince Hal's 'Thou owest God a death', where, as we found earlier, he simply substituted the word 'Nature' for that of the deity. There is no sign, however, that Freud ever milked Milton's epic for the symbolic and ethnological implications he sought to draw out in *Totem and Taboo.*

One religious notion for which Freud sought hard to find a secular equivalent is that of Original Sin; and critics as distinguished as Lionel Trilling have found in his work the influence of Milton's depiction of the Fall in Books IX and X of *Paradise Lost.* But Freud hardly needed Milton for that — he knew his Bible well, and could have absorbed much Christian doctrine from his Catholic nurse, his long residence in Catholic Vienna, and his study of Christian writers in many lands. It is, however, striking that this avowed enemy of all religion should count one of the greatest Christian epics among his favourite books. But then, as we have just seen, Freud found spokesmen for his own feelings among Milton's devils rather than the unfallen angels. Ever since he had had a vision of hell when he saw gas-jets in the streets during an early journey, hell had always been nearer to his thoughts than heaven. Like Milton himself according to Blake, Freud was of the Devil's party rather than Nobodaddy's.

As always, however, Freud's thinking developed in more complicated ways than might at first appear. Another dimension is opened by a passage in an as yet unpublished letter to Martha Bernays to which the Director of the London Freud Museum has kindly drawn my attention. The letter is dated 12 July 1883:

> I don't know how it occurred to me today that everyone should choose some great and powerful individual as his domestic god and protective patron, to whom he turns in dark and solemn hours. I seized on Milton and his sublime magic, which can waft me away like nothing else out of the silent unsatisfying present, so that the earth lies in the universe like a tiny point and the wide heaven opens itself.

Does that not sound like that 'oceanic feeling' which Romain Rolland saw as the basis of all religious feeling and which Freud, in later years, denied having experienced himself?[26] Does it not lend substance to the view that the later Freud deliberately stifled such impulses in himself, deflecting them into feelings like that which he had in the face of Leonardo's paintings, when he said that they 'breathe a kind of mysticism into whose mystery one dare not penetrate'?[27] Deflecting them above all into Freudian psychoanalysis itself, with its surrogates for confession and original sin, its disciples clustering around a prophet, its conclave for watching over heresies, its passionate denunciations of 'heretics' like Jung and Adler? I have argued this case against more orthodox commentators in another place,[28] where I have also sought to relate these stifled feelings to Freud's pervasive sense of the demonic which the opening chapter of the present book has already documented and which Freud's stress on the sayings of Milton's fallen angels has served to confirm. For even when Freud has a mystical sense of being wafted into the high heavens and seeing the universe beneath him as a tiny point, his vision is akin to that of Satan at the very end of Book II of *Paradise Lost*:

> Far off the Empyreal Heav'n, extended wide
> In circuit, undetermined square or round,
> Of living Saphire, once his native Seat;
> And fast by hanging in a golden Chain
> This pendant world, in bigness as a Star
> Of smallest Magnitude close by the Moon [. . .]

Freud's sympathies are with the angel expelled from 'his native Seat' because he was not content to 'serve in Heaven', rather than with those who blithely continued singing hymns of praise to the Lord.

There was a further reason why Freud should have felt so drawn to the poet who made Satan the most charismatic figure in this tale of the loss of paradise — an idyllic region whose inhabitants were forbidden to taste the fruit that would give them a knowledge of good and evil. The poet who defined his purpose as justifying the ways of God to men was also a man of political action, championing Oliver Cromwell against Charles I and playing a prominent part in the Commonwealth as an essayist and pamphleteer. *The Interpretation of Dreams* proclaimed Cromwell one of Freud's culture heroes, calling the man who facilitated the return of Jews to England after centuries of banishment 'a great historical personality, who had powerfully attracted me in my boyhood, especially after my stay in England'. Self-identification with Cromwell, he goes on to say, was part of a repressed longing for greatness ('unterdrückte Größensensehnsucht'), which he transferred onto his children.[29] We have already heard him speak of the Commonwealth that followed the execution of Charles I as 'the Great English Revolution'; and he devalued the restoration of the monarchy by characterizing Charles II, in *Totem and Taboo*, as 'zuchtlos' — licentious and undisciplined.[30]

⋆ ⋆ ⋆

It has often been noticed that Freud's ultimate view of life had affinities with that which Thomas Hobbes (1588–1679) advanced so memorably in his *Leviathan, or The Matter, Form and Power of a Commonwealth, Ecclesiastical and Civil* (1651). We do not know if he ever owned and studied a copy of *Leviathan*; but two key passages from this book found their way into his work by courtesy of later authors, shedding light on the charge of being 'zuchtlos' we have just heard him bring against Charles II. The first of these is John Stuart Mill, whose 'Notes on Socialism' included the famous passage in which Hobbes characterized what Rousseau and others would later glorify as the 'State of Nature'. In such a state, Hobbes maintains, 'men live without other security than what their own strength, and their own invention, can furnish them withal':

> In such condition, there is no place for industry; because the fruit thereof is uncertain; and consequently no culture of the earth; no navigation, nor use of the commodities that may be imported by sea; no commodious building; no instruments of moving, and removing, such things as require much force; no knowledge of the face of the earth; no account of time; no arts; no letters; no society; and which is worst of all, continual fear, and danger of violent death; and the life of man, solitary, poor, nasty, brutish and short. (*Leviathan*, Part I, ch. 13)

Freud will have remembered this well, for he translated it in 1880 for Volume XII of Theodor Gomperz's edition of German versions of Mill's works. His version tightens the passage up even more and transposes some of its components, so that the famous list of adjectives in the final sentence is now headed by 'Kurz' ('short'). He also prefers Germanic to Latinate words, 'regelmässige Arbeit' to 'Industrie'. The German word 'Industrie' had acquired a specialized meaning in the nineteenth century, which distinguished it from 'Arbeit' and might have misled Freud's contemporaries in associating it with later industrial developments. The efficacy of Freud's translation in no way lags behind Hobbes's powerful original.

> Unter solchen Verhältnissen ist kein Raum für regelmäßige Arbeit, weil die Früchte derselben unsicher sind, und demgemäß gibt es keinen Anbau des Bodens, Schiffahrt, keinen Verbrauch von Gütern, welche zur See eingeführt werden, keine behagliche Wohnstätte, keine Werkzeuge, um Dinge, welche viel Kraft erfordern, in Bewegung zu setzen oder von der Stelle zu rücken, keine Kenntniß von der Oberfläche der Erde, keine Zeitrechnung, keine Wissenschaft, keine Kunst, keine Gesellschaft, und was das Schlimmste ist, beständige Gefahr und Furcht vor einem gewaltsamen Tode in einem kurzen, einsamen, armseligen, ekeln und thierischen Leben.[31]

This view of a state of nature far removed from that inhabited by Rousseau's noble savage, of a chaos that called for a strong authority capable of mastering it, bears a striking resemblance not only to Freud's darker view of society, but also to a chaotic Id held in check, sometimes painfully, by a strong Superego. The translation also allows a glimpse of Freud's masterly command of idiomatic and rhythmically distinguished German.

The other quotation from *Leviathan* enters the later editions of *The Interpretation of Dreams* via Havelock Ellis's 'The World of Dreams' — one of the many articles Ellis devoted to a subject of such great interest to Freud. 'If', we read in Section VII of *The Interpretation of Dreams*, 'we call the direction the psychic process takes from the Unconscious into a waking state "progressive", we may say that dreams have a "regressive" character'. A footnote is added to this; it shows, among other things, how Hobbes's *Leviathan* anticipated this view of contrary motion in a single lapidary sentence: 'In sum, our dreams are the reverse of our waking imaginations, the motion, when we are awake, beginning at one end, and when we dream at another'.[32]

* * *

This chapter has attempted to show how Freud's interest in English writings of the sixteenth and seventeenth centuries led him to a great poet, John Milton, who served as spokesman and pamphleteer to the government of an English statesman Freud particularly revered: Oliver Cromwell. What made the most lasting impression on him, however, was *Paradise Lost*, which yielded Satanic figures that could be made spokesmen for his own feelings and concerns in the same way as Goethe's Mephisto. *Paradise Lost* also ministered to a sense of the mystical, an 'oceanic feeling' that had been fostered by a Czech nurse in Freud's childhood, and had been sporadically reawakened by conversations with the philosopher Franz Brentano, the 'aura' of Notre Dame de Paris, and the paintings of Leonardo, but had been deliberately stifled by his programmatic hostility to religion.

The chapter has also shown how two great thinkers of the time could be enlisted in support of Freud's developing world-view, while strengthening, at the same time, his respect for the expressive power of the English language: Francis Bacon, seen as the fountainhead of British empiricism, and Thomas Hobbes, whose dark vision of the 'state of nature' could be a wholesome corrective of Rousseau's vision of the 'noble savage'. Georg Brandes's book on Shakespeare led Freud to Raphael Holinshed, whose chronicles satisfied further an interest in British history that began with his delight in Shakespeare's history plays and his veneration of Oliver Cromwell. Reading Brandes's book, and struggling with differing interpretations of Shakespeare, led Freud to a conclusion which not only readers of imaginative literature but readers of Freud's own writings would do well to remember: that no interpretation tells the whole story, that literary texts no less than dreams and neurotic symptoms are polyvalent and will reveal facets to some interpreters which their predecessors ignored or missed. This did not, however, lead Freud to the conclusion that all interpretations were equally valid. Even Goethe, he found, had failed to detect the deeper springs of Hamlet's inaction. Like all previous interpreters Goethe had only revealed a partial truth in *Wilhelm Meister's Apprenticeship*: a deeper solution had to wait, Freud believed, for psychoanalysis and the 'discovery' of the Oedipus Complex. That this 'discovery' led so many of Freud's followers into a wearisome hunt for the same complex in whatever works of whatever literary merit came under their scrutiny should not blind us to the partial illumination it brought, in analyses by Freud and Ernest Jones, to the ever-fascinating mysteries of *Hamlet*.

Last but not least: admiration of Cromwell and the 'English Revolution' led Freud, in a letter to Martha Bernays dated 16 August 1882, to eloquent praise of England's 'sober industriousness and sensitive feeling for justice'. His visit to England, he explains, had a 'decisive influence' on his life, bringing enthusiasm for 'the history of the island' and 'the works of the men who were my real teachers — all of them English or Scotch'.[33] Here Freud is clearly speaking from the heart, without the need to demolish idols or adopt Satanic spokesmen.

Notes to Chapter 2

1. *GW* II/III, 272
2. *GW* II/III, 272.
3. 14 and 30 January 1912, *Freud/Jones*, pp. 124 and 130.
4. Ernest Jones, *On the Nightmare* (London, 1931), pp. 78–79.
5. *On the Nightmare*, p. 79. The transcriptions are those made by Jones.
6. *On the Nightmare*, p. 169.
7. *Freud/Jones*, pp. 404, 407.
8. *GW* II/III, 217.
9. *GW* IX, 54.
10. *Reisebriefe*, p. 253.
11. Sigmund Freud and William C. Bullitt, *Thomas Woodrow Wilson, Twenty-eighth President of the United States. A Psychological Study* (London, 1967), pp. xi–xvi.
12. Freud and Bullitt, *Thomas Woodrow Wilson*, p. xiii.
13. Freud and Bullitt, *Thomas Woodrow Wilson*, p. iv.
14. Freud and Bullitt, *Thomas Woodrow Wilson*, p. iv.
15. *Jugendbriefe*, p. 36.
16. 15 August and 7 September 1877, *Jugendbriefe*, pp. 188, 190.
17. *GW* VIII, 131.
18. *GW* IX, 102.
19. 'On Friendship'.
20. *Freud/Jones*, p. 215.
21. *Jones*, III, 459.
22. *Briefe*, p. 400.
23. *GW* X, pp. 428–46.
24. *Briefe*, p. 54.
25. 6 September 1896, *Reisebriefe*, p. 66.
26. *Civilization and its Discontents, GW* XIV, 421–22.
27. *GW* VIII, 189.
28. S. S. Prawer, 'A Change of Direction? Sigmund Freud between Goethe and Darwin', *Publications of the English Goethe Society*, 76 (2007), 109–10.
29. *GW* II/III 450.
30. *GW* IX, 54.
31. Gompaz's edition of Mill's works, translated into German (1880): XII, 220.
32. *GW* II/III, 547.
33. Quoted by Peter Gay in *Reading Freud: Explorations and Entertainments* (New Haven and London, 1980), pp. 67–68.

CHAPTER 3

❖

Enlightenment

Freud's reading of eighteenth-century British texts continued the interest he had shown in British empiricist traditions. This led him to John Locke (1632–1704), whose *Essay Concerning Human Understanding* (1690) had prepared the way for the British Enlightenment of the next century. It also provided a good example of a gentlemanly style — it had, after all, originated, as Locke explained, in conversations and discussions between like-minded friends. As Freud explained in a letter to Silberstein dated 15 March 1875, he had been alerted to Locke's writings by the philosopher Franz Brentano, whose lectures he had attended in the University of Vienna, and with whom he had also had some private contact. Brentano had declared Locke's argument 'höchst geistreich' — spirited, intelligent, and ingenious. He followed up the interest Brentano had aroused by buying a copy of Locke's *Essay* and underlining some passages in its opening section — the section that set itself to refute the notion that there were 'innate principles in the mind'. Whether Freud, who stressed the imprinting of the human mind not only by experiences in infancy but also by the experience of previous generations, could wholly assent to Locke's conception of the neonate mind as a *tabula rasa* is difficult to make out, though his stubborn adherence to the Lamarckian belief in the heritability of acquired characteristics and his views on predisposition to homosexuality might argue against it. His psychoanalytic practice and the theories based upon it were not materially affected by the epistemological problems Locke's *Essay* had raised.

The interest in John Locke which Brentano had stimulated remained sufficiently strong to make Freud curious about Locke's physical likeness when he visited the National Portrait Gallery during his stay in London in 1908. He coupled his notes on the portrait he saw with notes on a portrait of Isaac Newton, whose theories of gravity, light, and colour Freud would praise as enduring feats of scientific investigation in his *New Introductory Lectures on Psychoanalysis*, first published in 1933.[1] Strangely enough, the portraits of these great British thinkers and writers prompted Freud to make the general observation that philosophers tend to be 'gauntly emaciated'.[2]

Before investing in his own copy of the *Essay Concerning Human Understanding* Freud had already acquired the *Essays Literary, Moral and Political* which David Hume (1711–76) had published in the early 1740s. He paid Hume's work the compliment of careful reading, marking it with underlinings and marginal lines. The opening sentences of the very first essay combine two qualities Freud valued particularly highly: psychological subtlety and a style easily accessible to the 'common reader' with whom Dr Johnson rejoiced to concur.

> Some people are subject to a certain *delicacy of passion*, which makes them extremely sensible to all the accidents of life, and gives them a lively joy upon every prosperous event, as well as a piercing grief when they meet with misfortune and adversity. Favours and good offices easily engage their friendship, while the smallest injury provokes their resentment. Any honour or mark of distinction elevates them above measure, but they are sensibly touched with contempt. People of this character have, no doubt, more lively enjoyments, as well as more pungent sorrow, than men of cool and sedate tempers. But, I believe, when everything is balanced, there is no one who would not rather be of the latter character, were he entirely master of his own disposition. Good or ill fortune is very little at our disposal; and when a person that has this sensibility of temper meets with any misfortune, his sorrow or resentment takes entire possession of him, and deprives him of all relish in the common occurrences of life, the right enjoyment of which forms the chief part of our happiness. Great pleasures are much less frequent than great pains, so that a sensible temper must meet with fewer trials in the former way than in the latter. Not to mention, that men of such lively passions are apt to be transported beyond all bounds of prudence and discretion, and to take false steps in the conduct of life which are often irretrievable.[3]

Freud knew, of course, from the philosophy lectures he had so assiduously attended during his time as a medical student, that Hume was a revered figure in the history of classical German philosophy: the thinker whom Kant had acknowledged as having 'awakened [him] from his dogmatic slumbers'; but Freud's sole mention of Hume in his published writings concerns his *Natural History of Religion* (1757). This happens in *Totem and Taboo*, where Freud tries to show that Hume anticipated Feuerbach's claim that it was not God who created man in his own image, but rather men who create their gods in their own likeness. He quotes from Section III of *The Natural History of Religion*: 'There is an universal tendency among mankind to conceive all beings like themselves, and to transfer to every object, those qualities, with which they are familiarly acquainted, and of which they are intimately conscious'.[4] Freud welcomed this passage as confirmation of his own view of the 'illusory' nature of religion, but failed to notice Hume's caveat in Section XIV of his treatise. Hume warned his readers that it was 'not sufficient to observe, that the people, everywhere, degrade their deities in a similitude with themselves, and consider them merely as a species of human creatures, somewhat more potent and intelligent'. Section XV elaborates this by distinguishing between human representations that 'disfigure' the deity, and what he terms 'genuine principles of theism': 'What a noble privilege it is of human reason to attain the knowledge of a supreme Being, and from the visible works of nature be enabled to infer so sublime a principle as its supreme creator?'. But then, Freud did not find the passage he quoted in his copy of Hume. He took it, instead, from a work by an author who had first engaged his interest when he had visited England in 1875. The author was Sir Edward Burnett Tylor (1832–1917), and the work in question was Tylor's *Primitive Culture*, first published in 1871, which stimulated an interest that was to find its fullest expression in Freud's *Totem and Taboo* of 1912–13.

The provenance of Freud's quotation from Hume should alert us to a danger that besets a study like the present: the temptation to assume that because Freud cites a sentence that chimes in with his own views he must have read and pondered the whole work in which it first occurs. This is analogous to the problem that confronted us when considering Freud's veneration *of Paradise Lost*: can we presume him to have read the whole work because he admired the first two books? Did he, as a literary scholar would be bound to do, look up the context of every quotation that engaged his attention? The answer, surely, is that he did not, and that he was sometimes learned in the beginnings of books he never read to the end. It is particularly unfortunate that his annotated edition of Hume's *Essays* which survives is in private hands and has been inaccessible to me. Freud did, however, define one aspect of his respect for Hume's major work at a meeting of the Vienna Psychoanalytical Society on 2 November 1909. What he stressed on that occasion was Hume's importance in the history of epistemology through his questioning of naive beliefs in causality. How do we know that one thing is the cause of another when all we actually experience is *succession*? Psychoanalysis, Freud maintained, had to face the same problem in its own way, and formulate a 'psychology of cognition' ('Psychologie des Erkennens') that would, necessarily, have to dig deeper than Hume.[5]

⋆ ⋆ ⋆

Freud shared his initial interest in British empirical philosophy with his friend Eduard Silberstein; and it was this same friend who presented Freud with an 1875 edition of *The Letters of Junius*, anonymously published between 1769 and 1772 by Sir Philip Francis (1740–1818). Freud preserved this classic example of Whig satire and invective, which acknowledged the influence of the political ideas of Hobbes and Locke, throughout his subsequent life; he still had it on his shelves when he died in London in 1939.

⋆ ⋆ ⋆

Another book which Freud acquired, like his copy of *The Letters of Junius*, in the 1870s, and which he again thought important enough to keep in his library throughout his life, was *An Inquiry into the Nature and Causes of the Wealth of Nations* by Adam Smith (1724–90). He read the 1812 reprint of this book first published in 1776, and pronounced it 'fundamental' — its author's principal, groundbreaking work.[6] It was, in fact, Freud's first contact with a body of thought that stressed the wealth-creating possibilities of the division of labour and free commercial enterprise, which underpinned many of Freud's social attitudes. He never modified them, however, by reading Smith's complementary *Theory of Moral Sentiments* — a book first published in 1759, in which Smith stressed the mutual sympathy that moderated mankind's natural egocentricity.

The *Wealth of Nations* even entered Freud's dreams; it appeared, in what has become known as the 'Hollthurn' dream described in *The Interpretation of Dreams*, alongside another English book: Clerk Maxwell's *Matter and Motion*, first published in 1876. Freud offered no gloss on Smith's book, but found literary and physiological reasons for the appearance of Maxwell's. He links *Matter and Motion*, alliteratively, to Molière's *Malade imaginaire* and both to the line: 'La *ma*tière est-elle laudable' and then builds another alliterative bridge to 'a *mo*tion of the bowels'.[7] I hope others find this explanation more convincing than I do; but I must bow to Freud's superior knowledge of his own thought processes.

No less important than Freud's reading of *The Wealth of Nations* was that of his study of the *Essay on the Principles of Population*, first published in 1798 and reissued in expanded form in 1803, by Thomas Robert Malthus (1766–1834). Malthus's views on the tendency of populations to increase faster than the means of subsistence, which dashed so many optimistic hopes in the nineteenth century, are caricatured by Freud in a letter to Silberstein, who had spoken lightly of kissing his girlfriend:

> It is my duty to refer you to a calculation by the famous statistician Malthus, who proved that kisses strive to increase in uncommonly rapid proportion; after the beginning of the sequence the small area of the face will no longer suffice, so that they will be forced to emigrate. For this reason Malthus is decidedly hostile to kisses — and a budding national economist should respect his authority.[8]

This playful passage shows how well Freud had assimilated the central part of Malthus's argument. He also, however, remembered Malthus's advocacy of celibacy and abstinence as a means of limiting population increase, rather than what he called 'vicious practices', among which he included artificial contraception. Freud agreed with this, believing ever more strongly as time went on that contraception may further the neuroses that drive couples to seek medical and psychiatric help. In 'Sexuality in the Aetiology of Neuroses', first published in a Viennese medical journal in 1898, Freud found that 'Malthusian' considerations increased the readiness of middle-class couples to adopt contraceptive practices either after the birth of their first child, or even at the outset of their marriage. Such 'Malthusian practices', Freud argues in this early essay, often become necessary in the course of a marriage; their increasing number might even prove

> one of the greatest triumphs of the human race, its most palpable liberations from the compulsions to which nature subjects our generation, if it becomes possible to raise procreation to a willed and intended act, freeing it from being linked to the satisfaction of a natural urge.[9]

Such 'triumphs', Freud will come to believe, bring neurotic costs; he will greet Zola's philoprogenitive novel *Fécondité* as a welcome ally in his warning about the supposed neurosis-inducing effects of contraceptive precautions.

Hume, Adam Smith, and Malthus appealed to Freud because their translucent, often elegant, English style increased their importance as pervasive cultural influences within their own country and (in congenial translations) abroad. The writings of the Reverend Sydney Smith (1771–1845) were less well known in Freud's Austria; but he acquired an undated copy of Smith's *Essays Social and Political* in 1879, and brought the book with him to England fifty-nine years later. He found their liberal views on game laws, prisons, transportation of malefactors, and toleration of deviance from Church of England doctrines the more congenial because they were lightened by the sort of humour exemplified by 'Noodle's Oration' in Smith's 'Bentham on Fallacies', with its parody of out-and-out conservatism:

> I profess myself, Sir, an honest and upright member of the British Parliament, and I am not afraid to profess myself an enemy to all change and all innovation. I am satisfied with things as they are; and it will be my pride and pleasure to hand down this country to my children as I received it from those who preceded me. [. . .] I shall end with the memorable words of the assembled Barons — 'Nolimus leges Angliae mutari'.[10]

What Smith is parodying here is exactly the kind of attitude Freud imputed to member of the medical establishment of his time who opposed his theories and practice.

Freud added two observations. The first of these shows that he did not just look at faces individually — he sought to trace resemblances between them that might lead to a useful taxonomy. Smith's face, he notes, resembles that of the Viennese comedian Josef Matras (1832–82). The second follows from this resemblance between two very different humorists: it is only humour, Freud notes, that so presses itself on a person's features, that it seems an integral part of that person's constitution.

When Freud came to translate some of John Stuart Mill's essays for their collected edition in German, he encountered a characteristically liberal-minded passage in Sydney Smith's essay for the *Edinburgh Review* which accorded more with Mill's views than Freud's own, but which he nevertheless translated faithfully into congenial German:

> A great deal has been said of the original difference of capacity between men and women, as if women were more quick and men more judicious — as if women were more remarkable for delicacy of association, and men for stronger powers of attention. All this, we confess, appears to us very fanciful. That there is a difference in the understandings of the men and women we every day meet with, everybody, we suppose, must perceive; but there is none surely which may not be accounted for by the difference of circumstances in which they have been placed, without referring to any conjectural difference of original conformation of mind. As long as boys and girls run about in the dirt, and trundle hoops together, they are both precisely alike. If you catch up one-half of these creatures, and train them to a particular set of actions and opinions, and the other half to a perfectly opposite set, of course their understandings will differ, as one or the other sort of occupations has called this or that talent into action. There is surely no occasion to go into any deeper or more abstruse reasoning, in order to explain so very simple a phenomenon.

Freud's version of the sentence which reads 'As long as boys and girls run about in the dirt, and trundle hoops together, they are both precisely alike' may give a fair idea of a translation that matches its original in solidity of specification, mellifluousness, and idiomatic quality: 'So lange Knaben und Mädchen sich im Strassenkoth herum tummeln and zusammen Reifen rollen, sind sie einander völlig gleich'.[11]

Freud could not have agreed with Smith's refusal to see any difference between male and female 'conformation of mind' that was not due to 'difference of circumstance' — a characteristic extension of Locke's concept of the human mind as initially a *tabula rasa*. As a fair-minded translator, however, he would not let such disagreements interfere with his determination to convey the original author's thoughts and feelings as faithfully as he could. Freud's boisterous 'sich in Strassenkoth herum tummeln' might even be thought an improvement on Smith's more restrained 'running about in the dirt', without distorting the original meaning or impairing the passage's rhythmic felicity.

* * *

We have no record of Freud's reading of any of the writings of either Pope or Dryden; but he was sufficiently aware of Pope's cultural importance to seek out his portrait in the London National Portrait Gallery. He found the painted face considerably less sympathetic than that of Sydney Smith, calling it 'asexual' and adding that it resembled 'the visages of refreshed ecclesiastics'.[12] Freud's phrase 'erquickte Geistlichengesichter' summons up the stereotype of the bibulous monk — I cannot find that this fits any of the four portraits of Pope in the National Portrait Gallery. Does Freud mean 'spiritually illumined', perhaps? Whatever the meaning, it is not based on any intimate acquaintance with Pope's work or the course of his life.

A study such as the present must never lose sight of the fact that Freud in a busy life focused on the creation of what he conceived to be a new 'science' of the mind, and preoccupied with clinical and organizational problems, had neither the time nor the wish to acquire the kind of comprehensive knowledge of English and American literature that one might expect to find in a scholar who made this subject his principal work. He was, however, sensitive to the verbal sound as well as the discursive meaning, of lines or stanzas he came across in his reading or heard recited by others. In his letter to Martha Bernays of 9 July 1883 he quotes such a stanza — a quatrain by Robert Burns (1759–96), taken from the poem which begins 'Ae fond kiss, and then we sever'. Freud makes the verse more palatable to Martha by substituting English 'so' for Scottish 'sae' in Lines 1 and 2:

> Had we never loved so kindly
> Had we never loved so blindly
> Never met and never parted
> We had ne'er been broken-hearted.

He seems never to have known the complete poem, having found this single stanza quoted by Byron; but though he had been impressed by it before meeting Martha, it seemed to him to express perfectly what he felt when having to be parted from her for long periods. And when he wanted to bring home to Eduard Silberstein his love of hill-walking, he quoted 'Mein Herz ist im Hochland', expecting his friend to recognize Burns's 'My heart's in the Highlands' under its popular German translation.[13]

Dreams were the royal road Freud found into the Unconscious: he analysed them in himself, in his patients' accounts, in novels, and in compilations like M. Simon's *Le Monde des rêves*, published in Paris in 1880. They often contained fragments of the dreamers' reading experiences, and they were likely to trigger literary reminiscences in the analyst too. One dream reported by Simon, which featured giants and horses, brought one of the English books Freud had read in his early years vividly to his mind: *Travels into Several Remote Nations of the World by Lemuel Gulliver*, first published in 1726, by Jonathan Swift (1667–1745).

> M. Simon tells of a dream, in which he saw gigantic figures sitting at a table and heard clearly the terrible clattering which their jaws made as they snapped to while they chewed their food. When he woke up, he heard the clatter made by a horse galloping past his window.

This brought to Freud's mind Gulliver's stay among the giants of Brobdingnag and the virtuous Houyhnhnms, and he consequently related Simon's dream to Swift's novel. He did this without help from Simon himself, and therefore came to regard his analysis as illegitimate — as a warning example of what an analysis should not be. The analyst, he commented, must not let his imagination play on the dream without the dreamer's own thoughts (Einfälle) confirming the interpretation.[14]

This warning about the possible misuse of literary associations, which makes such an important point in *The Interpretation of Dreams*, is countered in the same work by a more 'legitimate' reference to *Gulliver's Travels*. Freud had dreamt of a stream of urine clearing away faeces and was reminded, on waking, of Gulliver's extinguishing a conflagration in Lilliput with a similar stream, an action that costs Gulliver the favour of the diminutive Queen. That, in its turn, reminded the analyst of the differently motivated action of Rabelais's giant Gargantua, who revenges himself on the Parisians by squatting on Notre Dame Cathedral and spraying his urine over the city.[15] The ultimate meaning of this dream, which incorporated images looked at in an illustrated volume of Rabelais the previous day, Freud would have us believe to be revulsion at excessive praise of his own work. An acquaintance had compared Freud's clearing away errors and prejudices to Hercules' cleansing of the Augean stables; he was conscious, however, of the dream's suggestion that he was forced to rummage in human filth whose clearing away required less savoury streams than those enlisted by Hercules in meeting the demands of his fifth labour.

And so, once again, Freud has placed his readings in English literature into the context of three different cultural ambiences: sixteenth-century France, eighteenth-century England, and the ancient world that conceived the myth of Hercules. He also downplayed the obvious sexual suggestions of the scenes described, as he often did when describing his own dreams. 'Irma's Injection', the analysis that sets the tone in *The Interpretation of Dreams*, is a case in point. Freud took the opportunity, however, to restore the missing dimension when he came to write *Civilization and its Discontents*, first published in 1930. He stressed the sexual associations of extinguishing fires by means of the male organ, referring once again to Swift's Gulliver, Rabelais's Gargantua, and the stables of King Augeas.[16] True to his doctrine of overdetermination, however, he added yet another facet in a letter to Marie Bonaparte dated 20 August 1938:

> There is an inner connection between urinating and writing, and assuredly not only with me. When I noticed the first signs of prostatic hypertrophy in my bladder, in 1909 in New York, I suffered at the same time from writer's cramp, a condition foreign to me until then.[17]

* * *

Ernest Jones tells us that Freud was 'particularly fond' of *Tristram Shandy* by Laurence Sterne (1713–68) — a work he used to bring home to readers of *The Psychopathology of Everyday Life* that it is not only *words* that betray their inner life. Dipping into the stream of Walter Shandy's learned eloquence, he quotes:

> [. . .] and I am not at all surprised that Gregory of Nazianzum, upon observing the hasty and untoward gestures of Julian, should foretell he would one day become an apostate; — or that St Ambrose should turn his Amanuensis out of doors, because of an indecent motion of his head, which went backwards and forward like a flail; — or that Democritus should conceive Protagoras to be a scholar from seeing him bind up a faggot, and thrusting, as he did, the small twigs inwards. — There are a thousand unnoticed openings [. . .] which let a penetrating eye at once into a man's soul; and I maintain it [. . .], that a man of sense does not lay down his hat on coming into a room, — or take it up in going out of it, but something escapes, which discovers him.[18]

Freud adds that however sane and 'normal' his readers conceive themselves to be, their everyday actions may betray their innermost selves no less than the neurotics and hysterics he observed in his professional life; and he used this passage from Sterne's novel, published between 1759 and 1767, to stress that imaginative writers, *Dichter*, anticipated the subtlest observations of psychoanalysis.[19] The icing was added to the cake when Freud discovered Darwin making the same observation. While Freud delighted in the sly games Sterne plays with his readers' expectations, he told Jones that he took equal pleasure in the more conventionally structured *History of Tom Jones, a Foundling*, by Henry Fielding (1702–54) — a novel, first published in 1749, which transposed the peripatetic mode that Freud had relished in *Don Quixote* onto a more realistic, and more picaresque, plane. During their courtship, however, in which he shared a good deal of reading matter with his fiancée and her sister, he did not think *Tom Jones* suitable for the young ladies' virginal eyes — no doubt because of the sexual freedom of some of its episodes (Jones I, 190). That Tom at one point thinks that he has bedded his own mother will not have escaped the attention of the later codifier of the Oedipus Complex. He justifies his reluctance to recommend the novel to Martha, because he found it

> so robustly outspoken in the older English manner that it would offend your fine feelings. It is, however, an honest and profoundly intelligent novel and contains many deep observations as well as some finely drawn characters, though it is a little old-fashioned in structure and design.

When Freud calls *Tom Jones* 'a little old-fashioned', he is comparing it with the nineteenth-century novels we shall find him reading around this time. He was never to relish literary innovations and experiments that went beyond those humorously employed by the incomparable Laurence Sterne.

* * *

Swift, Sterne, and Fielding span the gamut of Freud's first-hand acquaintance with eighteenth-century British fiction. The published evidence does not allow us to suppose that the writings of Tobias Smollett ever came to his notice; and he had heard just enough about those of Oliver Goldsmith (*c.*1730–74) to seek out his portrait when he visited the National Portrait Gallery during his stay in London in September 1908. The notes he made at that time show that he sought in many of these portraits traces of 'race' and constitutional disposition, on which his psychological interest centred. Most of them disappointed him, however, because they revealed far too little of the temperamental cast that led their subjects to choose particular professions, and — he felt — of their life-experience. He went on to speculate on such topics:

> It seems, however that [some] heroic and conquistadorial natures have to content themselves with becoming imaginative writers and artists (*Dichter und Künstler*) because they do not find their paths unimpeded. Those born to be imaginative writers (*Dichter*) seem to be those who have remained childish.[20]

As illustrations of this last observation, in which 'childish' seems to encompass such meanings as 'childlike' and 'keeping a taproot into their childhood', Freud cites the portraits of Goldsmith and Percy Bysshe Shelley. Neither Goldsmith nor Shelley have left discernible traces in Freud's writings, though his own practice conformed to that of the Vicar of Wakefield who chooses a wife 'as she did her wedding gown, not for a fine glossy surface, but such qualities as would wear well'. Freud was to meet a counter-example in the Lydgate episodes of George Eliot's *Middlemarch*.

⋆ ⋆ ⋆

Freud relished the British writers of the eighteenth century because he saw them as part of the great European movement known as *Aufklärung* or Enlightenment, whose principal German standard-bearer was Gotthold Ephraim Lessing (1729–81). He saw himself as a great enlightener, who 'built out into the dark'.[21] That image comes from *The Interpretation of Dreams*, where it is joined by terms suggesting enlightening, explaining, uncovering, solving puzzles — such words as *aufklären*, *aufhellen*, *aufdecken*, *enthüllen*, *Rätsel lösen*.[22] The same work also commends the 'sharp eye' of imaginative writers ('scharfes Dichterauge').[23] 'Enlightening' unites the British philosophers of the age with its realistic novelists; but it can also play a part in playful subversions of established forms like *Tristram Shandy*. His strong appreciation of humour made Freud delight in Sterne no less that Fielding, the *Letters of Junius* no less that the writing of Sydney Smith. At the same time, eighteenth-century British writers helped to wean Freud away from a heavy German expository style towards an idiom accessible to the 'common reader', reinforcing lessons he had already learnt from Lessing, Lichtenberg, Börne, and Heine — fellow 'enlighteners' all. He was sufficiently man of his time, however, to wish to keep literary depictions of sexual freedom away from the virginal eyes of well-brought-up young ladies like his own fiancée.

Notes to Chapter 3

1. *GW* xv, 187.
2. 'ausgemergelt mager' (*Reisebriefe*, p. 251).
3. See Hume's 'Of the Delicacy of Taste and Passion'.
4. GW IX, 95–96.
5. *PWAV* III, 303.
6. 10 August 1879, *Jugendbriefe*, p. 201.
7. *GW* II/II, 524.
8. 13 March 1875, *Jugendbriefe*, pp. 114–15.
9. *GW* I, 506–08.
10. *Reisebriefe*, pp. 252, 255.
11. John Stuart Mill, *Gesammelte Werke*, ed. by Theodor Gomperz, XII (Leipzig, 1880), p. 12.
12. *Reisebriefe*, p. 255.
13. 6 August 1873, *Jugendbriefe*, p. 40. Twenty years later Freud quotes a line from the *Irish Melodies* by Thomas Moore (1779–1852) in its original English: 'Go, where glory waits thee' (*Fliess*, p. 36 – Manuskript C, c. April 1893). The lines that follow are significant: 'But, while fame elates thee/ Oh! still remember me'.
14. *GW* II/III, 31–32.
15. *GW* II/III, 72.
16. GW XIV, 449.
17. *Jones* III, 252.
18. *The Life and Opinions of Tristram Shandy, Gent*, Book VI, Chapter 5.
19. *GW* IV, 237–38.
20. *Reisebriefe*, p. 254.
21. *GW* II/III, 525.
22. *GW* II/III, 97, 118, 258, 315, 419, 463, 515.
23. *GW* II/III, 252.

CHAPTER 4

Imperfect Sympathies

In 1883, irritated at what he felt to be his lack of professional advancement, Freud came across a version of a poem Sir Walter Scott (1771–1832) had inserted into his novel *The Bride of Lammermoor*, first published in 1819.

> In passing through a huge Gothic anteroom, Sir William Ashton heard the sound of his daughter's lute. Music, when the performers are concealed, affects us with a pleasure mingled with surprise, and reminds us of the natural concert of birds among the leafy bowers. The statesman, though little accustomed to give way to emotions of this natural and simple class, was still a man and a father. He stopped, therefore, and listened, while the silver tones of Lucy Ashton's voice mingled with the accompaniment in an ancient air, to which someone had adapted the following words: —
>
> 'Look not then on beauty's charming, —
> Sit thou still when kings are arming, —
> Taste not when the wine-cup glistens, —
> Speak not when the people listens, —
> Stop thine ear against the singer, —
> From the red gold keep thy finger. —
> Vacant heart and hand and eye, —
> Easy live and quiet die.'
>
> The sounds ceased, and the Keeper entered his daughter's apartment.[1]

The version Freud came to know, or concocted for himself, has been preserved by Ernest Jones:

> Look thou not on beauty's charming,
> Keep thee still when kings are arming,
> Speak not where the people listen,
> From the red gold keep thy finger;
> Easy live and happy die,
> Such shall be thy destiny.

Freud felt that this was just the kind of advice he needed — though peacefully accepting whatever destiny decreed, hardly suited his temperament. Throughout his life, however, Freud often wondered about his 'destiny' — a concept he imported into Lucy Ashton's song. He essayed a German version, in which 'destiny' ('das Loos') again figured in the final line:

> Lass dich nicht nach Schönheit lüsten,

Halt dich fern, wenn Könige rüsten,
Sprich nicht wo die Volksgunst winket,
Greif du nicht wo Gold dir blinket;
Stille leb und stirb in Frieden;
Dies werd dir als Loos beschieden.

Freud playfully describes this effort of his as a 'free and clumsy' translation by 'a more recent poet [. . .] evidently lacking in practice'.[2] It reads very well, however, and finds interesting equivalents which underline but do not distort Scott's meaning, as when 'where people listen' transmogrifies into 'where the popular favour (*die Volksgunst*) beckons'. He always distrusted people in the mass; the term 'Gesindel' (rabble, riffraff) often found its way into his letters and conversations.

What we have here is another example of Freud's fastening on a single verse by an author of whom he had read little, because it spoke to him of his own current problems and concerns. I was surprised to find that as far as the current state of publication allows there is no sign that Freud read either *The Bride of Lammermoor* as a whole, or any of the other Waverley novels which were still at the height of their fame in his day. Had he never come across *Ivanhoe*, for instance, which had so much to appeal to him? Be that as it may, he did know something of Scott's life; and when he was faced with the prospect of sinking some of his own savings into psychoanalytic publications, he took warning from the misfortunes that had attended the publishing and printing ventures of Scott's later years. He wrote to Max Eitingon on 11 November 1929 that

> this would not be the first case in the history of literature in which an author lost all he had earned in a publishing venture. This happened to Walter Scott and Mark Twain — and I am not a professional writer who can recoup his losses through new exercises of his imagination.[3]

* * *

By September 1896 Freud's fortunes had improved sufficiently to allow him a holiday in Italy. In Ravenna he put up in the Hotel Byron, where, as he proudly reported home, Byron had stayed for two years.[4] Neither this, nor many other historical reminiscences, could reconcile him to the discomforts of the hotel, and after a day of sightseeing he decamped to Florence before nightfall. Like that of so many Europeans, his interest in Byron was predominantly biographical; in one of the margins of his copy of Albert Moll's *Libido sexualis*, published a year after that brief stopover in Ravenna, he marked a passage about the precocious loves of famous poets, which included the information that Byron had fallen in love with Mary Duff when he was eight years old. He used this snippet when he addressed the Vienna Psychoanalytic Society on 3 January 1902, mentioning Byron as being among those 'who are mentally and sexually precocious, and fall sexually in love before their time'.[5] In Byron's portrait in the National Portrait Gallery he saw a reflection of the poet's vanity. 'Byron', he commented, 'has obviously dressed himself up to the nines for this occasion' ('hat sich offenbar sehr hergerichtet').[6]

Freud owned a copy of the five-volume Tauchnitz edition of *The Works of Lord Byron*, published in 1842 under licence from John Murray; but his interest in these writings centred more on the plays than the poems. The paranoid Judge D. G. M. Schreber, to whose delusional autobiography Freud devoted a study first published in 1911 ('Psychoanalytic Remarks on an Autobiographically Described Case of Paranoia'), revived this interest. Schreber adduces Byron's *Manfred*, alongside Goethe's *Faust* and Weber's *Der Freischütz*, as a case of 'soul murder' by an evil deity which Schreber identifies with the 'Ariman' of Persian mythology. Freud could detect no trace of 'soul murder' in this play, any more than the 'devil's pact' Schreber had found in it. There is no such pact there, he says, and cites Manfred's words to the demon who seeks to snatch him away:

> my past power
> Was purchased by no compact with thy crew.

For Freud, the 'core and secret' of Byron's play is incest with a sister; and that brings him back, not only to Schreber's history and secret desires, but also those of Byron himself:

> It is easy to relate this theme at the heart of *Manfred* to the poet's frequently asserted incestuous relationship with his half-sister; and it is striking that Byron's other play, the magnificent *Cain*, deals with the primal family within which no blame can attach to incest among siblings.[7]

Freud is not usually free with adjectives like magnificent ('grossartig'), and *Cain* does indeed touch on problems at least as interesting to him as the incest theme central to *Totem and Taboo*. Byron's play stresses a double rebellion against a father: Cain's physical father, Adam, who got himself expelled from paradise, and the Father-God who planted forbidden trees. Above all, it featured a demon as plausible as Milton's Satan and Goethe's Mephisto, who formulates a kind of anti-theology that culminates in praise of 'the joy | And power of knowledge'. No other six words could have penetrated so well to the core of Freud's being; but he was sufficiently aware of the aesthetic shortcomings of Byron's plays not to list him among 'the most magnificent (*grossartigsten*) works of world literature' that included Goethe's *Faust*, or among his 'favourite books' (*Lieblingsbücher*) that placed *Paradise Lost* alongside Heine's *Lazarus*-cycle.[8]

I would like to have been able to report that Freud's interest in the incest-theme in English literature had directed him towards Shelley's *The Cenci* as well as Byron's *Manfred* — Otto Rank, for one, might easily have called it to his notice. The only reference to Shelley, however, which I have been able to find concerns his portrait in the National Portrait Gallery, where Freud lists him alongside Goldsmith as retaining childlike traits.[9] No work by Coleridge seems to have swum into Freud's ken, despite Hilda Doolittle's efforts to interest him in 'The Ancient Mariner', a psychoanalytic view of which might have yielded some interesting insights.

Some members of Freud's family took a closer interest in Byron's poetry than Freud himself. Among these were his sister-in-law Minna, whose wish to have a copy of Byron's works he satisfied in June 1894, and his daughter Anna, who at the age of nineteen, delighted him by translating some of Byron's *Hebrew Melodies* better, in his view, than Gildemeister had managed in what had become the standard German version. Freud had himself drawn her attention to this collection, which must have been of special interest to him; but I have found no comment on it in his writings. He did, however, confess to Theodor Reik, on 18 November 1929, that outside Shakespeare and Milton the only English poetry he read to any extent was that of Byron.

★ ★ ★

While we have no evidence that any of Coleridge's writings ever came before his eyes, it is pleasing to find that among the excerpts from biographies, memoirs, and private papers fed to him by William Bullitt, his collaborator on the misconceived 'psychological study' of Woodrow Wilson, was just one stanza from 'The Character of the Happy Warrior' by William Wordsworth (1770–1850):

> Who is the happy Warrior? Who is he
> That every man in arms should wish to be
> — It is the generous Spirit, who, when brought
> Among the tasks of real life, hath wrought
> Upon the plan that pleased his boyish thought:
> Whose high endeavours are an inward light
> That makes the path before him always bright:
> Who, with a natural instinct to discern
> What knowledge can perform, is diligent to learn;
> Abides by this resolve, and stops not there,
> But makes his moral being his prime care [. . .][10]

This Wordsworthian equivalent of Kipling's 'If' did not, alas, cause Freud to delve deeper in Wordsworth's writings — notably *The Prelude*, whose autobiographical subtleties would have offered him more interesting material to work on than 'The Character of the Happy Warrior'.

Freud was made aware of the work of Alfred Lord Tennyson (1809–92) when he heard it alluded to in family banter on his first visit to the Manchester branch of his family in 1875. 'A connection of thoughts', he writes in *The Interpretation of Dreams*, 'leads me to England, to the home of my brother who used to tease his wife with the words "Fifty years ago", after the title by Tennyson, which the children used to correct to "Fifteen years ago" '.[11] The poem refers to long-lasting married love; its actual title is 'The Roses on the Terrace':

> Rose, on this terrace fifty years ago,
> When I was in my June, you in your May,
> Two words, '*My* Rose', set all your face aglow,
> And now that I am white and you are gray,
> That blush of fifty years ago, my dear,
> Blooms in the past, but close to me to-day,
> As this red rose, which on our terrace here
> Glows in the blue of fifty miles away.[12]

The children's 'correction' playfully reminded the parents that they had not been married as long as the protagonists of the poem, and that their courtship therefore did not lie as far back. Freud may well have had a subliminal memory of the poem's true title, 'The Roses on the Terrace', for a chain of association soon leads him to the English 'Wars of the Roses'.[13]

Nine years after the first appearance of *The Interpretation of Dreams* Tennyson's portrait served Freud as an element in the strange taxonomy of British faces he sketched out after a visit to the National Portrait Gallery in London. 'Great heroes', his notes read, 'often have childlike faces — Nelson, for instance, and Wolfe. Authentically heroic expressions, like that on Phidias' Zeus, appear on the faces of artists — Lord Leighton, Tennyson, Bulwer'.[14]

Ernest Jones always regretted that Freud, who took such delight in German and classical poetry, never came to share his taste for Victorian poetry — particularly that of Robert Browning (1812–89). He tried more than once to win Freud over to his view that Browning's insights matched those of Freud himself. On April 1909, for instance, he sent Freud a copy of lines from Browning's 'Cleon', in which he had underlined two words:

> Thou canst not think a mere barbarian Jew
> As Paulus proves to be, *one circumcised*,
> Hath access to a secret shut from us?

Jones thought that these lines might whet Freud's appetite for Browning's poetry because they supported something Freud had said to Jones at some point: that 'penis reasons' underlay 'contempt for Jews'. He made clear that in 'Cleon', Browning was not overtly speaking for the poet himself; but he thought it worthwhile to tell Freud:

> Browning was an orthodox Christian, and although none of his writings are anti-semitic still he may have been annoyed that his Saviour was a Jew. Much of his writing shews strong masochistic tendencies. I wonder what the explanation might be?[15]

Freud did not respond to this appeal for his interest.

Three years later, on 30 October 1912, Jones tackled Freud again. Browning, he declared, was one of Britain's best poets; he and his wife, Elizabeth Barrett Browning (1806–61), belonged to a 'select company of great writers that included Milton, Wordsworth, Keats, Swinburne and Ruskin'. 'They sing of Italy', Jones continued, appealing to Freud's passion for that country, 'as of heaven, with a love they give no other country on earth'. And in order to elicit a response from Freud this time, Jones sent him some lines from one of Browning's most lyrical poems, entitled 'By the Fireside':

> O woman country, wooed, not wed,
> Lov'd all the more by earth's male lands,
> Laid to their hearts instead.

Freud was not to be tempted, however. He felt no need to read British poets who praised Italy, he told Jones; 'we have our own enthusiasts'.[16] Goethe was no doubt foremost in his mind, supported, perhaps, by Heine and Platen.[17]

On 13 December 1937 Jones tried just once more. 'There is a wonderful picture of Moses' psychology in the wilderness, particularly in regard to the ingratitude of his followers, in stanzas IX, X, and XII of Browning's poem "One Word More". I rather think I presented you with a copy of Browning's poems years ago, but if you have not one I should be pleased to send you a copy of the poem'. Freud took no notice, however, and his writings on Moses — or indeed any others — make no mention of Browning and show no sign that Freud ever followed up Jones's reference.[18]

In January 1912 Jones did manage to interest Freud in some lines of English poetry by sending him one of the poems in which James Thomson (1834–1912) had formulated thoughts and feelings about sexuality and creativity under the title 'Art'. Freud replied on 14 January 1912: 'I like the little poem very much, and if you will present me with it, I am very glad'. He added that he had sent it to the *Zentralblatt für Psychoanalyse*, whose editors refused it 'as they wanted translation'.[19] A letter from Jones dated 30 January 1912 explained that the poem had been meant for Freud's 'personal interest', not for the *Zentralblatt*, but that a patient who had first drawn Jones's attention to it had, in fact, offered to translate it into German.[20] No poem by James Thomson ever appeared in the *Zentralblatt*, or in any publication in which Freud had a hand; in a later chapter we shall see 'The City of Dreadful Night' engage his attention again — but even there he never set himself to fathom the psychological depths of that fascinating poem. Jones's copy of Thomson's lyric has not survived, but what Freud read may have been Part III of a cycle Thomson published in 1867 under his pseudonym 'B.V.':

Singing is sweet; but be sure of this,
Lips only sing when they cannot kiss.

Did he ever suspire a tender lay
While her presence took his breath away?

Had his fingers been able to toy with her hair
Would they then have written the verses fair?

Had she let his arm steal round her waist
Would the lovely portrait yet be traced?

Since he could not embrace it flushed and warm
He has carved in stone the perfect form.

Who gives the fine report of the feast?
He who got none and enjoyed it least.

Were the wine really slipping down his throat
Would his song of the wine advance a note?

Will you puff out the music that sways the whirl,
Or dance and make love with a pretty girl?

Who shall the great battle-story write?
Not the hero down in the thick of the fight.

Statues and pictures and verse may be grand,
But they are not the Life for which they stand.

Though Freud told Jones that he liked the poem very much, he never specified what it was that appealed to him.

Jones could claim one other small victory. In the aftermath of the First World War, when Freud was depressed not only by the senseless slaughter of that war and the psychological damage it had done, but also by its aftermath of ruin and impoverishment, private griefs that included the death of a dearly loved daughter, as well as what Jones calls the 'antagonistic' attitudes of influential people to Freud's work — in face of all that, Freud was cheered, Jones reports, by the last stanza of the poem by Arthur Hugh Clough (1819–61) which begins with the words 'Say not the struggle nought availeth':

> And not by Eastern window only
> When daylight comes, comes in the light;
> In front the sun climbs slow, how slowly!
> But westward, look, the land is bright![21]

In the dark days of the Second World War Prime Minster Winston Churchill gave hope to his nation by quoting this same verse.

Throughout his life Freud preserved an enthusiasm for the history and literature of classical Greece and Rome which he had first conceived in his schooldays. 'Ages long past', he wrote in *The Man Moses and the Monotheist Religion*, first published as a whole in 1939,

> exert a great and often mysterious influence on people's imagination. Whenever they are discontented with their present — and they are that often enough! — they turn to the past and hope that this time they can make the never extinguished dream of a golden age come true.

A footnote then refers the reader to a group of Victorian poems which had impressed themselves on his memory in the way neither Tennyson nor the Brownings had been able to do: the *Lays of Ancient Rome* by Thomas Babington Macaulay (1800–59). The poet, Freud wrote, founded his work on a situation that mingled discontent and hope. He assumed 'the role of a bard who, saddened by the chaotic partisan struggles of the present, confronts his hearers with the courage, self-sacrifice, unity, and patriotism of their forefathers'.[22] But is Freud not ascribing to Macaulay his own discontent with his present? There is no hint of an admonitory purpose in Macaulay's Preface; and the image of ancient Rome that emerges from the Lays as a whole is far from Utopian. True enough, the ballad of Horatius keeping the bridge is an adventure story of heroic patriotism, calculated to induce admiration of Roman virtues; but the rest of the collection, with its tale of treachery, tyranny, and bloodshed, is anything but favourable to the Roman past, and more likely to make the Victorian reader feel comfortable in prosperous and peaceful Britain than yearning to remodel it in the image of the past. As for the victims of the capitalism that fuelled Victorian prosperity, and those who advocated their cause, they were more likely to look towards a socially fairer future than long for a return to the virtues and vices of the ancient world.

★ ★ ★

The main task Freud set himself in the course of his life was searching for the springs of human action in the depths of the mind and the detritus of memory. The Unconscious he postulated spoke to him first in his dreams, whose analysis became the key to unlocking its secrets. A visit to the London Portrait Gallery, however, also tempted him to seek clues to the constitution and temper of monarchs and writers in physiognomic images constructed by painters. His tentative steps in that direction led Freud to an interest in Francis Galton's experiments with photographic superimposition, and to intense study of Italian painting and sculpture. A re-examination of his explorations of the art of his beloved Italy, however, would transgress the bounds set for the present book.

An all too diffident feeling of inadequacy in the face of poetry written in languages other than his own caused Freud to bypass the glories of English poetry from Coleridge and Keats to Browning and beyond. Yet we can watch him responding with delight to the language of Shakespeare and Milton, and to English stanzas he encountered along his way. We can also see his interest in the classical world lead him to Macaulay's *Lays of Ancient Rome*, and his Jewish concerns to Byron's *Hebrew Melodies* — these latter he must have got to know well enough to compare his daughter's translation with Gildemeister's authorized one. He was especially intrigued by Byron's *plays*, with their rebel and outsider figures and their surmised relation to the poet's life. What remains true, however, is that no lyric poetry produced in Britain or America engaged his sympathies as fully as the poems of Goethe and other lyric poets writing in German which, along with the Greek and Roman classics, had formed his literary tastes in his earliest days.[23]

Notes to Chapter 4

1. Sir Walter Scott, *The Bride of Lammermoor*, ch. 3.
2. *Jones*, I, 190.
3. Transcribed from Freud's unpublished letter by Michael Molnar.
4. *Reisebriefe*, p. 60.
5. Cf. F. J. Sulloway, *Freud, Biologist of the Mind. Beyond the Psychoanalytic Legend* (London, 1979), p. 302.
6. *Reisebriefe*, p. 255.
7. *GW* VII, 279–80.
8. Letter to Hugo Heller, 1 November 1906 — *Briefe*, pp. 267–68.
9. *Reisebriefe*, p. 254.
10. *Thomas Woodrow Wilson, Twenty-eighth President of the United States. A Psychological Study* (London, 1967), p. 27.
11. *GW* II/III, 217.
12. *Demeter, and Other Poems* (1889).
13. *GW* II/II, 217f.
14. *Reisebriefe*, pp. 250–51.
15. *Freud/Jones*, p. 22.
16. *Jones* I, 364.
17. Cf. *Freud/Jones*, p. 166.
18. *Freud/Jones*, p. 166.
19. *Freud/Jones*, p. 125.
20. *Freud/Jones*, p. 130.
21. *Jones*, III, 11.
22. *GW* XVI, 175–76.
23. I was disappointed to find that Thomas de Quincey (1785–1859), whose opium-induced visions should have interested Freud, entered his writings only by dint of a single coinage: the word 'anecdotage'. Freud owed this reference to A. A. Brill. (*The Joke and its Relation to the Unconscious*, *GW* VI, 20.)

CHAPTER 5

Cultural Community

As has just been seen, Freud sought to illustrate the 'great, often mysterious attraction' the long-distant past exerts on human beings discontented with their present, by invoking the poems Thomas Macaulay devoted to subjects from the history of ancient Rome. Unlike any of the other British poets treated in the last chapter, Macaulay figures in the list of favourite writers Freud sent to Hugo Heller on 1 November 1906; he does so, however, not as the bard of *The Lays of Ancient Rome*, but as the author of the *Critical and Historical Essays* of which an edition published by Tauchnitz in 1850 remained among Freud's books until his death. Freud had, indeed conceived an enthusiasm for these writings early in his life, and a letter to Eduard Silberstein, dated 7 September 1877, had singled out two of them for especial praise:

> I have read through the volume of Macaulay [. . .] at least four times, opening the book somewhere in the middle and carrying on reading until I was too exhausted to continue. The essays on Bacon and Temple are quite magnificent ('ganz herrlich') [. . .][1]

In an earlier letter to the same correspondent he had called the essay on Bacon 'the most perfect in existence'.[2] It met, as has already been seen, a pre-existing interest in Bacon, especially his *Novum Organum*; it also, however, strengthened Freud's respect for the achievements of the Elizabethan and Jacobean ages, and encouraged forays into new intellectual as well as geographic regions. Moreover, the essay reinforced Freud's sense of the complexities of authorship by setting Bacon's world-historic contribution to scientific induction and experiment, clarity and elegance of style, and admirable maxims for the conduct of life, against his less admirable personal traits and political manoeuvrings.

Freud's interest in the essay on Bacon is easily understood: but what, apart from his admiration for Macaulay's style of exposition, can have attracted him to that on Sir William Temple? One factor was, no doubt, the sheer contrast between Sir William's attitudes and his own. Temple, Macaulay tells his readers, 'seldom went beyond the surface of any question', preferring 'security, repose, leisure to the turmoil and anxiety which are inseparable from greatness'. It may have been this very difference from his own temperament which attracted Freud's psychological curiosity. Macaulay's essay, however, also named and commended qualities Freud valued in himself. These included what Macaulay called 'the power of reading things of high import that to others were invisible or unintelligible' — which is, of course, precisely the power on which Freud prided himself from *The Interpretation of Dreams* onwards. Great writers of the past had provided hints; but the ultimate formulation, Freud thought, bringing clarity where there was darkness before, was his own. Much of this light, he believed, had come from his power of self-analysis; he would therefore feel that he had in full measure what Macaulay praised as a mind 'habituated to reflect on its own operations'. And did not his work with his patients confirm Macaulay's statement, so surprising in a nineteenth-century historian at the centre of an expanding empire on which the sun never set: 'the mutual relations of the two sexes seem to me at least as important as the mutual relation of any two governments in the world'? The essay on Temple also provided a model of how to situate a subject's individual life and work in his or her historical and social context. No wonder, then, that Freud counted Macaulay's essays among his favourite works, and that they led him to purchase the same writer's *History of England, from the Accession of James the Second*, which can still be seen, alongside a volume of the *Essays*, in the London Freud Museum.

★ ★ ★

Freud's translations from the French of Charcot and Bernheim showed him as a talented translator, who kept close to the original meaning of his texts without distorting idiomatic German usage. He saw translation, as Gerhard Fichtner has stressed, as part of that process of *Übertragung*, carrying over from one sphere of being, activity, or consciousness to another, which in its various meanings plays so large a part in his psychoanalytic work. He was given a chance to exercise this talent further when Theodor Gomperz commissioned him, in 1879, to contribute translations of essays on Socialism, Female Emancipation, and Plato, to the final volume of Gomperz's German edition of the works of John Stuart Mill (1806–73). Freud welcomed this commission, not only as a necessary boost to his finances, but also as an opportunity to hone his skills as a translator from English as well as French, and to delve further into the kind of Utilitarianism he had heard expounded, with reference to Mill, by Franz Brentano. Brentano's lectures, he told Silberstein on 22–23 October 1874 and 7 March 1875, had interested him in Mill's thoughts on education, distribution of goods, and different forms of the Struggle for Existence — interests further stirred by his reading of Adam Smith, Malthus, and, of course, Darwin. Utilitarian thinking percolated into Freud's later theories — his conception of the Pleasure Principle, and its limitation by the Reality Principle, has a distinctly Benthamite ring. His intensive engagement with Mill's texts further strengthened, however, Freud's opposition to at least one of the causes dear to Mill's heart: gender equality in the workplace. This becomes clear in his letter to Martha Bernays, dated 15 November 1883, in which he blamed an account by Georg Brandes of Mill's life and work for failing to situate Mill within the cultural and political ambience of his time. What Freud here missed in Brandes was the kind of 'placing' he had so admired in Macaulay's *Essays* — qualities which made him list these *Essays* among 'ten good books' he most valued. Neither Mill nor Bentham figured in that list.[3] Freud was not, at first, attracted by Mill's style, which he found 'lifeless' because it lacked pithy maxims and phrases that imprinted themselves immediately on the reader's memory: 'but later on I read a philosophical work by him which was witty, epigrammatically precise, and lively. He was perhaps in our century the man who was best able to free himself from vulgar prejudices'. All this, however, Freud continued, went together with what he considered a crippling deficiency: Mill lacked, he thought, 'a sense of the absurd'. This lack, he told Martha Bernays in 1883, showed itself most clearly in Mill's views on 'the woman question'; and as Freud warms to his subject his own bourgeois Victorian values assert themselves in a way which many of us feel unable to accept today:

> We will pretty well agree, surely, [Freud tells Martha] that keeping a household in order, and looking after the care and education of children, takes all the strength of a human being, and precludes almost all gainful employment outside the home, even when conditions are simplified to the point of relieving the wife of such tasks as dusting, clearing up, and cooking.

Mill 'forgets' all this, Freud continues, because he disregards the divisions caused by human sexuality. In this respect, he says, Mill must be pronounced

> simply not human. His autobiography is so prudish and unearthly, that one could never learn from it that mankind is divided into men and women. His relations with his wife are similarly inhuman. Nothing emerges from his whole disquisition to suggest that a woman differs from a man. I am careful not to say that she is inferior — rather the contrary.

What, then, has Freud to say about Mill's analogy between the oppression of women in England and that of black slaves in America?

> Every girl whose hand is kissed by a man who dares all for love of her could set him right — even if she lacks the right to vote or become a judge. There is no life in the idea that women should be thrust into the struggle for existence alongside men. Should I, for instance, see my dear delicate girl as a competitor [. . .]?[4]

Freud goes on in this patriarchal way quite a bit longer, lamenting a future in which Mill's views might prevail and destroy 'our idea of woman'; but he comforts Martha with the thought that Nature had bestowed on women a measure of beauty, grace, and goodness of heart, which would ensure them a fair destiny different from that of the men who struggled to provide for their families in the hurly-burly of the marketplace.

The texts Freud read took their place in a hierarchy of earlier reading experiences that had impressed and influenced him. Macaulay's essays renewed his interest in Francis Bacon, Mill's disquisition on socialism led to more intensive scrutiny of a key passage of Hobbes's *Leviathan*. In just the same way his translation of Mill's comprehensive review of George Grote's *Plato* reawakened his early interest in Greek philosophy. He had been struck, when preparing *The Interpretation of Dreams*, by 'Plato's observation that the virtuous man only dreams what a wicked man does in reality';[5] and it is fascinating to see 'the Eros of the divine Plato' leaping to his mind when sublimations of the libido come into question.[6] The yearnings and self-divisions he observed in his patients brought to mind the famous passage in the *Symposion* in which Aristophanes is made to speak of a longing for the restoration of a unity lost when the gods split mankind down the middle 'as one splits an egg with a hair'.[7] This led, indirectly, to Freud's introduction of a 'death drive' into a concept of mankind's instinctual life — which effectively made Thanatos a companion of Eros.[8] In the autobiographical sketch known as 'Selbstdarstellung', Freud presents his discovery of the sexual roots of hysteria as a continuation of Plato and a return to the earliest periods of medical diagnosis.

⋆ ⋆ ⋆

In John Stuart Mill and Macaulay Freud found not only stimuli for his own thinking, and reminders of earlier writers of great significance for the formation and reinforcement of his world-view, but also, after initial doubts about Mill, models of clear expository exposition and felicitous phrasing that helped to shape his own admirable prose style. But the influence of neither of these could match that of the scientist whom Freud, in his autobiographical sketch,[9] associated with Goethe in determining his future course of study and the principal direction of his interests: Charles Darwin (1809–82).

The professors under whom the young Freud worked in the University of Vienna were convinced Darwinists, and Freud agreed with them. He never changed his mind; and one only has to open one of his later writings to find how completely Darwinism had entered his thinking. Successive pages in *Civilization and its Discontents*, for instance, speak of 'Natural Selection', 'primal man in his monkeylike prehistory', 'our animalian ancestors', 'Mankind's earlier animalian existence'.[10] Freud took over Darwin's central notion of evolution of the species and saw it mirrored in the development of individuals from conception onwards, ontogeny mirroring phylogeny. Darwin's 'struggle for life', supplemented by the phrase Darwin took over from Herbert Spencer, 'survival of he fittest', became indelibly part of Freud's *Weltanschauung*. Most of his efforts as a practising psychoanalyst were devoted to fitting neurotic patients for survival and practical functioning amid the struggle of life. He welcomed in Darwin a thinker who had usefully shattered naive belief in the divine creation of invariant species, and could therefore claim him as an ally in his fight against established religion. He encountered, in *The Descent of Man*, references to a primal 'band' or horde of gorillas that offered, he thought, parallels to tribal conditions among primitive men — a dubious notion Freud elaborated, with the help of now largely discredited sources, into speculations about inherited memories of the murder of a primal father who then came to be reimbodied in the totem of the tribe. Besides *The Origin of Species* and *The Descent of Man* Freud cherished particularly Darwin's *The Expression of Emotion in Animals and Men*, with its insistence on non-verbal means of expression through facial and body language and cries. As Freud puts it in the course of that much-discussed piece of patient-bullying which he entitled 'Fragment of an Analysis of Hysteria' but which has become best know as 'the Dora Case': 'Whoever has eyes to see and ears to hear can convince himself that mortal man can never conceal a secret. When lips are silent, the fingertips prattle; betrayal oozes from every pore'.[11] Sterne's Walter Shandy, Freud knew, had made the same observation.

Darwin saw all this as governed by 'an overflow of excitation' — a view that led into Freud's Helmholtz-inspired conception of the flow, ebb, and conservation of psychic energy or libido. Darwin also gave him an example of how minute observation could go hand in hand with a constant concern for fitting each detail into a partly anticipated theory, along with a style of presentation that strove for lucidity without becoming pedestrian — a style suited to the 'sober way of thinking' (nüchterne Denkungsart) he admired in Darwin.[12] Darwin's 'scientific honesty' and 'psychological acuity' are praised in *The Psychopathology of Everyday Life*, where Freud quotes a passage from Darwin's autobiography which Ernest Jones had brought to his attention, and which constituted, he thought, 'a golden rule for workers in the scientific field':

> I had, during many years, followed a golden rule, namely, that whenever a published fact, a new observation, or thought came across me, which was opposed to my general results, to make a memorandum of it without fail and at once; for I had found by experience that such facts and thoughts were far more apt to escape from the memory than favourable ones.[13]

Freud introduced this maxim, which his practice did not always follow, by speaking of '*great* Darwin' ('der grosse Darwin'); and though, as Freud wrote to Oskar Pfister on 16 February 1929, Darwin had acknowledged the human right to irrationality by attending church on Sundays, part of his greatness lay in dispelling some of mankind's self-flattering illusions. In this respect, Freud thought, he had himself the right to a place alongside Copernicus as well as Darwin: as Copernicus had shifted mankind from the centre of the universe to its periphery, and Darwin had demonstrated man's kinship with, and indeed origins in, lowlier species, so, Freud believed, he himself had shown, once and for all, that man's conscious reason, source of so much of his pride, was subject to darker forces working below the threshold of his self-awareness.

Darwin, it should be said, did not see his own work as likely to depress mankind's consciousness of its own worth and importance. A passage from *The Descent of Man*, which is also worth quoting as an example of the well-balanced prose style that made reading Darwin's work such a pleasure to Freud, leaves the reader in no doubt of his views on that subject:

> Man may be excused for feeling some pride at having risen, though not through his own exertions, to the very summit of the organic scale; and the fact of his having thus risen, instead of having been aboriginally placed there, may give him hopes for a still higher destiny in the distant future. But we are not here concerned with hopes or fears, but with the truth as far as our reason allows us to discover it. I have given the evidence to the best of my ability; and we must acknowledge, as it seems to me, that man with all his noble qualities, with sympathy which feels for the most debased, with benevolence which extends not only to other men but to the humblest living creature, with his god-like intellect which has penetrated into the movements and constitution of the solar system — man still bears in his bodily frame the indelible stamp of his lowly origin.[14]

Darwin's admiring reference to man's godlike intellect takes in Copernicus too, along with Galileo, Kepler, and Newton; he sees their penetration 'into the movements and constitution of the solar system' as cause for pride rather than depression at man's rise from 'lowly origins'.

★ ★ ★

The *Interpretation of Dreams* refers repeatedly to experiments by the British eugenicist Francis Galton (1822–1911), which used superimpositions of the portraits of several members of the same family onto one photographic plate in order to detect heritable family traits. Freud used this on four distinct occasions to illustrate the process by which dreams merge several persons into one.[15] In *The Man Moses and the Monotheistic Religion* Galton's 'Mischphotographien' appear again: they provide an analogy for the construction of a composite 'myth of the hero' by combining common features of hero-figures in a wide variety of folktales, sagas, and myths.

There is however, as D. M. Forrest pointed out in *Francis Galton: The Life and Work of a Victorian Genius*,[16] also a way in which Galton anticipated Freud's clinical procedures, and may indeed have influenced them. Galton developed a series of association tests, and in an article published in the British journal *Brain* in July 1879 he asserted that putting a number of people through such tests led him to a better understanding of

> the multifariousness of the work done by the mind in a state of half-unconsciousness, and the valid reason they afford for believing in the existence of still deeper strata of mental operations, sunk wholly below the level of consciousness, which may account for such mental phenomena as cannot otherwise be explained.[17]

Freud subscribed to *Brain*, and may well have found Galton's description of accessing a 'state of half-consciousness' helpful in his own association experiments. After abandoning the practice of hypnotizing patients he found, for a time, that word-association helped in his constant endeavour to reach the less conscious regions of the human mind.

By applying Darwin's evolutionary principles to psychology and psychiatry, Freud believed himself to have taken a step further in the history of human thought that placed him as an equal by Darwin's side. Whatever one may think of this claim, the inspiration he sought, and the kinship he felt, with Goethe and Darwin, a German poet and an English scientist, enabled him to create a subject *sui generis*, psychoanalysis, which drew on insights from the humanities and natural sciences alike. At the same time his looking to English as well as German models of thought and style helped to validate his claim, made in his 'Timely Thoughts on War and Death' in 1915, when Britain and Austria were at war, that he was a 'cultural citizen of the world'.[18] Ten years later, in an autobiographical sketch he later augmented, Freud explained the origin of such 'cultural' self-consciousness by pointing to the denial, by anti-Semites among the students of Vienna University, that Jews could ever be part of the Germanic 'folk-community':

> I was affected above all by the claim that I should feel myself inferior, and not part of the folk-community. I refused to acknowledge the first; I have never understood why I should feel ashamed of my origins or (as people were beginning to say) my race. Exclusion from a particular folk-community I did

> not view with great regret: I thought that an assiduous worker could claim his place in humanity as a whole without particular classification. These first impressions formed at the university had, however, an important consequence: they accustomed me, early on, to the fate of one who stands in opposition and is ostracized by the 'compact majority'. A certain independence of judgement was prepared in this way.[19]

Such 'cultural citizenship' included all who knew, and responded to, an international canon of literary texts, from which individual taste made its own selections and to which it might add new or unfairly neglected works. Such a community also responded to scientific paradigms that were periodically 'shifted' by outstanding thinkers and experimenters originating in different parts of the world: the Pole Copernicus, the Italian Galileo, or the Englishman Darwin. What mattered, in this transnational community, was neither race nor creed, but education, taste, cultural awareness, and creativity.

Notes to Chapter 5

1. *Jugendbriefe*, p. 90.
2. 15 August 1877, *Jugendbriefe*, p. 188.
3. 1 November 1906, *Briefe*, p. 267.
4. 15 November 1883, *Briefe*, pp. 81–82.
5. *GW* II/III, 625.
6. e.g. *Three Treatises of the Theory of Sexuality* (1905), *GW* V, 32.
7. *Beyond the Pleasure Principle*, *GW* XIII, 62–63.
8. *GW* XIII, 69; cf. 'The Two Drives', in *The Ego and the Id*, *GW* XIII, 268ff.
9. 'Selbstdarstellung', *GW* XIV, 49.
10. 'natürlisch Ausleses', 'der Urmensch in einer affenähnlichen Vorzeit', 'unsere tierischen Ahnen', 'frühere animalische Existenz' (*GW* XIV, 447ff.).
11. *GW* V, 240.
12. *Beyond the Pleasure Principle*, *GW* IV, 164.
13. *GW* V, 164.
14. *The Descent of Man and Selection in Relation to Sex* (London: 1871), p. 405.
15. *GW* II/III, 144, 299, 498–99, 662–63.
16. D. M. Forrest, *Francis Galton. The Life and Work of a Victorian Genius* (London, 1974), p. 8.
17. Quoted in Ronald W. Clark's *Freud. The Man and the Cause* (London, 1980), p. 120.
18. 'Kulturweltbürger' (*GW* X, 327).
19. 'Selbstdarstellung', *GW* XIV, 34–35.
20. I am grateful to the Council of the English Goethe Society for incorporating into this chapter some passages of a paper published in the Society's *Proceedings* in 2007. The paper is listed under my name in the Bibliography on p. 137 below.

CHAPTER 6

❖

Adventures of Body and Mind

In a letter to Martha Bernays dated 7 February 1884 Freud recalled the early years of his friendship with Eduard Silberstein and his friend's youthful addiction to 'Redskin-Poetry' and tales about sailors.[1] In the former category he mentions particularly the 'Leatherstocking' cycle by James Fenimore Cooper (1792–1851); he does not specify an author in the second one, but will have had in mind novels of naval adventures by Captain Frederick Marryat (1792–1848), whose German translations and adaptations have delighted generations of German children, catering to a taste for adventures on land and sea also fired by native German authors ranging from the ever-popular Karl May to the more selectively known Friedrich Gerstäcker. We shall find that Freud, in later years, found equivalent pleasures in the tales of explorers, missionaries, and folklorists, gathered in the course of his researches for *Totem and Taboo*.

One work by a writer in whose National Portrait Gallery effigy Freud detected 'heroic' features[2] stimulated youthful imaginations in just the same way: *The Last Days of Pompeii* by Edward Bulwer-Lytton, First Baron Lytton (1803–73). This was almost certainly the unnamed novel by Bulwer which Freud sent to Eduard Silberstein on 4 September 1874; it met Freud's long interest in archaeology, first awakened by Heinrich Schliemann's search for Homer's Troy. He drew an analogy, later, between his own activity of delving into hidden strata of the mind and the archaeologist's excavation of cities long concealed by the passage of time or natural disasters. His *Delusions and Dreams in Jensen's 'Gradiva'*, first published in 1907, discussed a German novel that has scenes set in Pompeii, bringing Freud's interests in psychology and archaeology fascinatingly together. It is the longest analysis of any work of literature in Freud's writings — he never analysed an English work with comparable thoroughness.

Two lines from Bulwer's play *Richelieu*, the second of which had acquired proverbial status in Britain, impressed themselves on Freud's memory:

> Beneath the rule of men entirely great
> The pen is mightier than the sword.

These lines, which had an easy application to Freud's hopes of affecting the world more powerfully and lastingly than men who were deemed 'great' because of their martial prowess, brought to his mind a related saying by the Oxford satirist John Oldham (1652–83): 'I wear my pen as others do their sword'. This in its turn brought memories of the use of the sword as a sexual divider, preventing intercourse, in the sagas of Siegfried and in Arthurian legend, and the similar use of a stethoscope by a doctor all too easily impressed by sexually attractive female patients. The patient from whose buried memories Freud excavated the quotation from Bulwer became, *The Psychopathology of Everyday Life* tells its readers, a prolific writer in his later days, and used an outsize fountain pen to jot down his thoughts. When Freud asked him why he chose such a large instrument, he replied: 'Because I have so much to express'.[3] An answer, surely, after Freud's own heart!

We have to rely on Ernest Jones's assurance that Freud read some of the novels of Benjamin Disraeli (1804–81) and that he relished *Vanity Fair* — a novel that reached a wider public, in Freud's day, than any other by William Makepeace Thackeray (1812–63). In an unpublished letter dated 10 November 1884, made available to me by courtesy of the Director of the London Freud Museum, Freud announces that he will be sending 'some Thackeray' as a present for his sister-in-law Minna Bernays. This will probably have been the edition of *Vanity Fair* in which Martha Bernays declared herself deeply absorbed in her letter to Freud dated 1 March 1885. In the same letter she speaks of a 'charming' edition of Thackeray's *The History of Henry Esmond, Esq., a Colonel in the Service of Her Majesty Queen Anne, Written by Himself.* This had been given to Minna by Freud's sister Rosa; the edition Minna and Martha liked so much is probably the 1852 edition, got up in the style and typography of the Queen Anne period in which the novel is set.

I can find no traces, in Freud's writings, of overt of subliminal effects of Thackeray's novels; but some of Disraeli's philo-Judaism found an echo in Freud's occasional acknowledgements of the advantages Jewish outsiderdom could bestow: it could give relative freedom from what Freud was wont to call, after Ibsen, the prejudices of the 'compact majority'. Disraeli was clearly one of the people he had in mind when he spoke, in *The Man Moses and the Monotheistic Religion*, of an eminent Briton whose name pointed to Italian-Jewish origins.[4] The name 'Moses', on the other hand, with its echo of Egyptian names, pointed to Egyptian rather than Hebrew provenance. This led to Freud's belief that Moses was not a Jew but an Egyptian, who threw in his lot with an enslaved people and was — Freud thought without a shred of supporting evidence — murdered for his pains by those he had liberated.

In constructing his picture of Moses and his world, Freud drew on a number of British sources — notably the 1907 edition of W. Robertson Smith's *Lectures on the Religion of the Semites* and J. H. Breasted's *A History of Egypt*;[5] and he used this opportunity to draw a parallel between the Jewish feeling of being exalted and uplifted by their faith in an all-powerful God, and the proudly secure feeling of a Briton who found himself in a foreign country in the turmoil of an uprising:

> The Briton counts on the fact that his government will send out a warship if a single hair of its citizen is harmed; and the troublemakers know that their country does not possess any such warships. Pride in the greatness of the British Empire is therefore partly rooted in a feeling of greater security, in the protection each individual enjoys. That may well resemble the idea of a magnificent God [. . .] pride in Whom coalesces with the feeling of being among the Elect.[6]

It would not be long before Freud had himself to call on the protection Britain extended not only to its own citizens but also to victims of persecution in their own countries. He was kindly received in England, settled in London, and only his death frustrated efforts to have British citizenship bestowed on him. His devotion to British writers — especially, of course, to Shakespeare — would have helped to make this change welcome to both sides.

* * *

Of the nineteenth-century American writers of fiction who have left traces in Freud's writings we have already met James Fenimore Cooper, whose 'Leatherstocking' became familiar to German children as 'Lederstrumpf'; they were then left to get their tongues round 'Natty Bumppo' and 'Chingachgook' as best they could. Cooper's fame was eclipsed, however, by the single work with which Harriet Beecher Stowe (1811–96) did more than any novelist or pamphleteer to rouse the world's conscience about the iniquities of slavery: *Uncle Tom's Cabin, or, Life among the Lowly*, first published in book form in 1852. Memories of this novel regularly surfaced in Freud's analytical sessions. Simon Legree and his black victims seemed to stir up phantasies of beating and being beaten, stimulating childhood sadism and masochism: 'In competition with books of this kind the children's lively phantasy began to invent a wealth of situations in which children are punished and chastised because of their naughtiness and bad habits'.[7] Hardly the effect the author of *Uncle Tom's Cabin* intended — but that is what makes it so interesting in Freud's context. Murdstone beating his stepson in Chapter 4 of Freud's favourite Dickens novel, *David Copperfield*, has had a similar perverse effect on some people — an effect made notorious in our time by Liliana Cavani's *The Night Porter*, with its 'sexy' black uniforms and sado-masochistic concentration camp fantasies.

What Harriet Beecher Stowe did for black slaves, Helen Hunt Jackson (1830–85) sought to do for 'American Indians' ('native Americans') and for oppressed Mexican Americans. This is the intention that resonates throughout her once immensely popular novel *Ramona*, first published in 1884. This historical romance with a tragic ending dealt with the love of an 'American Indian', named Alessandro, for the eponymous heroine, who is hounded to death by covetous and unsympathetic whites. The author intended this novel, which had a long afterlife on the stage and in the cinema, to assure the equitable treatment of Native Americans which her tract *A Century of Dishonour* (1881) had advocated in more discursive form. Beyond telling Paul Roazen that Freud read this novel and talked about it with her, Freud's analysand Edith Jackson did not reveal what Freud thought of it — a gap not filled by any other source.[8]

More surely than Helen Hunt Jackson's life and work, those of Edgar Allan Poe (1809–49) were bound to excite psychoanalytical speculations. As a young man, Freud had read some of Poe's *Tales of Mystery and Imagination*, and had himself written, with a bow to E. T. A. Hoffmann too, a 'shudder-inducing night-piece' ('schauderhaftes Nachtstück').[9] The German term 'schauderhaft' has an element of humorous self-deprecation too; it can mean 'ghastly' or 'awful' in a pejorative sense. Many years later Freud had come across Poe's poems, and quoted, in conversation with George Sylvester Viereck, a line from Poe's poem 'For Annie', in defence of controversial speculations about a universal human 'death drive'. 'Secretly', Freud told Viereck, 'every living being, no matter how intense Life burns [in] him, longs for the cessation [of] "the fever called living"'.[10] The opening stanza of this once famous poem reads:

> Thank Heaven! The crisis —
> The danger is past,
> And the lingering illness
> Is over at last —
> And the fever called 'Living'
> Is conquered at last.

Freud's closest involvement with Poe was brought about when he read Marie Bonaparte's book *Edgar Poe. Étude psychonalytique*[11] and composed a Preface for its French edition, whose German version appeared in the Internationaler Psychoanalytischer Verlag a year later, in 1934. In this Preface Freud praised the way his 'friend and pupil' had allowed the light of psychoanalysis to fall on the work of 'a great and pathologically conditioned poet'. Thanks to her interpretation

> one can now understand how profoundly the character of his work has been influenced by this man's individual psychological makeup. One can also understand, however, that this disposition was itself the result of strong emotional ties and painful experiences in his early youth.

Studies of this kind, Freud continued,

> are not meant to explain the poet's genius; what they show are the impulses that awakened it and the themes these burdened him with. Studying the laws of the human soul in outstanding individuals holds a special fascination.[12]

What Freud, understandably, does not mention in this credo are the perils that await the psychoanalyst, who analyses a writer's work along Freudian lines without being able to call on the 'patient' to validate his interpretations. There can be few readers of Marie Bonaparte's book who are not startled by the arbitrariness of some of her exegeses — a problem that rears its head all too often when Freudian critics try to deal with works of imaginative literature. But then, how many of us, in this post-Freudian era, will not be tempted to discern sexual symbols in the very title of *The Pit and the Pendulum*, and reflect that among writers of fiction in the nineteenth century, Poe is more likely than most to trigger superficially 'Freudian' interpretations?

* * *

In 1927 Karl Federn, a prominent member of the Vienna Psychoanalytical Society, presented Freud with a German translation of the travel narrative by Herman Melville (1819–91) whose original bore the enticing title:

> TYPEE;
> or, a
> Narrative of a Four Months' Residence
> Among the natives of a valley of

THE MARQUESAS ISLAND
or, a
PEEP AT POLYNESIAN LIFE

The German version, published in Stuttgart in 1927, gave the main title a German acoustic slant and abbreviated the subtitle: *TAIPI. EIN SÜDSEE ERLEBNIS* (*An Experience in the South Seas*). Freud kept the book in his collection, where it could feed his love of adventure literature along with the anthropological and ethnographic interest evidenced in *Totem and Taboo*, which had seen three further editions since its first appearance in 1913.

⋆ ⋆ ⋆

Freud's analytic practice reminded him of yet another American, remembered by posterity for just one book: *Ben Hur*. This was the lawyer, politician, and officer in the Union army, Lew Wallace (1827–1905), whose other works include *The Boyhood of Christ* and *Prince of India*. The full title of the novel, published in 1880, which has attracted not only readers but also filmgoers in the silent as well as the sound era, is: *Ben Hur: A Tale of the Christ*. In *The Psychopathology of Everyday Life* it figures in Freud's example of a case of collective amnesia. A group of students from different disciplines are shown discussing the cultural place of the Christian religion when a female philosophy student recalls an 'English' novel she has recently read, in which she found an attractive presentation of the religious movements that agitated the first century AD. That novel, she recalled, depicted the whole of Christ's life, but try as she might, she could not recall its title. The other participants, predominantly male, thought that they knew the novel in question, but they too could not recall its title. The student tried some associations that might help her remember — *Ecce homo, homo sum, quo vadis* — but the right name would not come; she added, perceptively, that she had forgotten the title because it contained an expression a young girl, especially in mixed company, did not like to use — a context in which the Latin word 'homo' could also stir sexual associations.

The young lady, Freud comments, unconsciously felt that the name which formed Wallace's title contained a word that meant 'whore' in German, and that the uttering of such a word in mixed company would amount to a sexual offer. The rest of the company, Freud continues, unconsciously realised the reason for their companion's forgetfulness and 'forgot' in sympathy with her. What should not be overlooked, however, though Freud does not draw explicit attention to it, is that the young woman's attempt to recover her memory led to the appearance of another literary reference: to a novel written fifteen years after *Ben Hur*, Henryk Sienkiewicz's *Quo Vadis*. The meaning of *that* title, 'Where are you going?', might hold a warning against going along the road of sexual allusion, allusions to prostitution and homosexuality, in nineteenth-century mixed company. Things have certainly changed since then.

⋆ ⋆ ⋆

The dreams described in *The Interpretation of Dreams* contained oneiric reminiscences of two minor English novelists. The first of these irrupts into the dreamer's vision of three women in a kitchen:

> As I analyse this dream there springs to my mind a novel I read when I was about thirteen years old; — my reading began with the end of its first volume. I never knew the novel's title or the name of its author, but I remember its conclusion vividly. The hero becomes insane and cries out constantly the names of three women who brought the greatest happiness and the greatest misfortune. One of these names is Pélagie.[13]

The novel whose title Freud claims never to have known is *Hypatia* by Charles Kingsley (1819–75), which he may have read in a French translation. The anguished cry Freud has in mind is Philemon's 'Pelagia, Pelagia, darling sister, think of the pains of hell!' — but he seems to have unconsciously transported Philemon and his courtesan sister into some other, more sensational novel, for Kingsley's hero does not become insane and he dies peacefully in an odour of sanctity. 'The greatest misfortune', however, points to Kingsley's sadistic but historically accurate description of the murder of the novel's titular heroine, the pagan philosopher and mathematician Hypatia, by Christian fanatics in fifth-century Alexandria.

The agonized cry of *Hypatia* may well have merged, in his oneiric memory, with the cry that forms the climax of another nineteenth-century English novel that invaded Freud's dreams: *She*, published in 1887 by Sir Henry Rider Haggard (1856–1925). 'She Who Must Be Obeyed' is a white queen who rules over a dusky population in an imaginary city. She has defied aging as well as death for some two thousand years, as she waits for the reincarnation of a lover lost in her long-distant youth. When Leo Vincey, the hero of the tale, arrives in her kingdom, she believes him to be that reincarnation; but as she seeks to renew her apparently eternal youth in a sacred flame, time catches up with her and she withers into an unimaginable old age and ultimate extinction — a process that is accompanied by shriek after shriek. One of his own dreams, recorded in *The Interpretation of Dreams*, links itself to an incident in Freud's waking life in which a lady had asked him for something to read. Freud had offered her *She*, which he described as 'a strange book, but full of hidden meanings', but the lady waived further explanations, since she knew the book already, and demanded something of Freud's own — some masterpiece he had not yet written. Since *The Interpretation of Dreams*, in which this dream-conversation is recorded, had obviously not yet been published, the lady's request spoke to Freud of his own hopes for a book that he would always think of as the most profound and important he was ever to write.

Freud records two further associations provoked by his dream of Rider Haggard's *She* — both, characteristically, involving Goethe's *Faust*. The imperious woman who seeks to defy the ageing process while awaiting the return of her lover comes to stand for what the penultimate line of Part Two of *Faust* calls 'das ewig Weibliche', the 'eternal feminine'. The question whether Freud believed, with the Goethe of *Faust*, that the 'eternal feminine' is likely to draw mankind upwards, is not resolved, any more than Freud's own question 'What does Woman want?', which he never quite managed to answer to his own satisfaction. What matters most is that the adventure recorded in *She* is associated with Faust's quest for knowledge and understanding. That brings in the second meaning which the dream of Ayesha suggests to its interpreter: the 'immortality of our emotions'. In what sense, the reader will ask, may our emotions be said to be 'immortal? Does this merely reiterate that our earliest emotional experiences are never obliterated by the rest of our life, and may exert their full power when reactivated by later experience? Such questions are met by a further quotation from *Faust* which Freud thought applicable enough to his own case to quote it several times in the course of his life and writings — the passage which expresses Faust's feeling that he may not tell 'the boys' the best he knows:

> Das Beste, was du wissen kannst,
> Darfst du den Buben doch nicht sagen.

Once again Haggard's 'strange book' (Freud stresses its strangeness by emphasizing the adjective in 's o n d e r b a r e s Buch') raises questions that reach far beyond Leo Vincey's adventures in the realm of 'She Who Must Be Obeyed'.[14] What can be the prohibition, or inhibition, that prevents 'the best' being said? Freud mentions his reluctance to reveal as much of his innermost self as his public self-analysis demands, but refuses to go further:

> The further thoughts that connect themselves with my conversation with Louise N. [the patient who had asked him for something to read] reach too deep to become conscious; they are diverted by material brought to mind by the mention of Rider Haggard's *She*.

'This book', Freud continues, 'and a second book by the same author, "Heart of the World", deserve to be called 's o n d e r b a r g e n u g' [strange enough], and many elements of the dream are drawn from these two phantastic novels'.[15]

The book Freud refers to here is Rider Haggard's *The Heart of the World*, published nine years after *She*. This tells of an expedition into deepest Mexico, to an imaginary Aztec region left untouched by the Spanish *conquistadores* in pursuit of wealth and dominion. In both novels, Freud comments, it is a woman who serves as a guide into the unknown (another part-answer to the 'woman question' Freud agonized over). Both feature a perilous journey, and *She* in particular takes the reader into previously unexplored regions — just as, in its own way, *The Interpretation of Dreams* sought to do. In his indispensable book *Sigmund Freud's Dreams*, published in 1980, Alexander Grinstein has listed significant details of Haggard's novel which surface in the oneiric reports of Freud's book. These include being carried over swampy ground, crossing an abyss over planks brought there by the explorers — obvious symbols of Freud's own perilous journey into unexplored regions of his own mind, and the minds of his patients. Other elements of his dream that derive from *The Heart of the World* include Mexican Indians, a female guide, and a wooden house. This last item immediately suggests a coffin, and associates itself with the end of *She* as testimony, once again, of the anxious calculations about the approach of his own death which are so characteristic of Freud — especially after encountering Wilhelm Fliess's eccentric theories about the rhythms that govern the sequence of human life. The perilous journeys bring tired legs — a reminiscence, Freud tells us, of the weariness with which the previous day had burdened him.

By disentangling, as the subject of my book demands, reminiscences of Rider

Haggard's novels from Freud's account of a dream that used some of their elements, I have necessarily ignored many other aspects of a complex whole — envisaging a dissection of the dreamer's body as well as his mind, the irruption of a revered university teacher, memories of an Etruscan tomb in Orvieto, which associates itself with the wooden house of *The Heart of the World*, and so on. But the essential point has been made. Freud's boyhood love of tales of adventure that transported their readers into strange and distant realms continued in later life, occupying not only his waking life but also his dreams with adumbrations of significant emotions and problems. These could be analysed and used to delve deeper into the emotions and psychic problems of other people. The authors of such novels drew on myths that had agitated humanity from its beginnings, on their own sexuality, on acknowledged or unacknowledged psychic problems, and on phantasies and ambitions characteristic of their times. They usually did this without the intellectual and moral distinction, innovative power, structural sense, and aesthetic distancing which characterizes the highest achievements of narrative art. They are able, however, to imagine figures and events that reach into the dream-life, and the conscious and unconscious fears and desires which they share with readers of different degrees of sophistication. That is why they could enter Freud's dreams, mingle with literature of another kind, help him towards insights into himself and others, and furnish symbols for his adventurous quest into the depths of the human mind.[16]

Notes to Chapter 6

1. 'Indianerpoesie [. . .] und Matrosengeschichten' (*Briefe*, p. 104).
2. *Reisebriefe*, p. 252.
3. *The Psychopathology of Everyday Life*, *GW* IV, 219–20.
4. *GW* XIV, 105.
5. J. H. Breasted, *A History of Egypt* (London, 1934).
6. *GW* VI, 200.
7. 'A Child is Beaten' (*GW* XII, 198).
8. Paul Roazen, *Wie Freud arbeitete. Berichte von Patienten aus erster Hand* (Giessen, 1999), pp. 105–06.
9. 21 February 1875, *Jugendbriefe*, p. 104.
10. 'Mean Men Explained by Freud', *London Weekly Despatch*, 28 July 1927.
11. Marie Bonaparte, *Edgar Poe. Étude psychonalytique* (Paris, 1933).
12. *GW* XVI, 270.
13. *The Interpretation of Dreams*, *GW* II/III, 211.
14. *GW* II/III, 456.
15. *GW* II/III, 457.
16. Freud supplemented his reading of fictional adventures by reading accounts of adventures in Africa by Sir Samuel White Baker (1821–93) and Henry Morton Stanley (1841–1904). (Letter to Eduard Silberstein, 14 April 1878–*Jugenbriefe*, 192). He does not specify which works he has in mind.

CHAPTER 7

❖

'Our Highly Interesting Family Novel'

Thackeray's *Vanity Fair* and *Henry Esmond* figured briefly in Freud's correspondence with the Bernays sisters, but while Martha confessed herself absorbed by the former novel, we have only Ernest Jones's assurance that Freud relished it too. But what about Anthony Trollope (1815–82)? Freud attended a talk on him, given to the Vienna Psychoanalytical Society on 22 December 1909, by Otto Rank, who focussed on Trollope's *Autobiography*. Freud took this as an occasion to say that psychoanalysts should take an interest in 'mediocre authors', not to look for solutions of artistic problems, but for the uncovering of a 'psychological core'. Retelling one's ordinary daydreams, he went on, 'would encounter only an indifference', which writers overcame by offering their readers a 'veiled' revelation of the unconscious. 'Inartistic writers' ('Unkünstlerische Dichter') show up the things we are looking for in a frequently obvious way.[1] Whether Freud took what he heard of Trollope's literary production methods as a sign that he was a 'mediocre author' in the Haggard mould is unclear; but so far no sign has surfaced that Freud ever sampled his work for himself.

Charles Dickens (1812–70), however, was a presence in his life as early as 1874. In that year he sent a copy of *The Posthumous Papers of the Pickwick Club* to Eduard Silberstein, hoping, as he said, to satisfy his friend's ravenous hunger for powerful monosyllabic English words'.[2] This perceptive remark shows how much Freud had learnt from his study of the English and German versions of Shakespeare, in which August Wilhelm Schlegel's great gifts as a translator had proved unable to match his author's expressive use of monosyllabic passages like this from Act IV of *King Richard the Second*:

> Your cares set up do not pluck my cares down.
> My care is loss of care, by old care done;
> Your care is gain of care, by new care won;
> The cares I give, I have, though given away,
> They 'tend the crown, yet still with me they stay.

Even the most resolute lopping of weak endings from German nouns, pronouns, and verbs fails to reproduce the effect of this speech as fully as Schlegel would clearly have liked to do:

> Durch Eure Sorg' ist meine nicht geborgen.
> Die mein' ist, daß mir alte Sorg' entrinnt,
> Die Eure, daß ihr neue nun gewinnt.

> Die Sorge, die ich gebe, hab' ich noch:
> Sie folgt der Kron' und bleibet bei mir doch.

Freud and his friend had learnt to appreciate the expressive possibilities of a language which also lets Caliban 'cúrse' where his German reincarnation can only 'flúchĕn'.

When Freud visited his English family in the following year he found himself reminded of *Pickwick* once again. He noted that a nephew whom he describes as 'sharp and deep' had been given the name 'Samuel', which not only had a biblical resonance but which he also shared with Sam Weller and the rather less sharp Samuel Pickwick.[3] And on 7 September 1877 he confesses that instead of studying his academic textbooks he has been reading, or re-reading, 'tutti quanti Pickwick'.[4]

Freud's letters to Martha Bernays commend shorter texts by Dickens which he judged suitable for her own reading and for discussion in her ladies' reading group. These turn out to be the least popular among the famous series of 'Christmas Books' which included *A Christmas Carol* and *The Cricket on the Hearth*. The first of these, *The Chimes*, Freud praises as 'charming and movingly beautiful', sparing Martha any allusion to the indignant and satirical depiction of Victorian poverty in that tale, before (as befits a Christmas Book) the horrified vision of nineteenth-century capitalism dissolves in sweetness and light. It is interesting to find, however, that in later years, when he included *The Chimes* in his celebrated public readings, Dickens found it difficult to summon up sufficient composure at some of the more affecting parts, to project them with the necessary force, the necessary distance. 'I must harden my heart like Lady Macbeth', he exclaimed.[5] That Shakespearean parallel Freud could not have known about, but he will have recognized the deliberate echo of Falstaff's 'We have heard the chimes at midnight, Master Shallow' in Dickens's title.

On second thoughts Freud judged the English style of *The Chimes* a trifle too hard for Martha, and commended instead rereading a Christmas Book she already knew: Dickens's *The Battle of Life*, whose subtitle *A Love Story*, along with its introduction of a medical student as its male protagonist, might have suggested a parallel with the young Freud's own battle to achieve an income sufficient to consummate his love through marriage with Martha. The central metaphor of Dickens's tale, that 'broader battlefield of life' in which, as one of the characters says, 'there's a great deal of slashing and firing into people's heads from behind; terrible trampling down, and trampling on', suggests not only Darwinian and Malthusian struggles to survive, but also Hobbes's dark view of a state of nature — though Dickens, characteristically, has another character lighten this darkness by pointing to opportunities the struggle opens for 'quiet victories, [. . .] great sacrifices of self, and noble acts of heroism'. As befits a Christmas tale we end focusing on the consolatory vision, embodied in a celebration of sisterly love, in which one sister sacrifices her own prospect of conjugal happiness for the sake of the other.[6]

Very soon afterwards, in April 1884, Freud found his own life precipitated into one of the more benevolent regions of a Dickens novel. 'It seems', he writes to Martha,

> That we are now in the second part of our highly interesting family novel ('Riches'). Just imagine — it really sounds like a chapter out of Dickens —

> Paneth and his fiancée have deposited fifteen hundred Gulden in my favour [. . .][7]

The novel whose second part Dickens entitled 'Riches' is, of course, *Little Dorrit*. Did Freud remember, as he rejoices in a windfall that will bring his long-desired marriage nearer, that the Dorrits' change of fortune leads them into a corrupt society that brings new temptations, and new troubles, into their lives?

The trouble that Josef Paneth's generosity brought into Freud's life is a heightened sense of the obligations his straitened circumstances loaded on him — the loans and gifts he had to accept from Samuel Hammerschlag, Josef Breuer, Ernst von Fleischl-Marxow, and other friends and colleagues. But, he added in his letter to Martha on 15 April 1884, is it not just 'that a rich man should seek to alleviate the injustices of birth and the wrongfulness of his advantages?'.[8] This is in the spirit of Dickens's Christmas Books — in particular that archetypal one, *A Christmas Carol*; but it also recalls the philosophy of life of the *Schnorrer*, the beggar who figures in so many of Freud's favourite Jewish jokes. What the *Schnorrer* relies on is the rich man's awareness of Jewish law, which makes almsgiving a religious obligation. He therefore acts as though it were he who confers a benefit on his co-religionist by giving him the chance to perform an act pleasing to God — a reversal of capitalist ways of thinking which has a social as well as a religious *raison d'être*.

Two years before this allusion to *Little Dorrit*, Freud had sent Martha a copy of *David Copperfield* which, as he told Ernest Jones, was his favourite among Dickens's works.[9] In *Freud, Darkness in the Midst of Vision* Louis Breger suggests that Freud saw in his own father the very image of 'Mr Micawber, the eternal optimist, who in the face of life's miseries, always believes that "something will turn up" '.[10] In a letter to Martha dated 5 October 1883, Freud compared *Copperfield* with *Bleak House*, which he found too full of Dickens's 'mannerisms':

> You must have noticed that all our writers and artists have a 'mannerism', a stereotypical series of motives and arrangements which indicate the limits of their art. [. . .] To these mannerisms belong, with Dickens, those flawless girls, selfless and good, so that they are quite colourless; then the fact that all good people immediately become friends as soon as they meet and work together throughout the whole book; then the sharp distinction between virtue and vice which doesn't exist in life (where should I be, for example?); finally, his easy toleration of feeble-mindedness, represented in almost every novel by one or two blockheads or crazy people, who belong to the side of the 'good ones', and so on. Oh, I had almost forgotten the philanthropist, who has such a frightful lot of money and is available for any noble purpose.[11]

'*David Copperfield*', Freud concludes, 'has least of all this. The characters are individualized; they are sinful without being abominable'. He seems to have forgotten that the 'feebleminded' characters he condemned included the divine Mr Dick, with whose obsession about King Charles's head he had compared his own obsession with thoughts of Martha.[12] In *Bleak House*, Freud found only the Mrs Jellyby episodes at all comparable to *David Copperfield*. In other respects he tells Martha on 5 October 1883, it 'ranks far below that incomparable work'. He thought it 'tendentious and hard, like most of Dickens's later writings, and [it] has so many of Dickens's mannerisms'. But, he adds, 'I don't want to spoil it for you; its beauties are obvious, while its faults have to be sought for'.[13]

Despite his objections, Freud had greatly enjoyed *Bleak House* while he was reading it; he felt so involved with the 'dear company' he met there that he found it difficult to write to Martha in German rather than Dickens's English.[14] He found it much more enjoyable than *Hard Times* by which he felt 'wounded deep down', and 'worn down as though scrubbed with a [hard] brush'.[15]

In 1920 Stefan Zweig sent Freud a copy of his book *Drei Meister — Balzac — Dickens — Dostoevski*. Freud acknowledged this on 19 October, praising its empathy and stylistic felicity; he thought its sections on Dickens and Balzac successful but found what Zweig had said about Dostoevsky less to his taste. Discussing Balzac and Dickens, he wrote, was not difficult — they were simple, straightforward types; but Dostoevsky was more psychologically complicated, 'vertrackt', and Zweig's treatment of him left too many 'gaps and residuary puzzles'.[16] One could object to this that neither Dickens nor Balzac is as 'simple and straightforward' as Zweig presented them; the complications of their psyche just do not reach the surface of their fiction as obviously as Dostoevsky's, and are therefore less immediately discernible.

⋆ ⋆ ⋆

The 'mannerisms' Freud had diagnosed in Dickens's novels had made them, he told Jones, 'easy to parody'.[17] 'Bret Harte', he added, 'has done so brilliantly'. The parodies by the American short-story writer and satirist Francis Bret Harte (1836–1902) which Freud had in mind were the *Condensed Novels*, first published in 1878, which included 'The Haunted Man. By Ch-r-s D-ck-ns':

> A knock on the door, and Boots entered.
>
> 'Consider your salary doubled instantly. Have you read *David Copperfield*?'
>
> 'Yezzur.'
>
> 'Your salary is quadrupled. What do you think of *The Old Curiosity Shop*?'
>
> The man instantly burst into a torrent of tears and into a roar of laughter.
>
> 'Enough! Here are five thousand pounds. Open a porter-house, and call it "Our Mutual Friend". Huzza! I feel so happy!' And the Haunted Man danced about the room.

That parodies effectively the sentimentalities Freud had criticized in Dickens, and the Cheeryble-type of financial generosity which strikes so excessively philanthropic a note amid the high capitalism of Victorian England — though Dickens had countered such criticism by claiming the the Cheeryble brothers accurately portrayed actual philanthropists of his time. Bret Harte's parody also strikes, of course, at Dickens's thirst for instant popularity.

Freud's interest in Bret Harte did not come out of the blue. In August 1877 the *Neue Freie Presse* of Vienna had drawn attention to Bret Harte's short stories of American mining life by translating, for the benefit of its readers, two stories, including his masterpiece of 1868, 'The Luck of Roaring Camp'. Freud commended these to Silberstein as 'well worth reading'[18] and showed himself sufficiently intrigued to seek out the *Condensed Novels* without newspaper prompting.

* * *

One of Freud's patients, an unnamed 'elderly lady', directed his attention to *Adam Bede* by George Eliot (1819–80). He read this with interest, and used it to exemplify the contrast between the appearance of a person and that person's character and disposition. George Eliot's novel, he claims, contrasts

> A beautiful but vain and totally stupid girl [. . .] with an ugly but noble one; an aristocrat who seduces the little goose, and a working man who feels nobly and behaves accordingly. The characters don't look what they are.[19]

That characterization fits Hetty Sorrel, Arthur Donnithorne, and Adam Bede himself, in a rough and ready way; but it surely does little justice to George Eliot's presentation of Dinah Morris. The men in the crowd Dinah attracts with her Methodist preaching describe her as 'pleasant looking' and 'the pretty preacher woman'; and the novel's narrator sums up the impression her face creates as that of 'a white flower with light touches of colour on their pure petals'. It will never do to force George Eliot's characters into the rigid scheme of contrasts Freud seeks to draw.

On 6 January 1885 Freud tells Martha Bernays that he has ordered a work by George Eliot, which he does not name, as a present for her sister Minna;[20] and he informs the same correspondent, on 6 August of the same year, that the has a four-volume version of *Middlemarch* in front of him while he is writing. Could that have been the delayed arrival of the present intended for his sister-in-law? He certainly read it himself; for, as he told Ernest Jones much later, *Middlemarch* appealed to him greatly; he found it illuminated important aspects of his relations with Martha.[21]

Middlemarch has, at its centre, two unhappy marriages; and as I have already shown, much of Freud's correspondence with his fiancée sought to make sure that her expectations of their future marriage tallied with his own. What happens in *Middlemarch*, therefore, could serve as a warning of what might happen if he had chosen less wisely, and if his temperament and Martha's, and their mutual expectations, had been less complementary. Dorothea's marriage to Casaubon is that of a wife who had hoped to help in a great scholarly enterprise but comes to realize that the enterprise is doomed to failure, and that her husband's temperament brings little warmth, and no hope of children, into the partnership. This sets up tensions that draw her to the sexually and vitally more attractive Will Ladislaw. There are moments in the life of everyone engaged in a great intellectual or literary enterprise when the work on which they are engaged seems as little capable of completion as Casaubon's Dictionary of Mythologies — George Eliot had, in fact, admitted her own kinship with this pitiable figure. Freud had sufficient confidence in his own capabilities to make prolonged identification with Casaubon unlikely, and sufficient understanding of Martha's disposition to know that she was neither a Dorothea Brooke nor a Rosamond Vincy. What he expected from the woman he had chosen as his wife was neither aspiration to share in his work nor mere sexual compatibility. He needed a smooth-running domestic household, and a warm family life that would make an affectionate setting within which he could accomplish the work he felt called to do. Martha complied, and provided a settled bourgeois existence without ever seeking to interfere in his professional life.

If Casaubon's life and circumstances offered Freud little material for self-identification, those of Lydgate offered all the more. Lydgate, like Freud, is born into the less affluent branch of a respectable family. Like Freud, he is seized by the passion to make a contribution to science that would be practical, helping patients recover from debilitating illness, as well as theoretical and fundamental. His daily work of observation and inference, he hopes, would lead to insights that would have a practical effect in the wider world. Like Freud, Lydgate finds powerful inspiration in Paris; like him again, he incurs hostility and suspicion from professional colleagues and other establishment figures with entrenched opinions who resent his innovations. Where Casaubon and Dorothea are independently wealthy, Lydgate and his wife have to rely on his professional earnings, and when these prove insufficient they must incur debts — as Freud so often did in his early life. Here, however, we come to the contrast which lends its force to Freud's contention that *Middlemarch* 'illuminated important aspects' of his relationship with Martha. He had made as sure as anyone could be that there would be no danger of the kind of spendthrift extravagance, mute incomprehension, and counterproductive interference that Lydgate had to suffer from the beautiful but spoilt and childishly obstinate Rosamond. The incompatibility in this fictional marriage sets up sexual tensions in which Will Ladislaw is once again the third party. We know of no similar tensions in Freud's (though few marriages lack them altogether); and though Martha took as little real interest in Freud's daily labours as Rosamond in Lydgate's, she was loyally supportive and offered what the central character of John le Carré's *Secret Pilgrim* calls 'the lure of domesticity to a man returned from the front line'. He had every cause to congratulate himself on having chosen more wisely than Lydgate, and to believe that his wife had less reason to bemoan her lot than either Rosamond or Dorothea.

Freud's reaction to George Eliot's *Daniel Deronda*, her last novel, published in 1876, is summed up in his letter to Martha dated 26 August 1882.

> I read it with mounting puzzlement and interest until an hour ago, discounting a few hours of sleep. My well-known impatience made me hurry to get to the end.
>
> I don't know whether you know this work; it is highly remarkable to find a non-Jew writing such a Messiah story. It contains a number of fine and bold observations about Jews, which we would mention only in very intimate circles; outsiders would consider them far too imprudent.[22]

The 'messianic' element which captured Freud's attention adheres to the figure of Mordecai Cohen, whose preaching induces Deronda to seek out his Jewish origins and convert him to Zionism — a Jewish nationalist creed proclaimed in Freud's Vienna by the journalist and playwright Theodor Herzl. The 'imprudent' element Freud alludes to may be seen in George Eliot's presentation of Mordecai's not unsympathetic but more down-to-earth relatives, the family of the pawnbroker Ezra Cohen, who seem to 'make their toilet with little water' and have fingers 'both naturally and artificially dark' — features that go well with the insanitary bathhouse jokes that Western Jews tell about their less assimilated brethren from Eastern Europe, of which Freud has given specimens in *The Joke and its Relation to the Unconscious*. George Eliot also attributes to Ezra's family a 'taste for money-getting [. . .] favoured by success which has been the most exasperating difference in the greed of Jews during all the ages of their dispersion', and depicts Daniel's instinctive shrinking away from 'queer-looking Israelites not without guile' speaking their 'Jew-dialect' in the Frankfurt *Judengasse*. What she has hit upon there is the distaste of many Westernized 'assimilated' Jews for the Yiddish language, in which they could see nothing but a 'jargon' distorting the 'pure' German they took pride in speaking. George Eliot has also given voice, in Daniel Deronda, to a species of Jewish self-hatred diagnosed in Freud's time by Theodor Lessing but disowned by Freud himself. One of the lesser characters in the novel speaks of Jews who have 'words on their lips which mean "I wish I was not born a Jew, I disown my bond with the long travail of my race [...]"'. The Jewish religion seemed to Freud no less an 'illusion' than any other; but however disaffected he might feel from the Yiddish-speaking masses of Eastern Europe, he was too proud, and too fond of his 'outsider' status, to indulge in the lacerating self-hatred of his Viennese compatriot Otto Weininger.

We have no means of telling whether Freud felt alienated by the priggishness of Deronda, the pseudo-biblical language in which Mordecai delivers his Zionist prophecies and admonitions, or the abjectness of Mirah's early attitude to the Gentiles who have taken her in. Whatever critical reservations he may have had, however, the letter to Martha already quoted leaves no doubt about his respect for George Eliot's insights and perspicacity.

* * *

It was Ernest Jones who directed Freud's attention to *The Egoist*, first published in 1879, by George Meredith (1828–1909). The central character of 'Comedy in Narrative' is the nearest English equivalent of Molière's Alceste, and the plot woven around him is recounted in some detail in *The Psychoanalysis of Everyday Life*. Freud found this necessary in order to highlight a subtle instance of Meredith's psychological finesse: two slips of the tongue which betray the true feelings of the novel's principal female character, Clara Middleton, of which she herself is only 'half-consciously aware'. Clara, Freud explains, is betrothed to Sir Willoughby Patterne, the principal though not the only 'Egoist' in this sophisticated 'comedy in narrative', which puts into practice the principles Meredith had deduced from Molière, Aristophanes, Cervantes, and Fielding in his classic 'Essay on Comedy and the Uses of the Comic Spirit'.[23] Clara is increasingly alienated from Sir Willoughby, whose admirable qualities she finds soiled by his narcissistic egoism. She remembers an earlier fiancée who had broken away from Sir Willoughby to marry a captain in the Hussars called Harry Oxford; and since she herself is unwittingly in love with a cousin of Sir Willoughby, Vernon Whitford, she is prone to slips of the tongue of a kind illustrated by utterances such as 'It is, as you say, of Mr Ox — Whitford, beyond me'. She makes similar slips between the two names later; and on another occasion, not picked up by Freud, she speaks of 'Vernon' in a context in which only 'Whitford' would have been appropriate. Freud uses these examples of 'Versprechen' or parapraxis to show that while superficially they only occur because both names end in the same monosyllable, Meredith suggests the deeper reason by making Clara 'profoundly embarrassed' at having unwittingly revealed what Freud calls a 'half-conscious complex'.[24] Sir Willoughby, on the other hand, misunderstands what is happening; he hears the conjunction of 'Ox' and 'Whitford', and 'bursting with laughter in his joyful pride, he called it a portrait of old Vernon in society'. His proud self-absorption makes him incapable of realizing that yet another woman might prefer another man to him.

★ ★ ★

Glad to follow up Ernest Jones's championship of George Meredith, Freud proudly pointed out that he did not need Jones's commendation of another great Victorian: Walter Pater (1839–94). 'It is exciting news', Jones writes to Freud,

> that you are writing on Da Vinci. What a superb subject! [. . .] Do you remember Walter Pater's essay on Da Vinci, published in his *Renascence*? You must quote his page of description of the Monna Lisa. For it is the most magnificent and beautiful passage of its kind in English literature. If you haven't it by now, I enclose a copy of it.[25]

Freud replied on 15 April 1910:

> You must not expect too much of Leonardo, who will come out next month, neither the secret of the Vierge aux Rochers nor the solution of the Monna Lisa puzzle; keep your hopes on a lower level, and it is likely to please you more. Many thanks for the page from Pater, I knew it and had quoted some lines out of the fine passage.[26]

The work Ernest Jones calls *Renascence* appeared first in 1873 under the title *Studies in the History of the Renaissance*; its reissue in 1877 was entitled, more simply, *The Renaissance*. Freud quotes from it in his *A Childhood Reminiscence by Leonardo da Vinci*, using a German translation of 1906. Freud takes from Pater the division of Leonardo's work into three periods, in the last of which he became so devoted to empirical scientific experiment and investigation that much of his energy was diverted from his art. This brings in once again thoughts of another British writer in whose tradition Freud saw himself to stand alongside Leonardo: Francis Bacon. When Leonardo dissected human and equine cadavers, designed flying machines, and studied the nourishment of plants alongside their reactions to poison, he became, in Freud's view, a precursor of Bacon, engaged in the same battle for the advance of valid scientific investigation.[27]

The bulk of Freud's essay, however, is devoted to the personal secrets he saw behind some mysterious female figures in Leonard's paintings, for which he sought clues in the artist's recollection of a dream he had in his youth. One of his principal examples is, of course, the Mona Lisa and the fascination of what Pater describes as 'the unfathomable smile, always with something sinister in it, which plays all over Leonardo's work':

> Besides, the picture is a portrait. From childhood we see this image defining itself on the fabric of his dreams; and but for express historical testimony, we might fancy that this was but his ideal lady, embodied and beheld at last. What was the relationship of a living Florentine to this creature of his thought?[28]

In his attempt to answer the question Pater raised at the end of this quotation, Freud points to the clues already contained in it: the connection Pater makes between Leonardo's female portraits, his childhood, and 'the fabric of his dreams'. In Leonardo's dream of a bird thrusting its beak between his lips Freud sees a recollection of the nurturing mother from whom he was snatched by his father's second marriage which consigned him to a second mother. Freud then quotes some lines from the famous passage in which Pater describes how Leonardo universalized his personal experience in the portrait of the Mona Lisa:

> The presence that rose so strangely beside the waters is expressive of what in the ways of a thousand years men had come to desire. [. . .] All the thoughts and experience of the world have etched and moulded there [. . .] the animalism of Greece, the lust of Rome, the reverie of the middle age with its spiritual ambition and imaginative loves, the return of the Pagan world, the sins of the Borgias. She is older than the rocks among which she sits; like the vampire she has been dead many times, and learned the secrets of the grave [. . .][29]

Freud sees the experience of love throughout the history of civilization encapsulated in the passage, whose 'vampire' image recalls that element of the 'sinister' in the Mona Lisa smile which Freud singled out for praise in Pater's description of it. Pater's view of Leonardo makes him a precursor of Freud himself: the psychoanalyst who made connections between the infant's experience of motherhood, the language of dreams, and the complexities of desire.[30] What Pater confirmed for Freud was that the tenderest of all relationships, that of a baby to its mother, can have something sinister in it when it becomes — as Freud believed it did in the special circumstances of Leonardo's childhood — too smothering. It is this sinister or uncanny element in the relationship which, Freud argues, skewed Leonardo's sexuality, invaded his dreams, and revealed itself in the ambiguous smiles of his female figures that Pater had so convincingly characterized in his justly famous essay.

Pater's essay on Leonardo is followed, in *The Renaissance*, by that on 'The School of Giorgione', which contains the famous observation, italicized by its author, that '*all art constantly aspires to the condition of music*'. Freud was himself unable to respond to music unless he had words and dramatic action or intellectually graspable themes to help him; but he did feel moved to reflect on this art to which all other arts were said to aspire, and to which so many Viennese enthusiastically responded. He unveiled his thoughts at a meeting of the Viennese Psychoanalytic Association on 6 March 1912. Music, he told his audience, might offer the possibility of depicting intensities of feeling tangibly (Affektintensitäten plastisch darzustellen) — a system, perhaps, capable of 'transposing psychic processes' into another medium.[31]

That reverses Pater's contention. It sees in music not something to which all other arts aspired, but a medium which itself aspired, like the other arts seen from a psychoanalytical perspective, to make men and women aware of what went on in the depths of their minds or — to use the word that bears so heavy a charge in Freud's German — their *souls*. In the letter with which Arnold Zweig inaugurated their correspondence, Zweig praised Freud for 'reintroducing the soul into psychology' — and so far from repudiating this, Freud took it, in his answering letter, as a sign of Zweig's 'true appreciation' of psychoanalysis.[32]

The mysteries of music into which we have here seen Freud attempting to delve were never quite cleared up for him. It remained a purely intellectual solution which did not send him into the concert halls to which all Vienna flocked so eagerly; and, as Herman Nunberg observed, when Freud mentioned opera at their Wednesday meetings, the 'themes' he isolated in Wagner's *Flying Dutchman*, Strauss's *Elektra*, or Mozart's *Don Giovanni* and *The Marriage of Figaro*, were literary rather than musical.[33] Earlier on he had found a satiric political analogy in Gilbert and Sullivan's *Mikado*, first performed in 1885. Czar Nicholas II had called, in 1898, for an international disarmament conference to be held in St Petersburg. 'It is fortunate for us,' Freud comments in a letter to Wilhelm Fliess dated 31 August 1898, 'that the young man suffers from obsessional ideas [...] and "can't see blood" like Koko in *The Mikado*. To top it all Koko is the Lord High Executioner.' Freud detects an egoistic subtext in this call for peace — what the Czar really hoped to achieve was a peaceful dismemberment of China.[34]

Experience of the other great mystery — the otherness of women and their secret desires — Freud could hardly avoid, considering how many of his patients, pupils, fellow-analysts, and family members were female. His psychoanalytic probe never reached deep enough; and Pater's description of the alluring and uncanny smile of the Mona Lisa echoed his own sense of that mystery and otherness. It thus became part, alongside protagonists in the fictions of Dickens, George Eliot, and Meredith, of the 'highly interesting family novel' of which Freud had spoken to Martha Bernays, in relation to *Little Dorrit*, in the early days of their relationship.

One British author seemed, to the young Freud, to bridge the gulf between fiction-writing and philosophy: Thomas Carlyle (1795–1881), whose *Sartor Resartus* of 1836 he praised extravagantly in a letter to Silberstein dated 13 August 1874. He saw in Carlyle a combination of Faust and Mephistopheles, satirist and philosopher, and in his central protagonist, Professor Teufelsdröckh, a fictional creation that at once covered and revealed 'open wounds' of mankind. The Professor's comic name, and the comic German names of other characters in the story, Freud told his correspondent, concealed profound wisdom, and his 'philosophy of clothes' suggested metaphysical truths about the spirit that hid itself shamefacedly in our bodily form. He resembled German writers like Jean Paul, and that, together with his metaphysical bent, made this Scottish writer a cultural member of a German 'family' whose language he caricatured so affectionately, and a supranational company to which Freud felt himself to belong.[35]

Notes to Chapter 7

1. *PWAV* IV, 62.
2. 4 September 1874, *Jugendbriefe*, p. 68. 'English words' appears *in English* in Freud's original letter.
3. 9 September 1875, *Jugendbriefe*, p. 143.
4. *Jugendbriefe*, p. 69.
5. Quoted by Peter Ackroyd, *Dickens* (London, 1990), p. 805.
6. Letter to Martha Bernays, 10 January 1884, *Briefe*, pp. 94–95.
7. 15 April 1884, *Briefe*, p. 110.
8. *Briefe*, p. 111.
9. *Jones* I, 190.

10. Louis Breger, *Freud. Darkness in the Midst of Vision* (New York, 2000), p. 26.
11. *Jones*, I, 190–91.
12. 5–6 August 1882 (transcribed for me by Michael Molnar).
13. Transcribed by Michael Molnar.
14. Letter to Martha Bernays, transcribed by Michael Molnar.
15. 'im Innersten wund davon [. . .] wie von einer Bürste aufgerieben', 13 September 1885.
16. *Freud/St. Zweig*, p. 165.
17. *Jones*, I, 190.
18. *Jugendbriefe*, p. 188.
19. *The Interpretation of Dreams*, *GW*, II/III, 296.
20. *Briefe*, p. 135.
21. Letter to Martha Bernays, 12 August 1885, *Briefe*, p. 171; *Jones*, I, 191.
22. *Jones*, I, 191.
23. First delivered as a lecture in 1877.
24. 'Essay on Comedy and the Uses of the Comic Spirit', *GW* IV, 109–10.
25. *Freud/Jones*, 30 March 1910, p. 49.
26. Freud/Jones, p. 51.
27. *GW* VIII, 132–34.
28. Walter Pater, 'Leonardo da Vinci. Homo minister et interpres naturae' (chapter 6 of *The Renaissance: Studies in Art and Poetry*, London 1873).
29. Ibid.
30. *GW* VIII, 134, 181, 182, 186.
31. *PWAV* IV, 62.
32. *Freud/A. Zweig*, pp. 9–10.
33. Introduction to *PWAV* I.
34. *Fliess*, p. 356.
35. *Jugendbriefe*, p. 60. Freud gained some knowledge of Carlyle's life and work from a history of English literature by Johannes Scherr (*Geschichte der englischen Literatur*, 1854) which he commended to Silberstein in this same letter.

CHAPTER 8

❖

'Just So' Stories

The selection of books from his Viennese library Freud brought with him to London and now on the shelves of the Freud Museum does not include most of the nineteenth-century English novels he is known to have read — in his own or borrowed copies — in the course of his life. There is no Dickens, no George Eliot, no Meredith. One novel, however, by a Scottish author, which has thrilled boys in many countries since its first publication in book-form in 1883, did find its way onto his London shelves: *Treasure Island* by Robert Louis Stevenson (1850–94). As his choice of works by Rider Haggard, Charles Kingsley, and Rudyard Kipling also shows, Freud shared his friend Silberstein's predilection for tales of adventure in far-away lands and on the high seas. The copy of *Treasure Island* he had acquired in Vienna was part of the Tusitala edition, published in 1925. He did not, however, have to wait for that acquisition before becoming interested in Stevenson's writings; he had already consulted *Across the Plains, With Other Memories and Essays*, first published in 1892, while preparing his *Interpretation of Dreams*. The item in this selection of earlier pieces which most concerned Freud was, not surprisingly, 'A Chapter on Dreams', in which Stevenson opens to the reader 'that small theatre of the brain which we keep brightly lighted all night long, after the jets are down, and darkness and sleep reign undisturbed in the remainder of the body'. Stevenson then introduces a number of plays performed in the interior theatre in the course of a single life, which he confesses, in the end, to have been his own. One of these proved to mark an important stage in the gestation of Stevenson's most memorable uncanny tale: *The Strange Case of Dr Jekyll and Mr Hyde* (1886).

> For two days I went about racking my brains for a plot of any sort; and on the second night I dreamed the scene at the window, and a scene afterward split in two, in which Hyde, pursued for some crime, took the powder and underwent the change in the presence of his pursuers. All the rest was made awake, and consciously, although I can trace in much of it the manner of my Brownies. The meaning of the tale is therefore mine, and had long pre-existed in my garden of Adonis, and tried one body after another in vain. [. . .]

A 'Brownie', in Stevenson's usage, is

> some Familiar, some unseen collaborator, whom I keep locked up in a back garret, while I get all the praise and he but a share (which I cannot prevent him getting) of the pudding. I am an excellent adviser, something like Molière's servant; I pull back and I cut down; and I dress the whole in the best words and sentences that I can find and make. [. . .]

In *Dr Jekyll and Mr Hyde* 'All that was given me was the matter of three scenes, and the central idea of voluntary change becoming involuntary'; 'all the rest was made awake'.

We have no proof that Freud ever followed up this account by reading the famous tale on which Stevenson's conscious self, shaped by experiences in nineteenth-century Edinburgh, collaborated with his dreaming self and the 'Brownies' that led his imagination to conjure up a seemingly wholly benevolent figure who manages to split off, into a separate personality, an evil element that dwelt within him. One might speak, in Freudian terms, of an Id confronting its Ego. Neither in *The Interpretation of Dreams* nor in any subsequent work does Freud discuss the psychological implications of the haunting tale of the 'good' Dr Jekyll letting loose the aptly named 'Hyde', the hidden part of his waking self. Even Freud's essay on 'The Uncanny' fails to mention this startling example of a tale of terror 'not of Germany, but of the soul', or Stevenson's account of its gestation: dreams worked on by a conscious mind.

A tale of this kind which Freud does mention, and commend to Wilhelm Fliess and his wife, is 'The Phantom Rickshaw' by Rudyard Kipling (1865–1936). He does this in a letter to Fliess of 21 October 1892.[1] First published in 1885, this short story, set in the India Kipling knew so well, had many of the classic ingredients of the Uncanny. One of these is uncertainty; are we, as several characters suggest, listening to the tale of a man driven mad by guilt and subject to a return of the repressed, or are the 'phantoms' that haunt him, which include a no longer extant rickshaw as well as a wronged woman and her dead *jhampanis*, real 'revenants' visible only to the guilty man they have come to haunt? That they appear in order to thwart the man's sexual conquest of another woman will have attracted Freud to this particular tale: he was to describe a similar obsession in his classic essay 'The Uncanny', first published in 1919.[2]

The Indian world into which these spectres irrupt is presented in minute particulars; it is therefore, as Freud learnt from Schelling, at once *heimlich* and *unheimlich*: the place in which even your most secret self should feel at home become un-homely, uncanny. Kipling is not sparing in descriptions of the terror felt by the haunted man at the appearance of something called, successively, 'the Horror', 'the Infernal Thing', 'It', 'that ghastly phantom'. His very epigraph opens a metaphysical dimension by speaking of 'Powers of Darkness' in league — as Freud will have noticed — with 'ill dreams'. The uncanny in Kipling's tale has, as so often happens in works of this kind, something of the comic about it — it again and again provokes the haunted protagonist to bitter laughter without lessening its terror for him, or its thrill for the reader. These are the complexities that confronted Freud as he responded to Kipling's presentation of a man who believes that 'Powers of Darkness' are breaking into his familiar world to punish him for heartlessly spurning the most ardent and genuine love he would ever know. A psychopathic study, perhaps, but not without its metaphysical *frisson*.

The letter to Fliess of 21 October 1892 which recommended 'The Phantom Rickshaw' also commended Kipling's novel *The Light that Failed*, whose definitive version was first published in 1891. Its depiction of an unhappy childhood, in which the central figure is constantly beaten and becomes sadistic in his turn, beating smaller boys 'cunningly and with science', looks forward to Freud's later study of sado-masochism, 'A Child is Beaten. Contribution towards an Understanding of the Inception of Sexual Perversions'.[3] The novel's protagonist serves as a soldier in the Sudan and becomes a painter in London, where he is inspired by James Thomson's 'The City of Dreadful Night' (1880) to create his masterpiece, emulating Dürer with a painting called *Melancolia*. Kipling inserts generous quotations from 'The City of Dreadful Night', introducing Freud to a study of resolute pessimism, a 'forehead charged with baleful thoughts and dreams', and a figure of whom it is said:

> Baffled and beaten back, she works on still;
> Weary and sick of soul, she works the more,
> Sustained by her indomitable will.

That is not unlike the feeling and attitude we have found Freud admiring in Milton's Satan; a *quand même* or *Dennoch* spirit he fostered in himself and encouraged in his wife and in his patients. The painter at the centre of Kipling's novel is rendered blind by an old wound, and his masterpiece is destroyed by a vengeful woman — a vandalism of which he remains ignorant at first. When he finds out, and his blindness renders him unable to recreate his *Melancolia*, he seeks and finds death among Britain's enemies in Egypt. Always aware of pluralities of meaning, Freud will have understood that Kipling's title referred not only to the tragedy of a painter's blindness, but also to failures in a love that promised so well, and an early loss of faith caused by a sadistic woman 'who made the child loathe her God as intensely as he loathed her'.

The Light that Failed also brought Freud an early encounter with Edgar Allan Poe. A sexually charged encounter at sea, with a woman the narrator describes as 'a sort of Negroid-Jewess-Cuban, with morals to match', inspires a painting prompted by recollection of lines from Poe's 'Annabel Lee':

> And neither the angels in Heaven above
> Nor the demons down under the sea,
> Can ever dissever my soul from the soul
> Of the beautiful ANNABEL LEE.

This serves Kipling to introduce, once again, a characterization that secularized religious terms to suggest mingled good and evil in a woman who 'served as a model for the devils and angels both — sea-devils and sea-angels, and the soul half-drowned between them'. Together with the narrator's reference to a 'naked, choking soul' this meets Freud's conviction that he was born to be a healer of *souls* as well as minds — that he was in his way as much a 'Seelsorger' as any parson. The painting that depicts the woman who united the qualities of angels and devils is said to have turned out 'very fine and creepy': a touch of the uncanny again, to be stored in Freud's memory.

In the letter of 1 November 1906, in which Freud acceded to Hugo Heller's request to name 'ten good books', Kipling figures among the authors of books that resemble good friends, books to which one owes some of one's knowledge of life and view of the world, without inspiring a shy veneration, a feeling of one's own littleness in face of such greatness.[4] The work Freud names, however, to represent a 'good friend' among Kipling's writings, is *The Jungle Book*. In a paper entitled 'Reading Freud through Freud's Reading' included in *Reading Freud, Explorations and Entertainments*[5] Peter Gay has pointed to Freud's paper on '"Cultural" Sexual Morality and Modern Nervosity' of 1908, and his later cultural criticism in *Civilization and its Discontents*, to explain the attraction of Mowgli's experiences among his animal family, friends and foes, concluding:

> When Mowgli goes among men for a time, 'he had to wear a cloth round him, which annoyed him horribly'. Kipling's lesson seems plain [. . .]: men cover up their libido and their aggressiveness behind bland and mendacious surfaces; animals are superior beings, for they acknowledge their drives. They can hate and hate well, but, as Kipling explicitly and emphatically observes, they can love no less. The stories he wove around Mowgli, then, are intended to lift the reader above the humdrum, mediocre, middle-class world into the realms of candor, of free experience, of heroism.[6]

Freud will have noticed, however, that for all his love of the animals who befriend him and his respect for the Jungle Law all virtuous creatures obey, Mowgli learns, as he grows up, that he is not one of them — that, as the controlling power of his eyes tells him, man is ultimately master; and it is among men that he has to find his place. Even in his darkest hours Freud could not think of animals as 'superior beings' in any but the most limited sense.

Freud had two further encounters with Kipling. The first of these occurred in 1910, when Hanns Sachs introduced himself by presenting him with a copy of his congenial translation of Kipling's *Barrack Room Ballads*. Freud deemed this worthy of being taken to England when he found his last refuge there: it still represents Kipling on the shelves of Freud's library in the London Freud Museum. And he showed himself amused when 'a not unkind English critic', R. R. Marett, called the central hypotheses of *Totem and Taboo* a '*Just So Story*' — a reference to Kipling's delightfully fantastic animal stories for children.[7] This shows that Freud was capable of self-irony and, occasionally, scepticism about his own hypotheses.

* * *

In the list of 'good books' Freud sent to Hugo Heller in 1906 Kipling is joined by Mark Twain (1835–1910) whose famous telegram to the Associated Press ('The report of my death was an exaggeration') had become a staple of Freud's own humorous reports on his wellbeing. He had told Martha Bernays on 25 February 1884 that he had bought a volume of Mark Twain in order to cheer himself up: but he regretted that Martha, 'like all other women', failed to share his taste for that author's work. He would therefore circulate the volume among male friends like Breuer and Hammerschlag: 'but if you were here, my darling, I would make you laugh with the same stories' (unpublished letter, transcribed for me by Michael Molnar). On 3–4 August 1885 he reports to Martha that he is reading *The Adventures of Tom Sawyer*, and Jones confirms his liking for that book (*Jones* I, 191). The book he numbers among his favourites in the letter to Heller, however, is neither *Tom Sawyer* nor the greatly superior *Huckleberry Finn*. The book he names, rather, is one he calls *Sketches* — by which he presumably means *The Celebrated Jumping Frog of*

Calaveras County, and Other Sketches (1876), or Mark Twain's *Sketches, Selected and Revised by the Author*, published by Chatto and Windus in 1903. Both are headed by the 'Jumping Frog' story, which Twain based on a folk tradition but made his own with its sharp characterization, deadpan narration, and memorable use of a form of rural American dialect which is comprehensible even to those who have never heard it spoken. Freud *did* hear it spoken, by the author himself, when he attended what has become know as Twain's 'Morals Lecture', which brought the author to Vienna in 1898 in the course of a world tour. At this early time Freud could already regard Mark Twain as an 'old friend' — an author, that is, whose writings were familiar to him and which he had thoroughly enjoyed. 'I have allowed myself the pleasure', he wrote to Wilhelm Fliess on 9 February 1898, 'to hear our old friend Mark Twain in person, and relished it thoroughly'.[8] Twain's ironic look at conventional morality, illustrated by trickster stories from his rich store of tall tales, burlesque biographies, demonstrations of the malevolence of objects, prickings of overblown reputations, satires on American tourists in Europe, and subversions of moral commonplaces, also found its way into the *Sketches* Freud prized so highly. Thirty-two years after hearing the 'Morals Lecture' Freud remembered its details clearly enough to illustrate, in *Civilization and its Discontents*, the phenomenon of what passes for a 'conscience' awakened by misfortune:

> As long as things go well with people, their conscience is mild and allows the Ego all sorts of latitude; but as soon as misfortune strikes, they look into themselves, recognize their sinfulness, heighten the demands of conscience, impose abstinence on themselves, and punish themselves with penances.

Freud follows this with a footnote:

> Such enhancement of morality through ill-luck Mark Twain treats in a delightful little story: 'The First Melon I Ever Stole'. The melon happens to be unripe. I heard Mark Twain himself recite this story. After he had read out its title, he asked himself, as if in doubt: 'Was it the first?' That said everything: the first, then, had not remained the only one.[9]

Uncharacteristically Freud has missed a nuance here: for Mark Twain has the thief turn the tables on the man he robbed by making *his victim* feel guilty:

> I was spiritually strengthened and refreshed and carried that watermelon back to that farmer — restored it to him, and told him he ought to be ashamed of himself going around working off green watermelons on people who had confidence in him; and I told him in my perfectly frank manner it was wrong. I said that if he did not stop he could not have my custom, and he was ashamed [. . .]. I restored the watermelon to him and made him give me a ripe one. I morally helped him, and have no doubt that I helped myself the same time, for that was a lesson which remained with me for my perfection. Ever since that day to this I never stole another one — like that.

The 'moral' lesson the narrator takes away is that he should not steal fruit 'like that' — i.e. unripe — in future. The implication is that he will have no such scruples when stealing *ripe* watermelons.

Twenty-five years before *Civilization and its Discontents*, Freud had used examples from Mark Twain to show the principles underlying the humour he relished so much in the 'Morals Lecture'. He uses once again his psychological analogy with the physical principle of 'conservation of energy' when he has Mark Twain relate grotesque misfortunes that befell his family: an explosion throws them all into the air, but the tale is told in such a way that the reader disregards the injuries such an event would cause and thus saves the 'affective energy' such a reader would have had to expend on compassion. Another tale works through comic exaggeration, and through the substitution of comic delight for annoyance one would feel at such happenings in real life. Yet another uses a fictive story about less than respectable ancestors to subvert the respect we might be inclined to feel when presented with a family tree that goes back to Columbus: an antidote to the common 'family romance' which makes our ancestry more estimable, or of higher social class, than happens to be the fact.[10]

When Freud looked back, in 1914, on the development of the psychoanalytic movement, he remembered Twain's ridicule of 'family romances', and applied it to claims made by Jung and Adler for their deviance from Freudian orthodoxy:

> One remembers Mark Twain's famous story of the fate of his watch, and the wonderment that concludes it: 'And he used to wonder what became of all the unsuccessful tinkers, and gunsmiths, and shoemakers, and blacksmiths; but nobody could ever tell him'.[11]

Because the Jungian and Adlerian defectors think the origins of Freudian psychoanalysis too 'low', they invent a more 'respectable' ancestry for themselves — one that does not recognize its roots in the sexuality and the 'Family–and-Oedipus-complex' acknowledged by Freud's more faithful followers.

Freud's essay on 'The Uncanny' finds room for Mark Twain once again. This time it is *A Tramp Abroad* which provides him with a welcome illustration of involuntary repetition ('Wiederholungszwang') when its protagonist describes wandering about in an unfamiliar room in the dark, and colliding again and again with the same piece of furniture. Humorous tone and grotesque exaggeration ensure, however, that the experience loses whatever shudder-inducing potential it might have had in another context and the work of a less amusing narrator.[12]

Mark Twain's *Sketches*, which Freud lists among his 'good friends' in his letter to Hugo Heller, feature one piece which Freud does not mention but which must have struck a sympathetic note in so dedicated a cigar-smoker. It comes in a section headed 'Answers to Correspondents', which contains Mark Twain's strictures on killjoys and 'moral statisticians' who

> never try to find out how much solid comfort, relaxation, and enjoyment a man derives from smoking in the course of a life-time [. . .] nor the appalling aggregate of happiness lost in a life-time by your kind of people [. . .]

The catastrophic effects of smoking, which Freud was to experience for himself in his later life, were not fully known when Mark Twain wrote this passage.

* * *

A political battle fought, in 1934, by Austrian Marxists against the government of Chancellor Dollfuss, brought to Freud's mind a story by one of Mark Twain's American contemporaries. The story, which Freud had discussed in 1933 with Hilda

Doolittle, was entitled 'The Lady or the Tiger?'. Its author was Francis Richard Stockton (1834–1912), who had published it in 1882.

> It cannot go on like this; something is bound to happen. Whether the Nazis will come, or whether our own home-made Fascism will be ready in time, or whether Otto von Habsburg will step in, as people now think. I have a story in the back of my mind which I cannot remember exactly; it's called 'The Lady and the Tiger' and in it a poor prisoner is waiting in a circus, not knowing whether they are going to let the wild beast loose upon him or whether the lady will appear who by choosing him for her husband will release him from punishment. The point of the story is that it ends without our knowing who has arrived, the lady or the tiger. This can only mean that for the prisoner it does not matter which has happened and that it is not worth telling us.[13]

Freud's recollection of the story's plot is reasonably accurate, but his comment is puzzling. Most readers will surely think that it matters greatly to the handsome youth, imprisoned because he had had the audacity to fall in love with the king's daughter, whether a beautiful maiden or a ravenous tiger is behind one of two doors between which he has to choose. When the narrator asks, at the end, 'Who comes out, the lady or the tiger?' Stockton is teasing the reader's expectation of a conventional resolution, daringly keeping the reader, and the young man in the story, in freeze-frame suspense. That suspense — which has made the story famous — is all the greater because the outcome *matters* to the character and the engaged reader.

⋆ ⋆ ⋆

One work by an English writer delighted Freud particularly because it offered an even stronger subversion of moral commonplaces than those he relished in Mark Twain. This was what Freud called, in a letter to Lou Andreas-Salomé dated 13 May 1924, 'Samuel Butler's brilliant phantasy': *Erewhon*, first published, anonymously, in 1872. Freud was particularly taken by this novel's tenth chapter, entitled 'Current Opinions', in which the traveller to this upside-down country (*Erewhon* inverts 'Nowhere') is told by his host Mr Nosnibor (an equally inverted 'Robinson') that the inhabitants equate morality with health and beauty, and consequently treat illness as a crime. Freud therefore tells Lou Andreas-Salomé, who had praised his bravery in bearing the painful operations necessitated by his cancer, that in Erewhon such a fellow as he would not attract praise; he would, instead, have been punished and incarcerated.[14] Freud was, of course, aware that what Butler is drawing out here are the full consequences of the doctrine of 'survival of the fittest' — a phrase Darwin had found in Herbert Spencer and adopted as his own. What Freud did not know was that Butler had, in fact, kept Darwin so much in mind that when he published the shorter piece out of which *Erewhon* was to grow — appropriately 'down under', in New Zealand! — he had entitled it 'Darwin among the Machines'.

⋆ ⋆ ⋆

A letter to Jung, dated 18 June 1906, shows Freud entering a fictional world that offered adventures of the imagination no less exciting than those he had found in the writings of Rider Haggard, Kipling, and Mark Twain. 'Fräulein Spielrein', he writes, 'confessed to me that you yourself were the person concerned. [. . .] I answered in an extraordinarily wise and acute fashion, puzzling out what the situation held in the manner of Sherlock Holmes'.[15] One of Freud's most famous patients, generally known as 'The Wolf Man', thought he was telling his analyst something new when he mentioned a fictional detective whose methods resembled those Freud habitually used — only to learn that Freud knew and relished the tales Conan Doyle had spun around Sherlock Holmes. It is not difficult to see how psychoanalyst and detective resembled one another. In both cases a keen observer focused on tiniest details, and used reason, experience, learning, and imagination to interpret them in such a way that they revealed things hidden in the past. The account of these exploits moved both forwards and backwards: forwards in describing the process of arriving at what is hoped to be the truth; backwards towards uncovering it. In fiction, of course, the 'truth' will turn out to be whatever the writer had predetermined. In psychoanalysis the pattern the analyst teases out must be confirmed by a patient, subject, alas, to a double bind: if he agrees, the interpretation is correct; if he disagrees, he is merely showing a 'resistance' that is another kind of confirmation.

The taste fostered by Conan Doyle (1859–1930) precipitated, in Freud's old age, a liking for more recent detective fiction. Jones tells us that Freud's recreational reading included the work of Dorothy Sayers, which means that he encountered Lord Peter Wimsey. It may be imagined — though I have found no documentary proof — that he did not neglect Agatha Christie either, and that he had some fellow feeling for the way Hercule Poirot exercised those 'little grey cells'. What has to be remembered, however, is that Conan Doyle, unlike Lord Peter and Hercule but like Freud himself, had qualified as a physician; he had, in fact, based the methods of his iconic detective on those of his teacher in medical school, Dr Joseph Bell. These involved the penetration of disguises assumed by different diseases, intense scrutiny of often tiny physical and mental indices, and the detection of something in the present that could be made to speak of the past — analogous to Freud's attentive examination of dream and memory fragments that might yield clues to earlier traumata. All this needs sharp observation coupled with imaginative insight, deductive powers, and an ability to detect and co-ordinate patterns — skills which Freud believed himself to share with Sherlock Holmes, along with experience of tobacco and cocaine. While this led in Freud's case to early discovery of the anaesthetic properties of cocaine (as well as some spectacular error in prescription), Holmes is presented as expert in different kinds of tobacco ash. Freud, alas, had to experience on his own body the cancer-inducing effects of tobacco which were so little appreciated in his time.

⋆ ⋆ ⋆

In the Victorian world that forms the setting of Conan Doyle's Sherlock Holmes tales reason triumphs in the end, and order, disturbed by error and crime, is restored. It is far otherwise in the fictional world of E. T. A. Hoffmann (1776–1822), which serves Freud as a classic example in his essay on 'The Uncanny' (1919). Such great Victorian tales in that shudder-inducing genre as Stevenson's *Dr Jekyll and Mr Hyde* and Wilde's *The Portrait of Dorian Gray* failed to make it into that essay; another work by Oscar Wilde (1854–1900) did make it, only to serve as an example of the potentially uncanny defused of its terror and made 'irresistibly comic':

> Even an 'actual ghost, like that in O. Wilde's tale 'The Canterville Ghost', must lose all claim to raising even a shudder if its author allows himself the fun of having it ironized and teased. The effect fiction has on its readers can be as independent of its subject as this example shows. In a fairy-tale world feelings of anxiety, including uncanny ones, can never be aroused. We understand that, and therefore ignore what might have stirred up uncanny feelings [in a different context].[16]

My own experience of certain *Märchen* by the Grimms and Andersen contradicts Freud's rather too sunny view of the whole genre; but he is surely right in the case of 'The Canterville Ghost'.

* * *

As a young man Freud had read one of the great Victorian autobiographies: that of John Stuart Mill, first published in 1873. In his letter to Martha Bernays of 15 November 1883, we found him concentrating not on Mill's account of his education, and his relation to his famous father, but on those with his wife. He called it 'prudish and unearthly', and complained, as we have seen, that Mill seemed to have known nothing of the love Freud and Martha felt for each other, the kind that results in the production of children; and that he compensated for this by making his wife out to be a more excellent person than she probably was. Freud's library shows that in later life he came across, and acquired for himself, one of the last of these classic autobiographies of people who grew up in the reign of Queen Victoria: Edmund Gosse's *Father and Son. A Study of Two Temperaments*, first published in 1907. Freud owned a copy published in 1912 in which he marked the opening paragraph:

> This book is the record of a struggle between two temperaments, two consciences, and almost two epochs. It ended, as was inevitable, in disruption. Of the two human beings here described, one was born to fly backward, the other could not help being carried forward. There came a time when neither spoke the same language as the other, or encompassed the same hopes, or was fortified by the same desires. But, at least, it is some consolation to the survivor that neither, to the very last hour, ceased to respect the other, or to regard him with a sad indulgence.

One would dearly like to have had Freud's take on what Harold Nicolson rightly called a 'masterpiece' whose author had been able 'to combine the maximum of scientific interest with the maximum of literary form'. The scientific interest lies in the father's struggle to reconcile the zoology in which he was an expert with his religious fundamentalism, after Darwin's onslaught on the biblical account. This was, as we know, a subject of great interest to Freud — but of even greater interest would have been the son's struggle with the father, which brought perceptibly more emotional ambivalence into the book than the sentence about their mutual 'respect' and 'sad indulgence' allowed. Freud's intense scrutiny of the psychological patterns of family relationships gives modern readers greater insight into typical aspects of Gosse's loving struggle with his father than would have been possible to the author's contemporaries — or, indeed, to the author himself.

* * *

Freud's adventures among British and American books, which from the first included novels read purely for recreation, led to encounters with sleuths whose method of detecting crimes resembled those he used in seeking to solve the secrets of the psyche.[17] They also led to the delighted discovery of humorists who questioned bourgeois moral certainties, and fabulists who shared his fascination with the uncanny — a region of uncertainty that might be, but never quite was, colonized by rational explanation. He welcomed a witty aphorism by Oliver Wendell Holmes (1809–84) as a paradox in which the second part effectively negated the first, citing it in *The Joke and its Relation to the Unconscious* as an example of American wit that defied translation into German.[18] He told Jung on 14 August 1910 that by reading J. L. Motley's *The Rise of the Dutch Republic* (1856) he learnt how 'something which seemed incredibly puny could become great by dint of determined effort and unshakable resolve'.[19] And after the highways of Stevenson, Kipling, Mark Twain, and Samuel Butler, he found in the byway of R. S. Stockton's gladiatorial fable a symbol for a political situation he views with apprehensive puzzlement; and he discovered for himself Edmund Gosse's account of a conflict with a loved and loving father that offered parallels with a defining conflict in his own life — that ambivalence of feeling which had led Freud into the great adventure of psychoanalysis and its 'Just So' stories.

Notes to Chapter 8

1. *Fliess*, p. 20.
2. *GW* XII, 244.
3. *GW* XII, 197–226.
4. *Briefe*, pp. 267–68.
5. Peter Gay, *Reading Freud, Explorations and Entertainments* (New Haven and London, 1990).
6. Gay, *Reading Freud*, pp. 104–05.
7. *Group Psychology and Ego Analysis*, *GW* XIII, 136.
8. *Fliess*, p. 327.
9. *Civilization and its Discontents*, *GW* XIV, 485–86.
10. *The Joke and its Relation to the Unconscious*, *GW* VI, 263f.
11. 'Towards a History of the Psychoanalytic Movement', *GW* X, 107.
12. GW XII, 250.
13. 25 February 1934, *Freud/A. Zweig*, p. 76. The translation is by William and Elaine Robson-Scott.
14. *Briefe*, p. 367.
15. *Freud/Jung*, p. 259.
16. *GW* XII, 267.
17. See *Fliess*, p. 443 — 11 March 1990: 'I surrender myself to my phantasies, play chess, read English novels; everything else is kept at bay.'
18. *GW* VI, 33: 'Put not your trust in money, but put your money in trust.' Freud owed this reference to A. A. Brill. His library contained Holmes's *The Autocrat of the Breakfast Table*, first published in 1857–58; Freud's copy, published in London, is undated.
19. *Freud/Jung*, p. 384.

CHAPTER 9

❖

Ideological Interlude

As a young man, Freud had been given a taste of the Victorian faith in progress by Heinrich Braun, a future socialist leader, who had advised him to read two popular British authors of the day. The first of these was Henry Thomas Buckle (1821–62), whose *History of Civilization in England*, first published between 1857 and 1861, Freud remembered reading on Braun's recommendation.[1] Buckle commended a great principle he called 'scepticism', by which he meant enquiry untrammelled by received opinion:

> To scepticism we owe that spirit of inquiry, which during the last two centuries has gradually encroached on every possible subject; has reformed every department of practical and speculative knowledge; has weakened the authority of the privileged classes, and thus placed liberty on a surer foundation; has chastised the despotism of princes; has restrained the arrogance of the nobles; and has even diminished the prejudice of the clergy [. . .] it is this which has remedied the three fundamental errors of the olden time: errors which made the people, in politics too confiding; in science too credulous; in religion too intolerant.[2]

In his autobiography and elsewhere, Freud prided himself on scepticism of this kind, crediting the outsider status Austrian anti-Semitism conferred on him for strengthening his independence of mind.[3] The other British author to whom Braun directed his friend's attention was William Edward Hartpole Lecky (1838–1903). Freud could not remember the title of the work in question; it was probably Lecky's popular *History of the Rise and Influence of the Spirit of Rationalism in Europe* (1865), in which Lecky celebrated 'the great critical movement which has renovated all history, all science, all technology'. This movement, he claimed,

> has penetrated into the obscurest recesses, destroying old prejudices, dispelling illusions, rearranging the various parts of our knowledge, and altering the whole scope and character of our sympathies. But all this would have been impossible but for the diffusion of a rationalist spirit obscuring or destroying the notion of the guilt of error. [. . .][4]

Freud had learnt about 'the guilt of error' the hard way, for he had more than once had to abandon a cherished theory under the weight of contrary evidence. In his early days he sometimes fled into denial and cooking the books — but in his more truthful prime he had accepted the Lord's dictum in Goethe's *Faust* ('Es irrt der Mensch, so lang er strebt') and stressed the positive value of errors: they could lead to necessary correction.

What Freud learnt from Buckle and Lecky took shape in his criticism of Georg Brandes's views on John Stuart Mill. Brandes's essay, he told Martha on 15 November 1883, only gives one a personal impression of the man while failing to appreciate Mill's position in the history of his times. Mill was perhaps, the young Freud believed, 'the one man in the century who managed to free himself from the tyranny of common prejudices' — a view Freud had to correct when he came to know and value such subversive classics as Butler's *Erewhon*. The young Freud goes on to temper his praise of Mill by asserting that he lacked a sense of the absurd; and as we have already seen, he found the 'absurdities' particularly in Mill's championship of female emancipation, and more generally in what the young Freud called 'die Frauenfrage': the question of the status of women in society. Here the young Freud's own failure to free himself from prejudice showed itself all to clearly; and as so may studies have shown, he never found a satisfactory answer to his perennial question 'Was will das Weib?' — what, precisely, do women want?

Freud's belief in the virtues which Lecky termed 'rationalism' was strengthened and confirmed by his reading of Bacon's *Novum Organum*; but during and after the First World War he grew increasingly aware of the forces that worked against enlightenment and of the stress which the demands of civilization inevitably caused in those caught up in its progress This set the Id against the Ego and Superego, and caused many of the neuroses whose miseries Freud attempted to alleviate in his patients.

It was in this mood that Freud set out to apply what he had gathered from self-analysis and the analyses of neurotic patients to world history, believing, as so many did at the time, that the development of individual human beings mirrored that of society as a whole — that 'ontogeny recapitulated phylogeny'. In particular he sought to ground such guilt-feelings as orthodox Christianity had ascribed to Original Sin to a historical event whose memory had been passed on to successive generations: the slaying of a father by a band of sons. He connected this with totemic beliefs, taboos, and prohibitions regarding marriage and family relationships, which Victorian missionaries, explorers, and investigators of early history, legends, and folklore were chronicling in ever increasing numbers. The systematizations of Auguste Comte and Herbert Spencer joined the evolutionary thinking stimulated by Darwin to produce a tripartite view of human progress which Freud, in his *Totem and Taboo* of 1913, described as animistic or mythological, religious, and scientific — placing himself, and psychoanalysis, firmly in the 'scientific' era. When describing these 'scientific' endeavours he frequently used analogies from physics and chemistry; but his search for roots and origins in the human psyche reminded him most often of the work of archaeologists which had fascinated him ever since he first read of Heinrich Schliemann's excavations in search of Homer's Troy. His own quasi-archaeological quest led him to question the provenance of religious and moral ideas and preconceptions that dominated the minds he set out to study — and for this he sought the help of a multitude of British writings. Among the works he studied were Herbert Spencer's *First Principles* (1862), E. B. Tylor's *Primitive Culture* (1903), Andrew Lang's *In Search of the Totem* (1905), V. Crawley's *The Mystic Rose* (1902), and J. J. Atkinson's *Primal Law* (1903). Some of his reading he found dull;

but there were two writers who fired his imagination and elicited an assent that few more recent anthropologists and ethnologists would give to their findings: Sir James Frazer (1854–1941) and his fellow-Scot William Robertson Smith (1846–94).

Two works of Frazer's which still occupy prominent places on the shelves of Freud's London library were of especial importance to him: *Totemism and Exogamy*, with its significant subtitle *A Treatise on Early Forms of Superstition and Society*, begun in the 1890s and finally published in two volumes in 1910; and the monumental *The Golden Bough*, published in ever-increasing bulk from 1890 to 1915, with its supplemental *Aftermath*, appearing as late as 1936. In *Totem and Taboo* Freud cites Frazer no less than eighty times, piling up laudatory adverbs and adjectives. He commends the 'seriousness' with which Frazer treats 'savage' customs; calls *The Golden Bough* a 'great' work and an 'excellent' collection; praises the honesty with which Frazer acknowledges that some of his arguments are not quite compelling; dubs a sentence he quotes from Frazer 'beautiful' — and frequently quotes Frazer's work in its original English, as if relishing his style sufficiently not to diminish it with his own translation.

Freud was not troubled by Frazer's all-too-easy assumption of 'the essential similarity in the working of the less developed human mind among all races, which corresponds to the essential similarity in their bodily frame and anatomy' and his all-too-glib passage from ancient Rome to modern Africa without a day's personal field-work and with little thought of the widely different tribal and temporal contexts in which the beliefs and practices he chronicled might be seen. Freud found in Frazer's compilations what he needed to draw parallels between 'savage' beliefs and practices and the obsessions of modern neurotics; to find in stories of slain kings, fathers, or tribal chiefs material for his own ramshackle construction of an ancestral crime that worked on in modern consciousness through Lamarckian inheritance; and to trace the primitive roots of religious beliefs he sought to devalue as fantasy or delusion. He also found useful units of classification in the 'law of similarity' and 'law of contact or contagion' according to which Frazer categorized 'sympathetic magic' — laws paralleling those of metaphor and metonymy which have played so conspicuous a part in more recent structural investigations.[5]

Freud's own stylistic ideal was not far from that of Frazer, who had praised Hume, Hutcheson, and other Scottish thinkers because they 'wrote like gentlemen in the language of polished society, and not like pedants in the uncouth jargon of the schools'; and Freud, who had relished Kipling's 'Just So' stories and not been displeased at having his own work compared to them was able to enjoy Frazer's work in the spirit of R. R. Marett, who had called *The Golden Bough* 'that golden treasury of stories for grown-up children' — though Freud had greater faith than Marett in the scientific value of that work. Last but not least; as a persistent classicist and lover of the visual arts Freud could not find a work 'formless' which resolutely kept its material relevant to the legend alluded to in the title of Frazer's gigantic compilation: a title that combined reminiscences of Virgil and Ovid with an allusion to one of Turner's most haunting paintings.

References to Frazer in *Totem and Taboo* are underpinned and supported by references to the work of writers of imaginative literature whose insights parallel *exempla* Freud extracted from Frazer's work. These include writers who externalize their own or others' opposing drives in dramatic figures embodying them — Goethe's *Faust* and *Torquato Tasso* will easily spring to mind. Vengeful ghosts are paralleled by the 'hallucinations' of Shakespeare's Macbeth and Richard the Third; and the ambivalent nature of the ceremonial surrounding kings and governors is illustrated, not only by those found in *The Golden Bough*, but also by the treatment Cervantes makes Sancho Panza experience as governor of Barataria.[6]

* * *

The other writer whom Freud quotes with conspicuous respect in *Totem and Taboo* is William Robertson Smith, whom he describes as a 'physicist, philologist, Bible critic and antiquary', 'many-sided, acute, and of independent mind'.[7] Before quoting from what he calls Robertson Smith's 'excellent book', *The Religion of the Semites*, first published in 1889, he issued a caveat: many 'often so attractive details' will have to be omitted, and what is left 'cannot possibly give the reader an inkling of the lucidity and power to convince characteristic of the original'.[8] Later in the book Robertson Smith is called 'a man of genius', and his insights are welcomed as 'valuable' contributions to our knowledge of how ritual sacrifice relates to totem-veneration; how totemism links up with notions of parricide and exogamy, and how the totem-meal anticipates the Christian Eucharist.[9] Anxious, once again, to give his readers a taste of the actual style of authors he respects, Freud quotes from Robertson Smith's *Religion of the Semites* in its original English; and once again he underpins his argument with references to imaginative literature. 'The most ancient Greek tragedies', he writes in *Totem and Taboo*, 'show remarkable resemblance to the scene of the totem–meal recognized by Robertson Smith'.[10]

Freud's *Timely Thoughts on War and Death*, inspired by experience of the First World War and first published in 1915, lists Robertson Smith, along with Darwin and J. J. Atkinson, among those who helped him towards his idea of parricide as humanity's oldest crime, reverberations of which reach into the lives and consciousness of later generations in the way Original Sin does in orthodox Christian thought.[11] This tribute to British writers is repeated in Freud's autobiographical sketch,[12] and *The Man Moses and Monotheistic Religion*, where Freud explains his use of Robertson Smith's writings:

> I am a psychoanalyst, not an ethnologist, and as such I had the right to extract from the ethnological literature whatever I could use in my analytical work. The writings of Robertson Smith, a man of genius, yielded valuable connections with material gained in psychoanalysis and suggestions on how it could be used [. . .][13]

I cannot share Freud's belief that Moses, an Egyptian by origin, was ultimately murdered by the Israelites with whom he threw in his lot; and that the descendants of these Israelites then bore the burden of this primal guilt throughout their subsequent history. Freud's principal English-language source, J. H. Breasted's *The Dawn of Conscience*,[14] gives no warrant for this idea of parricidal murder; that came from speculations in a German book by Eduard Sellin, published in 1922, and an idea casually thrown out by the young Goethe.[15] It came above all from Freud's obsession with ambivalent father–son relationships and his desire to project what was gleaned from neurotic patients on the psychoanalytical couch into world-history in general and the history of the Jewish people in particular.

★ ★ ★

For Andrew Lang (1844–1912) Freud could not muster the praise he lavished on Frazer and Robertson Smith, whom he obviously enjoyed reading; but *Totem and Taboo* reveals close study of Lang's *Social Origins* (1903), and especially his *The Secret of the Totem* (1905). Freud draws on Lang for acknowledgement that enquiries into the origins of totemism are bound to be conjectural;[16] commends Lang's psychological account of how and why the totems of particular clans are given animal names;[17] upholds his critique of Frazer's assumption that the Arunta of Australia were crudely 'primitive';[18] agrees with Lang's Durkheimian derivation of totemism while noting that he also put forward an incompatible alternative which he later withdrew;[19] relies on him for an account of J. F. McLennan's pioneering *Primitive Marriage* (1865) and 'The Worship and Animals and Plants' (1869–70);[20] and pays him the compliment of citing Lang's writings in their original English. He gives no hint, however, that Lang contributed to the store of imaginative literature with poetry and fiction, and that he made a lasting contribution to British culture with his collection of fairy tales, charmingly retold or invented, in a series of books that began with *The Blue Fairy Book* of 1899 and continued with further compilations each of which bore the name of a different colour.

★ ★ ★

Reading British philosophers from Hume to Mill, scientists from Darwin to Thomas Huxley, ethnologists like Frazer, Bible critics like Robertson Smith, and psychologists like Ernest Jones and Havelock Ellis, helped to hone Freud's literary style and manner of presentation. Francis Galton (1822–1911), however, influenced Freud's writings not so much through his literary style or advocacy of eugenics as through his use of photography. Galton, as we have seen, had tried to highlight family resemblances and inherited traits through superimpositions of photographs in such a way that resemblances appeared clearly while differences faded into the background — a procedure that helped Freud to convey a vivid impression of the fusions and condensations characteristic of dreams.[21] 'Galtonesque technique' also allowed Freud to construct, with help from Otto Rank, an overriding super-myth which 'superimposed' a large variety of stories dealing with the birth of a hero — bringing out, for the benefit of readers not so steeped in the mythologies of many nations, the features they all had in common.[22]

Superimposition yields place, in Freud's narrative, to juxtaposition. He places side by side, for instance, a story gleaned from Frazer featuring taboos surrounding a Maori chief with an account of obsessions he had come across in his psychoanalytic practice in order to prove that 'modern obsessive prohibitions involve just as extensive renunciations and restrictions in the lives of those who are subject to them as do taboo prohibitions'.[23] Franz Baermann Steiner, who quotes this example in his *Taboo*, first published in 1956, goes on to refute the principal notions Freud took from Frazer and Robertson Smith, concluding with Freud's assumption that 'taboo is older than the gods and dates back to a period before any kind of religion existed'.

> The assumption of such a [pre-religious] age is part of Freud's reconstruction of human history, which includes also the assumption of a primaeval horde which slew its father and originated religion. Moreover, these crude assumptions are at the same time a way of discussing the structure of human drives and, in that capacity, concomitants of certain methods of healing neuroses. There is consequently no point in discussing in sociological terms theories so differently contrived. If, however, Freudian teaching comes to follow that attitude of the younger disciples, it is difficult to see why the hypothesis of a pre-religious age should be maintained. For most of these younger disciples have discarded the myth of our murdered *Urvater*, and the ensuing bad conscience of mankind, as a construct unnecessary for the analysis of drive structures. [. . .][24]

Freud found reinforcement for his dubious conclusions in Theodor Reik's *Problems of the Philosophy of Religion* published in 1919. He contributed a Preface to it, whose final paragraphs read:

> Scholarly investigation has led to the conclusion that in far-off times family life was quite differently organised from that we know — a finding that has been confirmed by data obtained from studying primitive peoples living today. If one subjects the prehistoric and ethnological material to psychoanalytic investigation an unexpected conclusion is reached: God the Father once walked bodily on the earth as chief of a primal horde, using the power this gave him to the full until his sons banded together and slew him. This liberating deed, and reactions to it, resulted in the first social ties, in fundamental moral restrictions, and in the oldest form of religion: totemism. It was also found that later religions have the same content. They try either to efface the traces of this primal crime, or to atone for it by finding other solutions to the struggle between fathers and sons; yet they cannot, on the other hand, avoid repeating the elimination of the father-figure. In myths we can also catch echoes of this primal event, which hovers like a gigantic shadow over the whole development of mankind. [. . .]
>
> Theodor Reik's studies of the Philosophy of Religion are based on this hypothesis, which is rooted in the insights of Robertson Smith and has been developed by me in *Totem and Taboo*. [. . .] Reik's work remains true to the techniques of psychoanalysis as it proceeds to illuminate hitherto uncomprehended aspects of the deepest assumptions and final goals of religion without ever averting the gaze from the relationship of earliest times to the beliefs of primitive people living today or the connection between cultural achievements and the formation of neurotic substitutes. [. . .][25]

The origins of the Oedipus Complex are here traced beyond its present embodiments to the early history of mankind, affecting subsequent generations as memories of a primal crime concept sufficiently like that of Original Sin to induce Freud to plunge deeper into that exploration of religious faith which was to find its final and most questionable form in *The Man Moses and Monotheistic Religion*.

* * *

Totem and Taboo, like *The Interpretation of Dreams* and *The Joke and its Relation to the Unconscious*, dutifully cites the work of Herbert Spencer (1820–1903). In *The Joke* Freud finds his theory of the discharge of energy confirmed in Spencer's essay 'The Physiology of Laughter', but modifies Spencer's version to such an extent that little remains of it.[26] There are a few vague references to Spencer's *Principles of Sociology* in *Totem and Taboo*, but the only concrete contribution to Freud's argument is an English expression Freud translates as 'Er ist nicht bei sich'.[27] I have not traced the original, which may have been 'he is not himself' or 'he is beside himself'; Freud sees it as a linguistic concentration of such fundamental dualisms as those of body and mind, or body and spirit, or body and soul. What becomes clear from this meagre representation of so important a Victorian thinker, and Freud's bypassing of such relevant works as Spencer's *Principles of Psychology* and *Principles of Biology*, is that Spencer did not inspire in Freud the enthusiastic interest he took in the writings of Darwin, Frazer, and Robertson Smith, or the milder one kindled by such investigators of myths and fairy tales as Andrew Lang. The reason, surely, is not far to seek. Spencer had none of the narrative gift of Frazer or Lang, nor did his diffuse work concentrate on one burning topic as did Robertson Smith's — the topic of religion which fascinated Freud even when he overtly rejected its consolations and promises. And Darwin, as I have tried to show earlier, was among the young Freud's formative influences, coupled in his mind with that of Goethe, and had kindled a veneration that never waned throughout Freud's life.

The invitation to lecture at Clark University in 1909 alerted Freud to American sympathy for his views. He met several influential figures and described them in his autobiographical sketch in a way that showed personal respect while allowing them no discernible effect on his work:

> G. Stanley Hall was a rightly respected psychologist and teacher, who had for years been introducing psychoanalysis into the university curriculum. He was something of a kingmaker who liked to set up authorities at one moment and dismiss them at the next. We also met James J. Putnam, the Harvard neurologist, who despite his advanced years gave an enthusiastic welcome to psychoanalysis. He brought the weight of his universally respected personality to bear on ensuring recognition for its cultural value and the purity of its intentions. What troubled us in this excellent man [. . .] was only his endeavour to bind psychoanalysis to a particular philosophical system, and to give it an ethical orientation. Meeting William James has left a powerful impression. I can never forget seeing James suddenly stop in the midst of a walk we took together; he handed me the case he was carrying and asked me to walk ahead, promising to catch me up when he had dealt with an attack of angina pectoris he felt coming on. He died of heart disease a year later; and ever since that little scene I have wished that I might meet the approach of my own death with equal fortitude.[28]

Other American psychologists inspired less respect; in Morton Prince, for instance, the chronicler of the dissociated personality, Freud saw a self-advertiser who had no serious contribution to make to the psychopathology he professed. He seems to have regarded Prince as a practitioner of 'the American method of ruthless propaganda' which he deplores in a letter to Stefan Zweig.[29] He tried to persuade Ernest Jones, who saw in Prince 'a thorough gentleman, a man of the world, and a very pleasant colleague', that this 'pleasant colleague' was not only 'rather stupid' but also a man whose 'pleasant speech' veiled 'bad intentions'.[30] He placed greater reliance on A. A. Brill, whose (not always adequate) translations, and fervent advocacy, spread orthodox Freudianism among English-speaking readers with little or no German.

* * *

Between 1899 and 1920 Freud frequently refers his readers to writings on dreams and the psychology of sex by the English researcher Henry Havelock Ellis (1859–1939), praising him, in 1920, as 'a psychological investigator of high merit, and an elegant critic of psychoanalysis'.[31] The adjective 'vornehm' that I have here translated as 'elegant', enshrines two further meanings, which explains the prominence Freud chose to give Ellis: that he could be seen as a 'principal' disseminator of Freudian views in Britain, and that his critique was 'gentlemanly' and therefore radically different from the heated abuse psychoanalysis so often encountered. At one time Freud even had a framed photograph of Ellis in the waiting-room of his Viennese practice. Privately, however, he confessed to Hilda Doolittle that he thought Ellis's work superficial, and that he failed to understand how a man could be so interested in every kind of sexual activity while showing so little interest in the deeper reasons why people behaved in the way he described. That helps to explain why references to Ellis fade out of Freud's writings after 1920, and contrasts with his greater delight in a work like Israel Levine's *The Unconscious*.[32] 'Who is Israel Levine?' Freud asked Ernest Jones on 7 April 1923; 'I was never so much pleased by a book on psychoanalytic matter as by his *Unconscious*. A rare bird if he is a philosopher. I want to know him better'.[33] Jones replied that Levine lectured in philosophy at University College, Exeter, and that he, Jones, had advised him during the writing of his book and had revised the manuscript before publication.[34] Freud remained so pleased with Levine's book (which the author had sent to him with the handwritten dedication 'To the Master. From a very grateful pupil') that he induced his daughter Anna to translate it for the Internationaler Psychoanalytischer Verlag and took a hand in the translation himself.[35]

* * *

The quest for the origins of religion attempted in *Totem and Taboo* had aesthetic implications which Freud spelt out at a meeting of the Vienna Analytical Society on 11 December 1911. Art, he told his hearers, used to have clear 'tendencies' but had lost these in recent times and become 'art for art's sake'. This psychic achievement had only become possible because something central to earlier times had been lost — and that lost element, Freud believed, was the *animistic* world-view. 'Nothing appears in our midst', he concluded, 'which can be explained without a look at its entire prehistory'.[36] The survey of human prehistory attempted in *Totem and Taboo* thus had an aesthetic as well as a religious dimension, and the thread which led into this labyrinth had been given to Freud by two Scottish writers: the armchair anthropologist Sir James Frazer and the analyst and historian of the Semitic religions William Robertson Smith.

★ ★ ★

Totem and Taboo, like most of Freud's works, is a dazzling piece of writing; but it raises in acute form those difficulties in the way of accepting his theories which the most fair-minded and knowledgeable of his adverse critics, F. J. Sulloway, has pinpointed in a contribution to Tod Dufresne's *Against Freud. Critics Talk Back*.[37] Under the heading 'Psychoanalysis and Pseudoscience' Sulloway declares his admiration for Freud's synthesis of ideas from the late nineteenth century, and his originality in building them into his system. He continues, however:

> If we lived in a Lamarckian world rather than in a Darwinian world, if the inheritance of acquired characteristics was really possible, and if energy really did circulate in the body according to a Helmholtzian, hydraulic model so that unused libidinal energy could become diverted and cause neuropsychological disturbances — in a word, if all these mistaken biological notions were true, it is quite possible that psychoanalytic theory would, in large part, be true.

The problem, Sulloway continues, is that these assumptions are not true, and that therefore the discipline created by the man whom Sullivan has dubbed 'a biologist of the mind' is built on quicksand.[38]

Few modern scientists would disagree with that, just as few more recent anthropologists and ethnographers would subscribe unquestioningly to the argument Freud based on the sources named in *Totem and Taboo* and *The Man Moses and the Monotheistic Religion*. He accepted uncritically Robertson Smith's argument, against the evidence, that the distinctive monotheism of the Old Testament was a late development and arose, largely, through the influence of the canonical prophets, out of a primitive religion of Israel which coincided with primitive religions the world over. He accepted the idea that all societies must have passed though some evolutionary process that began with animism and advanced to totemism until it reached the present state of belief and knowledge. Most modern scholarship holds instead that Old Testament monotheism arose much earlier, and that one must not start from the comparatively sophisticated society which confronts us in the Old Testament to speculate what *must* have been its primitive origins. It is surely illegitimate to think that there must have been one universal pattern of religious and social development, and to attempt generalizations — as Frazer and Robertson Smith tended to do — about *primitive* society on the basis of the reports missionaries and explorers brought back from expeditions into regions *of their own time* that had developed their own kinds of native culture.

Freud's aesthetic sensibility, his sheer delight in the storytelling and structuring power of Frazer and Robertson Smith, led him to accept their theories too readily. Interest in their speculations about the mind-set of earlier societies fed into Freud's belief that archaeological exploration offered analogies to his own delvings into deeper and older regions of the mind. This is attested by his passion for collecting antique figurines, which can still be seen in the London Freud Museum, and the many books of archaeological interest that remained in his library after his death. The admirable catalogue of these books, compiled by J. Keith Davies and Gerhard Fichtner, lists many by English-speaking authors. These include the compilers of specialist collections in the British Museum; the *Cambridge Ancient History*, edited by J. B. Bury and others; Ernest Budge on Egypt and Howard Carter on Tut'Ankh'Amun; Arthur Evans on Crete, A. H. Layard on Ninevah and Babylon, Percy Hancock on Mesopotamia, Albert Olmstead on Assyria, as well as books by Leonard Woolley, the discoverer of Ur, and Henry Stuart, the chronicler of classical Rome. Many of these volumes bear marks of close reading; they take their place in a collection that includes many books on similar themes in other European languages. Here too Freud shows himself 'a cultural citizen of the world'.[39]

Notes to Chapter 9

1. Letter to Julie Braun-Vogelstein, 30 October 1927, *Briefe*, p. 393.
2. Henry Thomas Buckle, *History of Civilization in England* (London 1857), Volume I, chapter VI.
3. e.g. *GW* XIV, 35.
4. Buckle, *History of Civilization in England*, Volume I, Chapter IV, Part I.
5. *Totem and Taboo*, *GW* IX, 102.
6. *GW* IX, 82, 49, 65.
7. *GW* IX, 161.
8. *GW* IX, 161.
9. *GW* IX, 165, 167, 171–72; XIV, 93.
10. *GW* IX,179, 183, 187.
11. *GW* X, 345.
12. 'Selbstdarstellung', *GW* XIV, 93.
13. *GW* XIV, 240.
14. J. H. Breasted, *The Dawn of Conscience* (London, 1934).
15. *GW* XVI, 135, 195.
16. *GW* IX, 132–33.
17. *GW* IX, 135–36.
18. *GW* IX, 141.
19. *GW* IX, 146, 154.
20. *GW* IX, 123, 133, 147.
21. *GW* II/III, 144, 299, 498–99, 662–63; XI, 175.
22. *GW* XIV, 107.
23. *GW* IX, 38.
24. *Totem and Taboo* (Harmondsworth, 1967), p. 87.
25. *GW* XII, 328–29.
26. *GW* VI, 163–64.
27. *GW* IX, 114.
28. 'Selbstdarstellung', *GW* XIV, 78–79.
29. *Freud/St. Zweig*, p. 213 — 17 December 1929.
30. *Jones*, II, 68–69.
31. *GW* XII, 309.
32. Israel Levine, *The Unconscious: An Introduction to Freudian Psychology* (London, 1923).
33. *Freud/Jones*, p. 519.
34. 13 April 1923, *Freud/Jones*, p. 520.
35. *Das Unbewusste* (Leipzig, Vienna, and Zurich, 1926).
36. *PWAV* III, 336.
37. J. Sulloway, 'Psychoanalysis and Pseudoscience', in *Against Freud. Critics Talk Back*, ed. by Todd Dufresne (Stanford, 2007).
38. Sulloway, 'Psychoanalysis and Pseudoscience', p. 58.
39. Freud's views on the analogies between his own work and that of archaeologists are conveniently spelt out in one of his last essays: 'Constructions in Analysis' (1937), *GW* XVI, 45–47. He also owed a considerable debt to the British neurologist John Hughlings Jackson (1835–1911), whose work played a crucial part in Freud's early attempts to relate the psychic to the physical and in the formation of his concept of regression. (See J. Sulloway, *Freud: Biologist of the Mind*, pp. 270–73, and *Gay*, p. 62.)

CHAPTER 10

❖

Old Wine in New Bottles

Freud faced the twentieth century with literary and artistic tastes formed by earlier masters. His cluttered home and study defied the aesthetic dicta of Adolf Loos. His musical tastes, such as they were, remained confined to Mozart and Offenbach; if he was even dimly aware of Schoenberg or Berg, he gave no sign of it. Mahler, who consulted him about a personal problem, never lured him into a concert hall to hear his music; and Hugo Wolf interested him only as a psychiatric case. In the visual arts he took no discernible notice of the Viennese Secession, of Klimt or Schiele; and he loathed expressionism, Dada, and even Surrealism, though that European movement acknowledged the inspiration of his work. He made an exception for Salvador Dali, who came to see him and produced a good likeness of his face, without adding ants or melting watches. He had no intellectual or social contact with Ernst Mach, Fritz Mauthner, or Ludwig Wittgenstein. Though Lou Andreas-Salomé engineered a visit from Rilke, and though his children loved Rilke's poetry, it made no visible impression on him, any more than that of Hofmannsthal; his love of lyric and ballad poetry was confined to Greek and Roman examples, to Goethe, Schiller, Heine, Uhland, and Lenau; and his epic poets were Homer, Virgil, and Milton. The many novels and short stories he analysed or praised for their psychological interest included no formal experimenters like Robert Musil, Alfred Döblin, or Hermann Broch; he respected but shied away from Arthur Schnitzler, whose psychological insights matched his own and in whom he feared a kind of *Doppelgänger*; and he found psychological interest in novels and short stories by writers ranging from E. T. A. Hoffmann to Carl Spitteler, Wilhelm Jensen, Stefan Zweig, and Arnold Zweig, without concerning himself with narratological or other aesthetic problems raised by their work. His ideal novel remained *Don Quixote*, though Goethe's narrative work (including his autobiography *Poetry and Truth*), and Thomas Mann's cycle of novels centering on the Biblical Joseph (*Joseph and his Brothers*, 1933–43), ran it close. In drama no-one could match the *Oedipus Tyrannus of Sophocles*, Goethe's *Iphigenia in Tauris*, and especially the plays of Shakespeare; but he also relished the humour and social criticism of Molière and Beaumarchais, the satiric wit and humanist philosophizing of Johann Nepomuk Nestroy, and Ibsen's take on rebels and outsiders in plays that made the past irrupt into the present — like Oedipus and Freud himself. He was interested in performers ranging from Sarah Bernhardt to Yvette Guilbert, and plays that raised contemporary problems in conventional form by Hermann Bahr or Theodor Herzl; but his aesthetic field of vision remained unclouded by such dramatic experimenters as Georg Kaiser, Carl Sternheim, Ernst Barlach, or Ernst Toller.

Freud did, however, come into contact with one significant figure in twentieth-century English and American poetry. Hilda Doolittle (1886–1961), who wrote under the pen-name H.D., sought Freud out, consulted him on her personal problems, and spent a little over one hundred sessions on his famous couch in 1933 and 1934. By then she had long been known as one of the creators of the Imagist movement which flourished between 1912 and 1917, aiming to produce short poems structured by a single image or metaphor, striving for clarity, concreteness, and economy of language. Her poem 'Oread' has joined Ezra Pound's 'In a Station of the Metro' as the most often quoted example of 'Imagist' poetry. Her book *Tribute to Freud* has been recognized, by Norman Holland and others, as the most enlightening account of Freud's methods of analysis ever penned by one of his patients. H.D. respected and admired Freud, but combined this with a clear-eyed perception of his weaknesses — including his frequent disregard of his own rules and his sudden rage at not being loved enough. Her comment 'The Professor was not always right' is a typically mild indication of her sense that she gained more from the general conversations she had with Freud, and the impact of his personality, than from an analysis she left incomplete. She also, however, noted the sly little jokes Freud allowed himself in conversation with partners likely to catch his literary allusions. When Hilda Doolittle told him that she was all too conscious of the onrush of time, Freud struck a theatrical pose and declaimed the answer Rosalind gives to her own question 'who Time gallops withal', when she tells Orlando: 'With a thief to the gallows; for though he go as softly as foot can fall, he thinks himself too soon there'.[1]

Before starting the analysis Freud had sent for some of H.D'.s books; he told her this, but declined to discuss them. A letter to H.D. under her married name, 'Mrs Aldington', dated 18 December 1932, explained his refusal:

> You will understand that I did not ask for your books in order to criticise or to appreciate your work, which I have been informed is highly praised by your readers. I am a bad judge on poetry especially in a foreign language. I wanted to get a glimpse of your personality as an introduction to making your personal acquaintance. Your books will be waiting with me for your arrival. (An American friend of mine brought me today 'Palimpsest'.)[2]

H.D'.s novel *Palimpsest*, published in Paris in 1926, and her novella *The Hedgehog*, in an edition published in London in 1936, stayed in Freud's library until the end of his life — but we have no record of his reaction to them.

The letter just quoted shows Freud's understandable reluctance to complicate the treatment of a new patient by revealing his reaction to works he had only recently read. It reveals at the same time why he resisted H.D'.s attempts to interest him in Coleridge, and Ernest Jones's to get him to read Browning: he distrusted his judgement of poetry not yet winnowed by time in a language other than his own. He felt no such distrust in the case of Shakespeare and Milton, hallowed by generations of worldwide fame.

Hilda Doolittle did, however, rekindle Freud's old enthusiasm for Greek drama when she drew his attention to the *Ion* of Euripides. He wrote to her on 26 February 1937:

> Dear H.D.,
> I have just finished *Ion*. Deeply moved by the play (which I had not known before) and no less by your comments, especially those referring to the end where you extol the victory of the reason over the passions. I send you the expression of my admiration and kindest regards.

'Victory of the reason over the passions' — here Freud had found one of his patients, who was also a poet, discover in Greek drama what he had so often tried to encourage in those who entrusted themselves to his healing care.

* * *

The diffidence inspired in Freud when it came to judging English poetry after Milton did not deter him from reading contemporary English and American fiction, so long as it did not depart too far from narrative conventions familiar to him from English novels of the eighteenth and nineteenth centuries. Suggestions for such reading came to him occasionally from one of his patients. In his *New Introductory Lectures on Psychoanalysis*, first published in 1933, he tells his readers of a patient who had spent some of his early life in England and had kept a passionate interest in English literature. 'He owned a well-stocked library of English books and used to bring me books selected from this'.[3] These included works by Arnold Bennett. Ernest Jones, in his biography of Freud, confirms Freud's acquaintance with Bennett's fiction;[4] but I have found no further allusion to Arnold Bennett (1867–1931) in Freud's published work or his letters.

Freud's sympathy with the narrative fiction of John Galsworthy (1867–1933) appears much more openly. In *The Psychopathology of Everyday Life* he uses an analysis by his friend and disciple Hanns Sachs to illustrate unconsciously motivated forgetting — a process related to what we now know as 'the Freudian slip' or 'parapraxis'. The story he quotes is Galsworthy's 'The Island Pharisees'. This tells of a university-trained young man belonging to those affluent middle classes which so often engaged Galsworthy's attentions. This young man reaches beyond bourgeois prudence and thrift when he learns of the plight of an acquaintance, whose very different lifestyle had led him into severe financial difficulties. Should he help him, as he had done on previous occasions? Class-specific reasons are against it: is it not just sentimentality to keep on propping up someone who can't manage his own financial affairs properly? One must call a halt somewhere! But as he murmurs this to himself his fundamental honesty protests that all he wants is to keep his money. He therefore writes a friendly letter ending with the sentence 'I enclose a cheque', and signs it with his name. Just then, however, his attention is distracted by a moth fluttering around his lamp; he catches it, releases it outside, and 'forgets' to make out and enclose the cheque. The letter, with its now empty promise, is sent off without it. The protagonist's selfish, class-specific, and capitalist motives have apparently been overcome; his unconscious, however, makes his action conform to his secret desire.

Civilization and its Discontents pays tribute to Galsworthy as 'a subtle and sensitive (*feinsinnig*) Englishman, whose work enjoys general approbation today' and suggests

Freud's own perspicacity because quite early on he relished 'a little story' by this author, entitled 'The Apple Tree' — one of the *Five Tales* Galsworthy published in 1918. That story, Freud maintains, shows in a particularly impressive way 'how in the life of civilized people today there is no room for the simple, natural love of two human beings'. The phrase I translate 'civilized people today' reads in German 'des heutigen Kulturmenschen'; it picks up the keyword in the original title of *Civilization and its Discontents*, *Das Unbehagen in der Kultur*, and thus moves Galsworthy's story into the very centre of Freud's cultural argument. The tale has many other features, however, which appeal to a taste formed by the conventions of nineteenth-century European narrative. It concentrates on its one central story, class-related like 'The Island Pharisees'. It tells of a young bachelor of independent means, laid up by a leg injury in a remote farmhouse; of his falling in love with a simple farm girl and his decision to elope with her and make her his wife; of a last-minute change of mind brought about by an accidental meeting with an old schoolfriend which draws him into a family of his own class; of his marriage into that family, and the abandoned farm girl's broken-hearted suicide. Its construction resembles that of a classical German *Novelle*, with its concentration on one powerful storyline; a central symbol (the apple tree which sees the lovers' meetings and the girl's later sorrow and despair); a turning point (the meeting with the fellow-student and the subsequent abandonment of a love that reached beyond class boundaries); and a strong conclusion which follows logically from its opening. There is also a framing action, set at a later time than the central story, which broaches a problem important in so much of Freud's work: the irruption of the past into the present.

One other feature of this tale was bound to appeal to Freud's long-standing affection for the Greek and Roman classics: its constant undertow of references to Gilbert Murray's translation of Euripides' *Hippolytus*. This begins with the tale's title and epigraph which point to the Hesperidean idyll painted by one of Euripides' choruses:

> To the strand of the Daughters of the Sunset,
> The Apple-Tree, the singing and the gold;
> Where the mariner must stay him from his onset,
> And the red wave is tranquil as of old;
> Yea, beyond that Pillar of the End
> That Atlas guardeth, would I wend;
> Where a voice of living waters never ceaseth
> In God's quiet garden by the sea,
> And Earth, the ancient life-giver, increaseth
> Joy among the meadows, like a tree;

continues with ominous references to 'the Cyprian' Artemis and the dangerous powers of 'Erôs, Erôs, who blindest, tear by tear, | Men's eyes with hunger. . .'; and culminates in a quotation from another of the choruses:

> For mad is the heart of Love,
> And gold the gleam of his wing;
> And all the spell thereof
> Bends, when he makes his spring;
> All life that is wild and young

In mountain and wave and stream,
All that of earth is sprung,
Or breathes in the red sunbeam;
Yea, and Mankind. O'er all a royal throne,
Cyprian, Cyprian, is thine alone![5]

The centrality of Eros in this Georgian rendering of Euripides reflects the importance Freud's writing gives to Eros in its narrower and its wider meanings. He could also find himself reminded of German *Novellen* from Tieck to Theodor Storm by the touch of the Uncanny in this primarily realistic tale: the imagination of its simpler characters is haunted throughout by a ghostly apparition known as 'the gipsy bogle'.

In his *New Introductory Lectures on Psychoanalysis*, published when Freud's cancer no longer permitted an oral delivery, he tells his readers that until his patient started lending him English books he had read little of either Bennett or Galsworthy. Now, however, he was able to read Galsworthy's *Man of Property* and later portions of *The Forsyte Saga*. These became, he says, part of a private language, between himself and P., the patient he met regularly in analytic sessions:

> The name *Forsyte* and all the typical features the novelist sought to embody in it, had played a part in my conversations with P, and had become part of the secret language which so easily forms itself between two people who meet one another regularly.[6]

The word I have translated 'novelist' is *Dichter* in the original; a term usually rendered 'poet', which has the wider connotation of 'imaginative writer', and is used by Freud to indicate writers in any genre who have a deeper than usual understanding of the human mind. The 'typical features' include the class-consciousness and economic power of the middle-class family at the centre of Galsworthy's saga, whose opening volume, Freud reminds us, is entitled *The Man of Property*. This, along with its non-experimental structure and narration, assimilates Galsworthy's novel-sequence with a genre familiar to Freud: the German *Familienroman* or 'family saga', whose greatest representative is Thomas Mann's *Buddenbrooks*.

The 'secret language' of which we have just heard Freud speak included a game of verbal associations that linked the name of 'Forsyte' with that of Freud's analysand 'David Forsyth' and both with the English word 'foresight' and its semantic meaning — associations that helped Freud uncover repressed memories at the root of a patient's neurosis. These included memories of Galsworthy's novel-sequence — particularly its first volume, whose title, *The Man of Property*, speaks so patently of the class-structure and capitalist values characteristic of the English society Galsworthy's fictional world seeks to reflect.

★ ★ ★

Ernest Jones lists Galsworthy, Bennett, Kipling, and Mark Twain as authors who occupied Freud's leisure hours and brought consolation into his pain-wracked existence. He read these alongside works like *Goodbye Mr Chips* and *Lost Horizon* by James Hilton (1900–54), though he did find that Hilton's work suffered because he wrote too much. Other books Jones saw in Freud's hand or heard about in conversation with him included the novels *The Edwardians* by Vita Sackville-West (1892–1962) and *Public Faces* by Harold Nicolson (1886–1968), as well as the already mentioned detective stories by Dorothy Sayers (1893–1957). The epigraph of Nicolson's novel also introduced him to a quotation from W. H. Auden which amused him greatly:

> Private faces in public places
> Are wiser and nicer
> Than public faces in private places —

But there is no sign that his amusement led him to seek out Auden's poetry or his other writings.[7] He was, however, sufficiently interested in the translations from the Chinese by Arthur Waley (1889–1966) to acquire instalments of his version of Lady Murasaki's *The Tale of Genji: The Sacred Tree*, published in 1926, which would have fascinated him because of its link with tree symbolism in *The Golden Bough*; and *The Blue Trousers*, published in 1928. These can still be seen on his shelves in the London Freud Museum. They are joined there by the Japan-based *Kokoro* by Lafcadio Hearn (1850–1904), in a German version by Bertha Franzos, published in the year of Hearn's death. In this way English writers became conduits through which knowledge of Far Eastern literature flowed into Freud's consciousness.

In 'Some Character Types Encountered in Psychoanalytic Work', first published in *Imago* in 1915, Freud followed up his analysis of Lady Macbeth with that of another character created by a writer for whom he had the greatest respect: Rebecca West in Ibsen's *Rosmerholm* (1866). Many years later, in 1933, Cecily Isabel Fairfield (1892–1983) who had adopted the pen-name 'Rebecca West' as an *hommage* to Ibsen, introduced herself to Freud by sending him her book *St Augustine* with a handwritten dedication: 'To Professor Freud with deep gratitude from Rebecca West'. Freud thought this book important enough to take it with him to London, where it can be seen in the Freud Museum to the present day. The pen-name must have intrigued him, but if he acknowledged the gift the acknowledgement is unrecorded, and there is no evidence that he ever read the book or any of 'Rebecca West's' other writings.

* * *

In April 1933, the year in which 'Rebecca West' obtruded herself on Freud's notice, he received a visit from another English writer passing through Vienna. This was Norman Douglas (1868–1952), whose travel book *Old Calabria* had enjoyably ministered to Freud's predilection for accounts of travel and adventure in exotic places. The visit seems to have satisfied both parties and Douglas followed it up by sending Freud a book whose main title might have seemed to outsiders to reflect Freud's principal preoccupation: *Paneros*. It bore the subtitle *Some Words on Aphrodisiacs and the Like*, and had been printed for subscribers in Florence in 1930. The dedication copy, still to be seen in the London Freud Museum, seems to have remained unread, and is not mentioned in the letter of 10 April 1933 in which Freud thanks Douglas for some (unnamed) books and continues:

> I would like to return the compliment and send you some of my books. You would only have to express the wish; but I fear that my books do not please

> readers — they annoy or frighten them. I submit to my fate in this respect, but not without envy.[8]

Bypassing discussion of Douglas's writings, Freud reveals that their conversation had touched on Hitler's recent assumption of the German Chancellorship. Seeking a parallel in German history Freud lights, unexpectedly on the medieval Emperor Frederick II (1194–1250) and comments: 'So the past always glimmers through the very last moment in time. It is the Messiah-belief of the Germans'.[9] Freud's constant quest for roots in the past has here found one of its rare political manifestations.

* * *

Three years after the visit from Norman Douglas, Freud received a visit from another English-speaking writer which he deemed important enough to mention in his correspondence with Arnold Zweig (14 August 1936),[10] as well as recording it in his diary entry for 13 October 1936.[11] This was the American author Thornton Wilder (1897–1975). Wilder was a welcome visitor because he had written a novel Freud valued highly: *The Bridge of San Luis Rey*, first published in 1927. He told Arnold Zweig, in a letter dated 13 October 1936, that he had found this book enticingly attractive ('reizend'); and he commended it to his son Ernst in even stronger terms on 14 October 1935: 'You must read it — it is extraordinarily beautiful'.[12] 'Etwas ganz ungewöhnlich Schönes': these are words Freud did not use lightly, and they entitle us to ask what special feature of this short book may have appealed to him so strongly.

The Bridge of San Luis Rey is set in eighteenth-century Peru — a geographical region akin to that which had attracted Freud to Rider Haggard's *Heart of the World*, where an older civilization irradiated the new. Wilder makes this explicit by having one of his characters stray 'through the ruins of the old race'. This could stir Freud's archaeological interests along with the taste for adventure stories that had drawn him to Haggard, Kipling, and Conan Doyle. The opening of the story introduces a character who sets out to discover what brought five people to the eponymous bridge whose collapse led to their deaths — a quest that seeks to draw the past into the present, like Sherlock Holmes, and like Freud himself. Unlike Sherlock Holmes, however, Freud does not seek in the past the facts behind a mysterious crime, but a psychological truth: what was it that moved these five characters to act as they did? This involves a presentation of different kinds of love — a subject whose range from Eros to Agape so often occupied Freud's own mind. It is therefore significant that Freud brought his conversation with Wilder round to the role of psychoanalysis in literature, praising Wilder's psychological perspicacity that had no need of clinical jargon. He liked his writers to show insights that confirmed his findings without aping the techniques and terms of professional psychoanalysts. He was always suspicious of writers who used these terms and described these techniques without having undergone analysis — preferably by himself.

It was again *The Bridge of San Luis Rey* which induced Freud to broach a second subject in his conversation with its author: the question of the nature of religion and its place in the consciousness, and the actions, of believers. The fallible investigator Wilder had introduced into the opening chapters of his novel is a monk, Brother

Juniper, who seeks to conduct an investigation that would, he hopes, ensure theology a place among the exact sciences:

> [. . .] this collapse of the bridge of San Luis Rey was a sheer act of God. It afforded a perfect laboratory. Here at least one could surprise His intentions in a pure state. [. . .] He knew the answer. He merely wanted to prove it, historically, mathematically, to his converts [. . .]

He fails, of course, for he 'never knew the central passion of Doña Maria's life; nor of Uncle Pio's, nor even of Esteban's'; and the narrator, who knows so much more, has to ask himself: 'isn't it possible that even I have missed the very spring within the spring?' What will have appealed to Freud particularly is that Wilder chose to express this ultimate human perplexity by alluding to contrasting words spoken by Gloucester in *King Lear* ('As flies to wanton boys are we to the gods | They kill us for their sport') and by Hamlet in the play that bears his name ('There is providence in the fall of a sparrow'). That Hamlet's words echo Matthew 10. 24 will have done the passage no harm in the eyes of the man who confessed in an extension to his autobiographical self-presentation[13] that early acquaintance with the Bible had permanently affected the direction of his interests; and also the man who in his conversation with Thornton Wilder had admitted the 'historical truth' adhering to the religious sentiment he had so resolutely sought to stifle in himself.[14]

Readers well acquainted with Freud's way of thinking will discover many details in *The Bridge of San Luis Rey* that could not fail to engage his interest. The chapter dedicated to Esteban asserts the reality of telepathic communication; that devoted to the Marquesa de Montemayor declares the main purpose of literature to be 'the notation of the heart'; and the chapter concerned with Uncle Pio presents him as a secular pendant to Brother Juniper. Where the monk has sought to delve into psychological motivation to justify the ways of God to man, Uncle Pio sought the friendship of beautiful women because he was 'insatiably curious about their minds and hearts'. Did not Freud's writings, from *Studies of Hysteria* onwards, show the same passionate curiosity, though his attitude towards his analysands inevitably differed from those of Uncle Pio towards his female friends? No wonder, then, that he preferred the succinct 'notation of the heart' in this minor classic to that in many a more elaborately plotted work of greater prestige among his contemporaries.

Freud was honest enough to confess to its author that he had disliked *Heaven's My Destination*, Wilder's tale of a holy fool making his way across America in the unlikely guise of a successful salesman while trying to model his life on Christ and Gandhi. An 'American fanatic' of this kind, Freud declared, did not strike him as a suitable subject for a work of fiction. The character's combination of successful capitalism with genuine unworldliness seemed highly unlikely; and the optimism of the central story seemed unwarranted and contrasted unfavourably with that of one of Freud's favourite works of world literature, Voltaire's *Candide ou l'Optimisme*, which it superficially resembles without reproducing its satiric thrust.

Freud was no better pleased with another novel of Wilder's, first published in 1926, which Freud's sister-in-law, Minna Bernays, had strongly urged him to read. It was entitled *The Cabala*, which might have held out the promise of a Jewish subject, but which turned out, instead, to precipitate its readers among a group of mostly tiresome, reactionary characters who had banded together in a society that took its name from seventeenth-century English political life. The original 'cabal' after which they had named themselves consisted of five ministers at the court of Charles II, whose surnames began with the letters C, A, B, A, L. Freud might have found a little solace when he found his own name on one of the fashionable books an Italian cardinal had heaped on his table, linking Freud's name with those of Spengler, Sir James Frazer, Proust, and James Joyce. The compliment this seemed to pay him is, however, negated by the Cardinal's outburst when asked to write a book himself:

> 'Yes, I could write a book better than this ordure your age has offered us' (and with a sharp blow he pushed over the tower of books . . .). But a Montaigne, a Machiavelli . . . a . . . Swift I will never be. . . . No, don't pick them up. Let the animals soil them. What is the matter with this twentieth century of ours?[15]

The reader is not, of course, invited to agree with the Cardinal's dismissal of twentieth-century literature; but Freud cannot have been pleased to have found the sole mention of his name in a motley assembly of writings dismissed by the character who has collected them as 'ordure'. That in the section called 'Marcantonio' psychiatry fails to prevent a character's suicide could further undermine Freud's liking for the book.

Richard Goldstone, whose *Thornton Wilder: An Intimate Portrait*[16] documents Freud's conversation with Wilder, also reports that it turned on the question whether psychoanalysis, in the state of development it had reached in 1935, was a fit subject for fictional treatment. Freud thought that the way writers of fiction such as Stefan Zweig, Arnold Zweig, and Franz Werfel used psychoanalysis made it appear too clinical and schematic, and that it could take centuries before psychoanalysis had so deeply penetrated the inner life of writers that it could enter into a proper novel. He was tactful enough not to mention Thomas Mann's sceptical use of it in *The Magic Mountain*; but Wilder objected that the kind of novel Freud envisaged already existed: *Ulysses*, by James Joyce. Freud took no notice, and never sought to obtain a copy of Joyce's novel. It would, in any case, not have been to his taste.

★ ★ ★

We have already met Freud's admission, in conversation with Wilder, that religion could lay claim to 'historical truth'. He defined this truth as 'the recapitulation and the solution of the problems of one's first years that have been covered over by amnesia'. That religion could be a 'solution' as well as a 'recapitulation' in human development is an admission that goes well beyond its out-and-out rejection in *The Future of an Illusion*. Religion might even be an ally of the psychoanalyst, as Freud's friend Oskar Pfister firmly believed. Could it also help to prevent the onset of a cancer which, Freud is said to have told Thornton Wilder, 'might some day be shown [to be] allied to the presence of hate in the subconscious'?[17]

★ ★ ★

Among the English books Freud acquired in Vienna was a novel entitled *When It Was Dark* by Guy Thorne — a pseudonym adopted by C. A. Ranger Gull

(1875–1923). This caught Freud's attention not least because it offered a variation on questions raised by the 'Grand Inquisitor' fable in Dostoevsky's *Brothers Karamazov.* In Thorne's fable enemies of the Christian faith spread the false news that an archaeological discovery in Jerusalem has disproved the Gospel account of Christ's resurrection. They maintain that a freshly uncovered tomb contains an inscription in which Joseph of Arimathea confessed that he had secretly removed the body of Christ three days after his burial, and had reburied it in this tomb in order to inspire the legend of the divine nature of Christ which showed itself in his apparent resurrection. The Dostoevskian consequence Guy Thorne's novel draws from this blow to a religious faith underlying European culture is an extraordinary increase of violent crime, which only abates when the forgers' plot is revealed.

In *Group Psychology and Ego-Analysis* (1921) Freud used Guy Thorne's fable — commended, he said, by the Bishop of London — to explain something of what he meant when he spoke later on to Thornton Wilder of the 'historical truth' of religion. Christianity, he explained, held in check inimical impulses against other believers by means of its Gospel of Love; but its downside, stressed by Freud but not by Thorne or the Bishop, is that the repressed impulses are then turned against those of a different faith. Other mass movements, Freud continues, such as socialism for instance, are likely to generate the same intolerance towards those outside their faith as that which had inspired the religious wars of the past — a prophecy more true of the Marxist-Leninist faith that had just inspired the Bolshevik revolution in Russia than the socialism of those who rallied under the Red Flag of the British Labour Party.[18]

Freud's interest in mass movements and crowd psychology was fired by his reading of Gustave Le Bon's *La Psychologie des foules* which he read in a German edition of 1912. The First World War had deepened this interest, and brought a brief resurgence of political awareness that led to his enthusiastic reception of a volume brought out by the American editor of the *Encyclopaedia Britannica*, Franklin Henry Hooper, entitled *These Eventful Years.*[19] He relished especially its introductory essay by J. L. Garvin (1867–1947). 'I wholeheartedly admire Garvin's introductory essay', Freud wrote to Hooper on 4 September 1924, 'and my warmest sympathy goes out to his attempts to correct judgments about the origin of the war and the results of the peace which have been distorted by party passions'.[20]

Freud steadfastly believed that the Versailles settlement after the First World War had grievously wronged Germany. In Garvin's essay he found confirmation of this belief — a confirmation he later sought in the story of the part played at Versailles by Woodrow Wilson, and in the arguments brought forward by Maynard Keynes in *The Economic Consequences of the Peace.*

Hooper and Garvin were joined, on Freud's bookshelves, by Montgomery Belgion (1892–1950), who sent Freud his book *Our Present Philosophy of Life* (London 1929) with a flattering dedication. I have found no sign that Freud ever read this treatise, though he kept it on his shelves. This contrasts with his attention to books and articles sent him by the journalist George Sylvester Viereck (1884–?) — a German who had made his home in the United States. Viereck published his writings under various pseudonyms as well as under his own name. The apologetics of *Days in Dorn*, in which Viereck presented the life of Kaiser Wilhelm II after his abdication, annoyed Freud so much that he put off acknowledging its receipt; but he made up for this by commending Viereck's later biography of the French statesman Georges Clemenceau, whom many Germans execrated because of his intransigent attitude at the Versailles peace conference of 1919. 'Your *Clemenceau*', Freud writes to Viereck on 20 July 1928,

> pleased me inordinately. One can feel — yes that's how this remarkable man is, so magnificently unconcerned with what people call 'greatness'. [. . .] Reading your interview I was astonished to notice that I could feel profound sympathy for this man whom I had hated as an enemy, that I did not find it difficult to empathize with him in a way I never could with other despots like Lenin or Mussolini. I think I felt bowled over by the identity of his view of life with mine, and did not resent his claiming never to have heard of psychoanalysis.[21]

Encouraged by such praise, Viereck sent Freud two novels he had written: *My First Two Thousand Years: The Autobiography of the Wandering Jew* and *Salome, the Wandering Jewess.*[22] Freud never acknowledged the second of these volumes and was circumspect in his acknowledgement of the first:

> The Memoirs of your 'Ewiger Jude' are certain to engage my fullest attention. I will make sure to study them along the lines you yourself suggest. My judgment, however, won't be worth much; I find literary valuing difficult anyway, and my sympathy for the author will surely falsify my critique.[23]

The sympathy of which Freud here speaks had been conceived when he had read Viereck's *Rejuvenation*[24] and admired, as he acknowledged in a letter to him dated 8 December 1923, 'a many-sidedness surpassing the kind of many-sidedness which is now trumpeted from the four corners of the world'. He therefore agreed to be interviewed by Viereck in 1926, and confessed to him: 'My language is German. My culture, my attainments, are German. I considered myself a German intellectually, until I noticed the growth of anti-Semitic prejudice in Germany and German Austria. Since that time, I prefer to call myself a Jew'.[25] The advent of Hitler strengthened this identification and rekindled the resentments aroused by *Days in Doorn* when Viereck defended another scion of the Hohenzollern dynasty in a contribution to the *New York Herald Tribune.* 'I am sorry', Freud writes to Viereck on 16 April 1933, 'that you have demeaned yourself by supporting the wretched lies contained in a letter [from the ex-Crown Prince of Germany]. These lies included the assurance that in the new Germany "non-one had to suffer injustice on account of his religion"'. Viereck's offence was compounded by his contention that those who opposed the regime in Germany were themselves guilty of 'racial prejudice'. Freud likens this to Neville Chamberlain's readiness to 'discount supposed atrocities' reported as being committed in the new Germany, believing official assurances that nothing of the kind was taking place. He adds that he wants these private opinions to be kept confidential and not used for journalistic articles.[26] Despite such disagreements, however, Freud thought well enough of Viereck's *Wandering Jew* novels, as well as four other publications Viereck had sent him between 1919 and 1932, to take them along with him when he emigrated to London in 1939; but he never commented on Viereck's work again.

* * *

The array of variously talented authors assembled in this chapter will stand as proof that Freud's well-known animus against the United States did not extend to American authors. One of these, H.D., came as a patient; before meeting her, Freud sought acquaintance with her work, without revealing his reaction to it either to her or to his readers. Her *Tribute to Freud* leaves no doubt of the friendly relations he managed to establish with her within the analyst–patient dependency. It was another American patient, a descendant of the original author, who had led him to Helen Hunt Jackson's *Ramona*, and thus acquainted him with a socially and racially tolerant work which sought to do for the American Indian (Native American) what *Uncle Tom's Cabin* had done for the black slave. Thornton Wilder, whose *Bridge of San Luis Rey* engaged his most serious attention, he came to meet personally. Freud engaged him in wide-ranging conversation, touching on politics as well as literature, but did not conceal from him that he found some of Wilder's other novels less to his taste than *The Bridge of San Luis Ray*. With George Sylvester Viereck he had more serious disputes; but ideological differences did not lead to expressions of personal hostility. Viereck intrigued him enough to tempt him into another confession of his difficulties in *valuing* works of literature, adding that in Viereck's case 'my sympathy for the author will surely falsify my critique'.[27]

Freud's growing fame brought him complimentary copies from other American authors — especially those like Ludwig Lewisohn whose novels had a Jewish theme which, they surmised, would have a special appeal for him. But though he kept works like Lewisohn's *Mid-Channel: An American Chronicle* on his shelves, alongside poetological works by F. C. Prescott, no comments on them have hitherto come to light. He was, however, sufficiently interested in a title that promised to relate poetry and dreaming to acquire two of Prescott's books; but there is no proof that he read them, or most of the books that came with the compliments of authors hitherto unknown to him.[28] He was interested enough in Prescott's book to acquire it for himself; but there is no proof that he even read most of the books that came to him with the compliments of authors with whose works he had no previous acquaintance.

Freud's interest in twentieth-century British writers discussed in the present chapter centres on John Galsworthy, whose fame reached its peak during his lifetime but was eclipsed later by more adventurous novelists like Joyce, whose experimental art fell outside the limits of Freud's literary tastes. Galsworthy was joined, in Freud's literary landscape, by minor figures in the history of British fiction such as 'Guy Thorne'; the travel writings of Norman Douglas, whose novel *South Wind* Freud never came to know; and political journalists such as J. L. Garvin, whose clear exposition satisfied Freud's tastes and whose liberal political stance was more akin to his than George Sylvester Viereck's.

Three more topics remain to be covered, all mediated by Ernest Jones: contact with the Bloomsbury Group and its associates; acquaintance with the 'scientific divination' of H. G. Wells; and Freud's reaction to some of the plays and prefaces of Bernard Shaw. These will form the subject of the final chapter.

Notes to Chapter 10

1. *As You Like It*, III, 2.
2. H.D., *Tribute to Freud*, rev. edn (Manchester, 1985), pp. 189–90.
3. *GW* xv, 52.
4. *Jones*, III, 485.
5. *Gilbert Murray's Euripides*, ed. James Morwood (Bristol, 2005), pp. 240, 230, 265.
6. *GW* xv, 51.
7. *Jones*, III, 458.
8. *Kürzeste Chronik*, p. 255.
9. *Kürzeste Chronik*, p. 255.
10. *Kürzeste Chronik*, p. 339.
11. *Kürzeste Chronik*, p. 339.
12. *Kürzeste Chronik*, p. 339.
13. 'Selbstdarstellung', *GW Nachtragsband*, p. 763.
14. *Kürzeste Chronik*, p. 339.
15. *The Cabala*, Book IV; 'Astree-Luce, and the Cardinal'; cf. *Kürzeste Chronik*, p. 339.
16. Richard Goldstone, *Thornton Wilder: An Intimate Portrait* (New York, 1975), pp. 147f.
17. *Kürzeste Chronik*, p. 339. This is Wilder's recollection of a conversation conducted in English.
18. *GW* XIII, 106–07.
19. Franklin Henry Hooper, *These Eventful Years* (London and New York, 1924).
20. *Briefe*, pp. 372.
21. *Briefe*, pp. 395–96.
22. George Sylvester Viereck, *My First Two Thousand Years. The Autobiography of the Wandering Jew* (New York, 1928); *Salome, the Wandering Jewess. My First Two Thousand Years of Love* (New York, 1930).
23. Letter to Viereck, 12 May 1928.
24. Viereck, *Rejuvenation. How Steinach Makes People Young* (New York, 1923).
25. Quoted in Peter Gay, *Freud. A Life for our Time* (London, 2006), p. 448.
26. *Briefe*, pp. 431–32.
27. *Briefe*, p. 396. I have discussed Freud's reaction to Jackson's *Ramona* on p. 63, and documented his enthusiasm for Mark Twain on pp. 84–87.
28. Ludwig Lewisohn, *Mid-Channel: An American Chronicle* (New York and London, 1929); F. C. Prescott, *Poetry and Dreaming* (New York, 1912); F. C. Prescott, *The Poetic Mind* (Boston, 1922).

CHAPTER 11

❖

Bloomsbury and Beyond

We have already seen that Freud was sufficiently interested in Vita Sackville-West and Harold Nicolson to read their best-known novels. Information about their stable and ultimately happy marital relationship permitting homosexual liaisons by both partners will have reached him through Ernest Jones and made him curious about the inner life conveyed in their literary work; but both novels introduced him to facets of British social and political life which he could not have derived from previous forays into English literature.

Nicolson's *Public Faces: A Novel*, first published in 1932, is a psychologically subtle satire on British political attitudes in which a number of fictional members of parliament, diplomats, and civil servants interact, at a time in the near future, with actual politicians of the early 1930s, including Winston Churchill, Oswald Mosley, Neville Chamberlain, Leslie Hore-Belisha, and Brendan Bracken. The plot is set in motion by an incident that anticipates the triggering event in Stanley Kubrick's *Doctor Strangelove: Or, How I Learned to Stop Worrying and Love the Bomb* (1963). In Nicolson's satire an out-of-control British Minister of Aviation launches a series of rockets over Europe and the United States and detonates an (atomic?) bomb that kills thousands of people. Nicolson is particularly good at showing how the public and private lives of politicians, civil servants, secretaries, and couriers interact, and how events belie, in the most unexpected ways, the intentions of those who think they are directing them. The satire is never so broad as to obscure Nicolson's insider view, and his shrewd assessment of the characters who made up the political establishment of the country that offered a home to Freud and assured the survival of the psychoanalytic movement he had founded.

Sackville-West's *The Edwardians*, which had become the Hogarth Press's bestseller two years before *Public Faces*, introduced Freud to another facet of the British establishment and a type of storytelling considerably less cool and distanced than Nicolson's. The novel allowed readers to share its author's daydreams as she parcelled out what she knew of her own characteristics, feelings, and aspirations between three characters: a charismatic, faintly Byronic young lord testing himself in a series of sexual affairs; his nonconforming sister, who rejects the life of the traditional aristocracy in their country mansion for a more Bohemian life in London; and an explorer who beckons both of them to adventures beyond the comfortable existence into which they were born. The novel's chief interest, however, beyond its often clumsy plot and snob-appeal, lies in its presentation of the lifestyle of English aristocrats at the beginning of the twentieth century with a wealth of intimate detail possible only to one who, like the author, had been born and raised in just such a family. It allows readers to dream themselves into an existence ministered to by a host of servants who re-enact downstairs the precedences observed upstairs; a community of forelock-tugging tenants with whom 'His Grace' and his family have a feudal relationship with strictly limited paternal aspects; and middle classes occasionally drawn into their periphery. Within the English aristocracy Sackville-West depicts, the reader is invited to observe careful gradations, ranging from great families with centuries of inherited wealth in their vast mansions and richly furnished town houses, to minor country gentry and a more raffish element introduced by a hedonistic king, Edward VII. Historically most useful is the notation of detail about male and female dress, hairstyle, jewellery, furnishings, garden designs, and so on, and the depiction of ceremonies in a society the author knew so intimately, ranging from coming-out parties and balls, to Christmas parties for tenants and their children. At the same time the reader invited to share all this vicariously is flattered by being shown how shallow, venal, sexually promiscuous, predatory, and hypocritical these aristocrats can be — an impression given greater force by the author's assurance: 'No character in this book is wholly fictitious'. The book's very title alerts readers to what the coronation ceremony at its end, and many hints in its middle portions, serve to reinforce: a sense that this type of existence is limited in time and will inevitably be modified, however many of its trappings survive. This 'good read' of 1930 retains its value as a social and historical document and *roman-à-clef* that could teach much about the stratification of the society which sheltered Freud in his hour of need.

Nicolson and Sackville West were closely allied with the Bloomsbury group of writers and artist with which Freud too came into contact. This was again mediated by Ernest Jones, who had received an offer from James and Alix Strachey to translate some of Freud's works into English. James Strachey prepared for his task by entering analysis with Freud, who reduced his fees to accommodate Strachey's slender resources. Strachey, together with Jones, persuaded Leonard and Virginia Woolf, who had founded the Hogarth Press in 1917, to publish English translations of Freud from 1924 onwards — a venture that ultimately led, after Freud's death, to the *Standard Edition of the Complete Psychological Works of Sigmund Freud*, edited by James Strachey with assistance from Anna Freud and Alan Tyson (1958–74).

The most illustrious member of the Bloomsbury set was Virginia Woolf (1892–1941), whose mental troubles might have predisposed her to seek help from the psychoanalysis whose influence in the English-speaking world her Hogarth Press helped to spread and deepen. This she refused to do, however, fearing that such treatment would 'reduce her to a whirlpool' or dry up the springs of her creativity. Her husband Leonard Woolf (1880–1969) had favourably reviewed Freud's *Psychopathology of Everyday Life*, together with *The Interpretation of Dreams*, as early as 1914; but Virginia refused for a long time even to read the works whose translation the Hogarth Press was publishing. She could not, however, escape the hum of psychoanalytic conversations all around her, and she made her doubts about its literary reverberations known in a review of J. D. Beresford's novel *An Imperfect*

Mother. Under the heading 'Freudian Fiction' this review appeared in *The Times Literary Supplement* on 5 March 1920. Novelists who make conscious use of Freudian theories, she maintains, cannot

> help adopting the professional manner of a doctor intent upon his diagnosis. A love scene interests us because something bearing significantly upon our patient's state of mind may emerge. [. . .] Yes, says the scientific side of the brain, that is interesting; that explains a great deal. No, says the artistic side of the brain, that is dull and has no human significance whatever. Snubbed and discouraged, the artist retreats; and before the end of the book the medical man is left in possession of the field; all the characters have become cases; and our diagnosis is now so assured that a boy of six has scarcely opened his lips before we detect in him unmistakable symptoms of the prevailing disease.

Virginia Woolf goes on to accuse Beresford of the principal sin of all those who hunt for Oedipus Complexes and the like in the most diverse works:

> We must protest that we do not wish to debar Mr Beresford from making use of any key that seems to him to fit the human mind. Our complaint is rather that in 'An Imperfect Mother' the new key is a patent key that opens every door. It simplifies rather that complicates, detracts rather then enriches. The door swings open briskly enough, but the apartment to which we are admitted is a bare little room with no outlook whatever. Partly, no doubt, this is to be attributed to the difficulty of adapting ourselves to any new interpretation of human character; but partly, we think, to the fact that, in the ardours of discovery, Mr Beresford has unduly stinted his people of flesh and blood. In becoming cases they have ceased to be individuals.[1]

By 1935, as we saw him reveal to Thornton Wilder, Freud had come to agree with this estimate of the dangers that beset the conscious use of psychoanalysis, in its early stages, by novelists — dangers, I would add, that menace literary critics even more. Freud came to think that it would take centuries before imaginative writers had so internalized the findings of psychoanalysis that they would not strike a clinical, over-schematic note in their work.[2]

In 1939 Leonard and Virginia Woolf visited the mortally ill Freud in his London home. Leonard was impressed by the personality that seemed to defy age and debility. He saw a courteous old man, with great gentleness and strength, and an aura not of fame, but of greatness', where his wife saw only 'a screwed up shrunk old man: with a monkey's light eyes'.[3] Freud recognized in Virginia a 'narcissistic personality', and presented her with a symbolic narcissus flower.[4]

Virginia Woolf's brother, Adrian Stephen, became a professional psychoanalyst, and Virginia herself could not hold out for ever against reading some, at least, of Freud's writings in their English translation. She then recognized that much of it corresponded to her own experience, ranging from ambivalent feelings about her father, Leslie Stephen, to seeing aggressive and destructive impulses breaking through the thin crust of civilization during the Second World War. She gave this realization a feminine twist, however. In her reading notes on Freud's *Group Psychology and the Analysis of the Ego* she described the aggression let loose by the war as 'specifically masculine'. The fascist state, she came to believe, was also a patriarchal state; the war against it, she wrote in her reading notes, could only be won if 'we destroy the male attributes. Thus the woman's part is to achieve the emancipation of man'.[5] Like so many other readers of Freud's writings, Virginia Woolf used them as springboards for ideas that were far from his.

James Strachey's brother, Lytton Strachey (1880–1932), sent Freud an advance copy of his book *Elizabeth and Essex*.[6] Freud felt sufficiently honoured to begin his letter of thanks, dated 25 December 1928, with a hyperbole he did not often use in addresses to correspondents: 'Hochgeehrter Herr!'. He thanked Strachey for 'the most enjoyable and surprising Christmas gift' he had received that year, and regretted that he had nothing suitable to send in return: 'I am old, do not feel strong, and will probably not produce anything more'. As usual these fears were premature: *Civilization and its Discontents*, *New Introductory Lectures on Psychoanalysis*, *The Man Moses and Monotheistic Religion*, and a number of shorter writings still lay ahead. He went on to assure Strachey that he had read all his previous publications with aesthetic enjoyment:

> This time, however, you moved me more profoundly, for you have yourself gone deeper. You confess what other historians so easily slide over: that it is impossible to be sure we understand the past, because we cannot guess people's motives, penetrate their inner being, their souls — and that therefore we cannot interpret their actions. [. . .] We confront human beings of the past in the way we confront dreams for which no associations have been given us — and only laymen can demand that we should interpret dreams of this kind. As a historian you therefore show yourself steeped in the spirit of psychoanalysis.
>
> After such reservations you approach one of the most remarkable figures in your nation's history; know how to trace the formation of her character in her childhood; and hint with boldness and discretion at her most secret motives, and — it is very possible that you have managed to reconstruct what really happened.[7]

Freud goes on to disclose that when he stood by Elizabeth's tomb in Westminster Abbey many years ago, he had the idea that this childless Queen had inspired Shakespeare to construct the figure of Lady Macbeth for which he had found so little evidence in the printed sources. Lady Macbeth's pangs of conscience may have derived, in Shakespeare's mind, from Elizabeth's remorse at the murder of a guest who had entrusted herself to her hospitality — Mary, Queen of Scots — and made that guilt cover the 'murder' of Essex. Shakespeare, Freud speculated, embodied parts of Elizabeth's character in Macbeth as well as his spouse: if she was really the kind of hysteric Strachey saw in her, the great psychologist Shakespeare was perhaps not wrong to divide her character between two persons. Divided selves always figured largely in Freud's thinking.

Freud had been unusually hesitant in putting forward this interpretation, asking Strachey not to treat it with too much contempt. He hedged his bets even more when he asserted again that he had found Thomas Looney's ascription of Shakespeare's works to the seventeenth Earl of Oxford convincing, but added, modestly:

> I know too little, of course, to be able to guess what those who really understand these times could bring against this new candidate for the authorship of Shakespeare's works. I don't know, and would dearly like to know. Edward de Vere resembles Essex in many respects [. . .][8]

Feeling that he had ridden his hobby horse somewhat too vigorously he ends his letter with an apology for having put forward this plea for information that might confirm or count against Looney's theory. He called for further speculations about de Vere's putative mother complex, his revealing himself, in *Hamlet*, as 'the first modern neurotic', and his supposed reflections that he might easily have shared the fate of the Earl of Essex.

Besides Lytton, James, and Alix, the Strachey family is represented on Freud's shelves by several volumes with introductory material by its communist member, John, one of which Freud has read with particular intensity. His marginal lines and underlinings have been transcribed for me by J. Keith Davies. The book John Strachey introduced on this occasion was Reuben Osborn's *Freud and Marx. A Dialectical Study*, published by Gollancz in 1937. Predictably, many of the passages Freud distinguished — often with a question mark — contained observations about his own work which he thought fallacious; but they also show his interest in the 'interaction of the social environment with certain subjective urges' which in Strachey's and Osborn's view linked Marxist preoccupations with Freud's. Freud underlines the word 'psychological' when Strachey maintains that 'as practical politicians Marxists need to find that correct *psychological* approach which will enable their audiences to grasp and act upon their message'. 'Such a new political technique, Strachey continues 'can [. . .] arise only upon the basis of a genuinely scientific psychology' towards which 'the psychoanalysts have taken the first difficult steps'.[9]

In Osborn's text, as opposed to Strachey's, Freud has marked in lead pencil just one passage:

> Man, says Marx, makes his own history, but out of material conditions ready to hand. In so far as the making of history demands revolutionary action, not until the material conditions exist, can this take place. At the time when the conditions are in process of becoming, their development overshadows the role of man in the making of history, but, at the point where these conditions become so mature that revolutionary action becomes necessary, the figure of man looms large in the role of the maker of history. There is an exchange of significance. History, which is always a process of interchange between subjective and objective qualities, between, as Engels puts it, the constitution of the individual and the economic conditions, shifts its emphasis from one to the other in accordance with the necessities of the historical process.[10]

Freud was obviously glad to have so succinct a statement of the views of Marx and Engels; but he remained sceptical of the political aims and methods of the Communist Party, whether in Russia (where the dangers exhibited themselves most clearly) or in the Austro-Hungarian empire. His scepticism in this regard shows itself in his *New Introductory Lectures on Psychoanalysis* (1933), where he levels at the writings of Marx precisely the criticism so often brought against his own work. These writings, he contends, have 'taken the place of the Bible and the Koran as sources of revelation, though they are no less free of contradictions and obscurities than these older sacred scriptures'. He follows this up with a detailed critique of 'practical Marxism', tempered only by the reflection that at least it had helped to do away with the Christian pieties against which Freud's own suspiciously overemphatic abjurations of religious sentiment were principally directed. The future might show, he concludes, whether the new order of society envisaged by Marxism 'not only banishes the material deprivations suffered by the masses, but also the cultural demands of individuals'.[11] Marx himself, who never witnessed what governments that paid lip-service to his ideas actually got up to, would have wholeheartedly agreed with that.

One work from the fringes of Bloomsbury came to assume special importance for Freud: it reinforced conclusions he had come to himself. This was the indictment of harmful effects springing from the harsh terms imposed by the victors of the First World War on the defeated enemy which the great economist John Maynard Keynes (1883–1946) published under the title *The Economic Consequences of the Peace* in 1919. Keynes was a friend of James Strachey, who lent Freud this book. Strachey confided this to Paul Roazen, who showed, in his 'Oedipus at Versailles',[12] how this book reinforced Freud's resentment at Woodrow Wilson's abandonment of his Fourteen Principles under pressure from the French and (to a lesser degree) the British victors.[13]

⋆ ⋆ ⋆

Ernest Jones, the original mediator between Freud and the Bloomsbury group, also drew his attention to the work of H. G. Wells (1866–1946). Writing to Freud on 15 February 1914, Jones sent along an excerpt from Wells's work which has not survived, but is likely to have been a passage on 'taboo' in Wells's book *Mankind in the Making*, first published in 1903.[14] Hanns Sachs, Jones reported, had been excited by this passage because it had arrived at conclusions about the concept of 'taboo' which conformed with Freud's own: conclusions about the 'partly instinctual' and 'partly developmental' nature of taboo at which, Jones believed, Wells had arrived 'accidentally' , without appreciating their significance. 'It is simply, he writes, 'one more proof of the inevitability of your theory'.

The passage to which Jones referred comes from a chapter intriguingly called 'The Cultivation of the Imagination' and speaks of 'Taboos' in modern times: inhibitions about tinkering with parts of the machinery of state that badly need overhauling. In these matters, Wells explains,

> there is something that is probably an instinct, a deeply felt necessity for Taboos. We know perhaps that our Taboos were not devised on absolutely reasonable grounds, but we are afraid of just how many may not collapse before a purely reasonable inquiry. We are afraid of thinking quite freely even in private. We doubt whether it is wise to begin, though only in the study and alone. 'Why should we — ? . . . Why should we not — ?' And the thought of a public discussion without limitations by a hasty myriad untrained to think, does, indeed, raise an image of consequences, best conveyed, perhaps, by that fine indefinite phrase, 'A Moral Chaos.'

Such fears, Wells continues on a later page, affect what we pass on to the next generation:

> we want the children to go through a serious educational process, and we find at once still further limitations coming in. We discover the necessity of

> deferring experience, of pushing back adolescence, of avoiding precocious stimulation, with its consequent arrest of growth. We are already face to face with an enlarged case for decency, for a system of suppressions and of complicated Taboos.

This leads on, inevitably, to a sceptical look at a subject of practical concern to H. G. Wells which was also, as Jones knew better than anyone, of theoretical as well as practical interest to psychoanalytic therapists. 'I very much doubt', Wells writes,

> when at last the days for the sane complete discussion of our sexual problems come, it will give us anything at all in the way of 'Liberty,' as most people understand that word. In the place of the rusty old manacles, the chain and shot, the iron yoke, cruel, ill-fitting, violent implements from which it was yet possible to wriggle and escape to outlawry, it may be the world will discover only a completer restriction, will develop a scheme of neat gyves, light but efficient, beautifully adaptable to the wrists and ankles, never chafing, never oppressing, slipped on and worn until at last, like the mask of the Happy Hypocrite, they mould the wearer to their own identity. But for all that — gyves![15]

Freud's reply referred only to Wells's explicit use of the word 'taboo' and was distinctly unenthusiastic: 'I find Wells missing on both points', he writes, in English, on 21 February 1914, 'the killing of the father and the origins of the taboo, but as a piece of scientific divination it may pass'.[16] Nineteen years later, however, in June 1933, Freud had what he described as an 'interesting 'visit from Wells, in which they discussed feelings about death. 'He did not', Wells reports, 'feel [about death] as I do. [. . .] He is older than I and in bad health, but seems to be clinging to life and to his reputation and teaching much more youthfully than I do to mine. But then he was probably just drawing me out'.[17] Wells continued to admire Freud, sent congratulations on Freud's eightieth birthday (in an illuminated address also signed by Virginia Woolf), visited him again after his arrival in England, and took steps to have British nationality conferred on the exiled Freud — a process aborted by Freud's death. Wells also sent Freud a copy, with an inscribed dedication, of his book *The Fate of Homo Sapiens* (1939) which is now in a private collection, and commended the conclusions of Freud's *The Man Moses and the Monotheistic Religion* as 'immensely probable' — a conviction not shared by many of its readers.[18] The shelves of Freud's London library still contain the eighth edition of Wells's *Outline of History*[19] in which Freud's work is acknowledged. Freud also owned an edition of *The Science of Life*,[20] which Wells had written in collaboration with Julian Huxley and G. P. Wells, and which had first appeared in 1931. There is no clue, however, to Freud's reaction to these works — his copies have none of his usual markings, nor have I found any sign that Freud ever read any of Wells's novels and short stories.

* * *

Ernest Jones's many literary enthusiasms included the plays of George Bernard Shaw; and he tried hard to make Freud share his liking for them. He had copies of Shaw's plays sent to Freud, and followed his gift up with a letter dated 11 March 1911:

> I hope they will arrive safely. I do not expect you to read them all, except possibly on a holiday. The ones worth reading are, in order: Man and Superman, Major Barbara, Caesar and Cleopatra, and The Devil's Disciple. The first (notably the Hell scene in it) I can specially recommend to you. [. . .][21]

Freud obliged by dipping into *Man and Superman* while preparing an essay for Volume 3 of the *Jahrbuch für psychoanalytische und psychoanalytische Forschungen*, in which he sought to distinguish between an Ego dedicated to the Pleasure Principle (*Lust-Ich*) and an Ego seeking to accommodate itself to the Reality Principle (*Real-Ich*): 'The Pleasure Ego can only *desire*, work towards gaining pleasure and avoiding un-pleasure, while the Reality-Ego seeks to strive for the *useful* and secure itself against harm'.[22]

The sentence Freud had pulled out of the Shavian bran tub presented to him by Jones is quoted at the bottom of the page, with an explanatory commendation: 'A preference for the Reality-Ego over the Pleasure-Ego is admirably expressed in the words of Bernard Shaw: "*To be able to choose the line of greatest advantage in the direction of least resistance.*"' The sentence in italics is cited in its original English, to which Freud adds its derivation: *Man and Superman. A Comedy and a Philosophy.* The subtitle was clearly important to him — he had always admired writers who combined the poet and the philosopher, from Plato to Schiller.

Jones was delighted. He wrote to Freud on 25 November 1911:

> I was enormously impressed by your choice of the quotation from Bernard Shaw. I know all his work and life very well, and think you could not possibly have selected a better passage for expressing the central and most fundamental point of his philosophy. In spite of his unconventionality he is at heart essentially an English Puritan of the ascetic type.[23]

On 14 January 1912 Freud replied: 'I was very much amused at your discovery of my quotation from Shaw, as it was pointed directly at you as an indirect means of expressing my thanks to the giver'.[24]

Striking while he thought the iron was hot, Jones directed Freud's attention to yet another of Shaw's plays by quoting Mrs Gilbey's speech in Act III of *Fanny's First Play* which, he thought, paralleled views on religion and conscience put forward in *Totem and Taboo*: 'We are all sinners, *what else is religion*?[25] Freud did not react to this supposed parallel, and subsequent references to Shaw are, more often than not, critical and disparaging. 'I believe', Freud writes in his *Introductory Lectures on Psychoanalysis*, 'it was Bernard Shaw who said that if there is someone an English lady hates more than her mother, it is her elder sister'. He finds this saying apt to alienate readers and spectators, who will 'find it far more offensive when there is no love between parents than between siblings'.[26] There can be, in Freud's view, no comparison between sibling conflict and that fundamental love-hate relationship which this passage of the *Lectures* helps to introduce — the Oedipus Complex.

In an Epilogue to *Group Psychology and the Analysis of the Ego* Freud finds a generalization he attributes to Shaw unduly cynical: that being in love meant over-estimating the difference between one woman and another. This applies only, Freud explains, to a state of regression to an earlier stage of relations between the sexes — one in which 'being in love' played no part and all 'sexual objects' were deemed of equal value.[27]

Freud's increasing distaste for Shaw shows itself most clearly in his reaction to the passage at the end of *Caesar and Cleopatra* in which Caesar, about to depart for Rome, suddenly realizes that he had forgotten to take leave of his Egyptian lover:

	Ah, I *knew* there was something.
[*To Ruffio*]:	How could you let me forget her, Ruffio?
[*Hastening towards Cleopatra*]:	Had I gone without seeing you, I should never have forgiven myself.

Freud cites this passage in the section on psychologically motivated forgetting in *The Psychopathology of Everyday Life*, objecting to its misrepresentation of the real historical situation in seeking to show that Caesar cared very little about the 'little Egyptian Princess'.[28] He explains his objection more fully in his *Introductory Lectures on Psychoanalysis*:

> The author's little stratagem is intended to ascribe to great Caesar a superiority he did not possess and which he did not aspire to. The historical sources will tell you that Caesar had Cleopatra follow him to Rome, and that she lived there with their little Caesarion at the time of Caesar's murder. After this she fled the town. [. . .][29]

A later letter to Arnold Zweig puts the case even more strongly:

> When B. Shaw makes his Caesar stand and gape at a stony Sphinx just as though he were a Cook's tourist and forget to take leave of Cleopatra when he leaves Egypt, he proves that a joke means more to him than anything else. The historical Caesar summoned Cleopatra to Rome after the birth of their son Caesarion and there she remained till her flight after Caesar's murder. It's true, the poets usually fail to keep these rules [about historical accuracy], e.g. Schiller in *Don Carlos*, Goethe in *Egmont* and *Götz von Berlichingen* etc., but it's frequently not an advantage to do so.[30]

Freud was, of course, well aware of anachronisms and distortions of historical facts in Shakespeare's history plays as well as Goethe's *Egmont* and Schiller's *Don Carlos*. He therefore sought a criterion that would define the extent of the dramatist's freedom to alter such facts. The view he expressed to Arnold Zweig[31] was that poets are free to fill lacunae in history: they are free to settle the creatures of their imagination in uninhabited regions. He also deemed it legitimate to alter facts that have to be dug for in specialized research and are unknown to the common reader. 'It's no objection to Shakespeare's depiction of Macbeth', Freud tells Arnold Zweig, 'that Macbeth was in fact, around the year 1000, a just and benevolent Scottish monarch' ('ein gerechter und volksfreundlicher König von Schottland'). When the historical facts, however, are well established and generally known, the writer should respect them — and it is with disregard of this ('admittedly conservative') rule that Freud charges Shaw's *Caesar and Cleopatra*. He is less critical of such disregard in Goethe and Schiller because of a distaste for Shavian levity which had grown in him over the years.

As Freud's cancer took increasing hold, he did find some comfort in a quotation from *The Doctor's Dilemma*. 'The uncertainty', he writes,

> which hovers over an old man of sixty-seven has now found a material expression. It does not bother me greatly; one will defend oneself for a while with the means of modern medicine, and will then heed Bernard Shaw's reminder: 'Don't try to live forever, you will not succeed'.[32]

In the meantime, however, Jones had tried again by directing Freud's attention to a work which contradicted this saying from *The Doctor's Dilemma*:

> It may interest you to know that Bernard Shaw has just written an epic play in which he attempts to deal with the origin of death, and also uses Plato's Idea of the origin of sex in connection with Lilith. I will bring the book with me.[33]

The play, of course, *is Back to Methuselah*, and the passage to which Jones refers comes towards the end of Part 5: 'As Far as Thought can Reach: AD 31,920'. Freud was unimpressed. 'I have very little affection for Bernard Shaw; his *Back to Methuselah* I found positively insipid'. He expressed his dislike publicly in *The Man Moses and the Monotheistic Religion*, where he explained that he felt himself unable to

> share the view of my coeval Bernard Shaw that people will only achieve something really worth while when they could reach an age of 300 years. Just lengthening the life-span won't achieve anything — this would have to be coupled with many other changes in the conditions of human life.[34]

Did Freud have the horrible senility of the ancient Struldbrugs in *Gulliver's Travels* in mind, as a more plausible effect of extreme old age? Among the 'changes' he wanted to see were an ultimate abolition of what he deemed the modern alliance between material progress and barbarism, and the tyranny of political and ecclesiastical power that inhibited the expression of unconventional opinions.[35]

He wrote this, of course, after the advent of Hitler and his hordes in Austria as well as Germany, and in a book that put forward opinions about the life and fate of the biblical Moses that went counter to Jewish and Christian orthodoxy alike.

Jones had to give in. In his biography of Freud he acknowledged that Freud 'never came to like Shaw's writing, probably because of their widely different conceptions of womanhood'.[36] Here, then, was another of Jones's enthusiasms which Freud found himself, in the end, unable to share; but he never spelled out the objections, which Jones here imputes to him, to Shaw's presentation of women as the ultimate expressions and embodiment of the life-force. What Goethe called 'das Ewig-Weibliche', the eternal feminine, remained a puzzle to Freud right up to the end.

Notes to Chapter 11

1. Virginia Woolf, 'Freudian Fiction', *The Times Literary Supplement*, 5 March 1920, pp. 199–200.
2. *Kürzeste Chronik*, p. 339.
3. Brenda Maddox, *Freud's Wizard. The Enigma of Ernest Jones* (London, 2006), p. 37.
4. Hermione Lee, *Virginia Woolf* (London, 1996), p. 713.
5. Lee, *Virginia Woolf*, p. 724.
6. Lytton Strachey, *Elizabeth and Essex. A Tragic History* (London, 1928)
7. *Briefe*, pp. 399–400.
8. *Briefe*,, p. 200.
9. John Strachey's *Introduction to Freud and Marx: A Dialectical Study* (London, 1939), p. 11.

10. *Freud and Marx: A Dialectical Study*, p. 167.
11. *GW* xv, 195–260.
12. *TLS*, 22 August 1922.
13. For a full discussion of Freud's collaboration with William C. Bullitt on *Thomas Woodrow Wilson: A Psychological Study*, see Chapter 2.
14. *Freud/Jones*, p. 262.
15. H. G. Wells, *Mankind in the Making* (London, 1904), pp. 291–93, 296.
16. *Freud/Jones*, p. 264.
17. Quoted in *Kürzeste Chronik*, p. 267.
18. *Jones*, iii, 219, 250, 259, 462.
19. H. G. Wells, *Outline of History* (London, 1937).
20. H. G. Wells, *The Science of Life* (London, 1938).
21. *Freud/Jones*, p. 94.
22. 'Formulations concerning the Two Principles of Psychic Events', *GW* viii, 235.
23. *Freud/Jones*, p. 121.
24. *Freud/Jones*, p. 125.
25. 30 October 1912, *Freud/Jones*, p. 166 (Jones's emphasis).
26. *GW* xi, 209–10.
27. *GW* xiii, 157.
28. *GW* iv, 170.
29. *GW* xi, 47–48.
30. *The Letters of Sigmund Freud and Arnold Zweig*, ed. by Ernst Freud, trans. by Elaine and William Robson-Scott (New York, 1970), p. 77 (12 May 1934); *Freud/A. Zweig*, p. 88.
31. 12 May 1934, *Freud/A. Zweig*, p. 88.
32. To Kate and Lajos Levy, 11 June 1923 (*Briefe*, p.361).
33. 6 September 1921, *Freud/Jones*, p. 439.
34. *GW* xvi, 156.
35. *GW* xvi, 156.
36. *Jones*, ii, 351.

RETROSPECT

❖

Freud's tastes in literature were largely formed in the latter part of the nineteenth century: a period in his life in which his schooling instilled in him a love of the Greek and Roman classics; when he was also reading Ludwig Philippsohn's 'Israelite Bible' and sampling Christian worship under the aegis of a Catholic nurse; when he conceived an enthusiasm for Goethe, revered in Schiller the union of poet and philosopher, learnt something of German Romantic *Naturphilosophie* (which was still in the air though increasingly devalued by a new breed of scientist), and stored his mind with melodious verses not only by Goethe but also by nineteenth-century poets such as Uhland, Lenau, and Heine. Heine was joined by Lichtenberg and Nestroy as favourite providers of quips and humorous observations on social, philosophical, and literary problems. Delight in Shakespeare, whom he read in German and English, led him to other British and American authors, in ways the present book has sought to document. These included not only writers of imaginative literature, but also the works of Darwin, empirical philosophers from Bacon to Hume, economists such as Adam Smith and Thomas Malthus, physicists like Clerk Maxwell, systematizers of science like Karl Pearson, archaeologists like Arthur Evans, as well as the eugenicist Francis Galton, whose experiments with composite photographs furnished him with analogies and metaphors for his own activities comparable to those he drew from his passion for archaeology. His adventures in thought found physical parallels and symbols in adventure stories by Rider Haggard and Kipling, which also seemed to offer confirmation of psychoanalytical findings, and in compilations of myth and fairy tale like those of Andrew Lang. A search for the origins of religions in totemism and primitive cults led him to Frazer's *Golden Bough* and Robertson Smith's *Religion of the Semites*, where he found ammunition for his polemic against contemporary religious beliefs as relics of the past which, whatever historical justification they might have had, now constituted a reservoir of harmful illusions. He thereby sought to stifle his own sense of the numinous carried over from childhood, which reasserted itself in feelings induced by poetry, painting, sculpture, and architecture, and found a haven in Freud's sense of the demonic, diabolic, and uncanny. It also found substitute gratification in the content and organization of the psychoanalytic movement, as well as the parallels he discovered between himself and biblical figures like Joseph, the interpreter of dreams, and Moses, the lawgiver and hero of his people. The endeavours of his later years to prove the non-Jewish origins of the biblical Moses reflect ambivalences in his attitude to the Judaism he continued to profess while repudiating its religious faith and practices.

If one accepts Tim Ingold's distinction,[1] which sees the objective of *anthropology* as 'a generous, comparative, but nevertheless critical understanding of human being and knowing the world we all inhabit', while *ethnography* seeks to 'describe the lives of people other than ourselves, with an accuracy and sensitivity honed by detailed observation and prolonged first-hand experience', Freud would have seen his work as akin to that of an anthropologist rather than an ethnographer. Even there, however, the lack of direct observation of living people in more 'primitive' societies, common to Freud and his major sources, vitiates the experiment of *Totem and Taboo*: to arrive at generalizations that would link the belief-system of people in the past to psychic predispositions and problems in the present.

The present book's attempt to document and bring into focus Freud's knowledge and use of imaginative literature, *Dichtung*, in Britain and the United States of America has not sought to minimize the inadequacies of his theoretical stance. He was well aware of these, and liked to stress that his concerns were those of the psychologist and not those of the professional literary critic. The most obvious failings are due to his notorious conception of literary 'form' as a sort of forepleasure to make 'themes' (*Motive*) and 'content' palatable; the parallel he drew between imaginative literature and daydreaming; and his tendency, made worse by some of his disciples, to pull a wriggling 'Oedipus Complex' out of the most diverse writings. None of this should, however, tempt us to ignore Freud's genuine aesthetic sensibility, his delight in works of verbal and visual art, beyond all theoretic concerns. A fine stylist himself and master of metaphor, he responded to verbal felicity and painterly values with an immediacy that contrasted with his inability to surrender himself to music without the help of words. Music could not give him what made him look beyond the immediate pleasure his reading gave him: illumination of his own problems and concerns, and those of his patients, and guidance into the darker regions of the mind he had set himself to explore. This included effects never intended by the author of a particular book — *Uncle Tom's Cabin*, for instance, feeding sado-masochistic fantasies in some of its readers. Freud had a sure sense of the qualitative difference between a Shakespeare and a Rider Haggard, and his ability to distinguish between the uniquely insightful and the meretricious in a great writer like Dickens. This did not blind him to the interest lesser writers offered to the psychologist — writers who unselfconsciously revealed a great deal of soul-stuff while spinning their yarns. And even literary critics aware of the weaknesses in the psychoanalytic approach to literature may find, with a shock of recognition, that many of the mechanisms Freud described as typical of dreams, jokes, and parapraxes — condensation, displacement, overdetermination, translation into the visual, symbolization — are close kin to literary devices they also seek to discern and describe.

The parameters of the present study have been set out in its opening chapter — for no English-speaking writer engaged Freud as fully, as constantly, and in so many ways, as Shakespeare. Only Darwin ran him close. His engagement with other British and American authors, however, recapitulated and extended many of the 'uses' Freud found for his reading, and it must be the task of this Retrospect to pinpoint the most important of them.

A good deal of Freud's reading, inevitably, was for research — his summaries of the work of his predecessors in such diverse fields as cerebral palsy in children, dream-interpretation, or the theory of wit and humour, induces respect for his ability to assimilate and summarize writings in several languages and varying disciplines. He also read for recreation and pleasure, however, and for ease and comfort in days of pain, without too much straining after 'significance': James Hilton for instance, or Dorothy Sayers, served him in this way. But as his dealings with Rider Haggard show, such stories could also yield potent symbols for the deeper elements of our being that surface, disguised, in our dreams.

The autobiographical impulse which governed so much of Freud's use of Shakespeare could also be recognized in his comments on other writers and their works. He makes Milton's Satan a spokesman for his own defiance of adversity, sees his scatological obsession and physiological reactions mirrored by Gulliver among the Lilliputians, finds a parallel for a sudden access of 'Riches' in *Little Dorrit*, and even discovers kinship with poor Mr Dick's inability to turn his thoughts away from King Charles's head. He contrasts his own marital choice and prospects with those of George Eliot's Casaubon and Lydgate, and sees a parallel between his methods of psychoanalytic probing and those employed by Sherlock Holmes on the trail of past crimes.

Freud sought and found in his reading anticipations and confirmations of his own theories: his Oedipal interpretation of *Hamlet* is joined by the convincing depiction of psychologically motivated forgetting in stories by Galsworthy and Meredith, contrasting with unconvincing forgetting in a play by Bernard Shaw. What is striking, however, is that with the exception of Shakespeare, no British or American author is subjected to the same intense psychoanalytic scrutiny as Conrad Ferdinand Meyer, Wilhelm Jensen, and Dostoevsky. Scientists from Darwin to Karl Pearson could be quoted in support of his views on the nature, function, and limitation of the search for scientific truth; but he could seriously deceive himself here. His methods were far less empirical than he thought, he was far less rigorous in testing his own hypotheses than Darwin, and psychoanalysis was *sui generis* in a way that precluded its classification as a 'science' akin to, or part of, biology.

Freud looked to British authors not only for confirmation, but also for extension, of his own experience. He was glad to learn about historical processes from writers ranging from Holinshed to Macaulay and Lytton Strachey, about slavery and discrimination from Harriet Beecher Stowe and Helen Hunt Jackson, about the English class system from Galsworthy and Victoria Sackville-West, about eighteenth-century politics from 'Junius', and modern politics from Harold Nicolson; and — alas — he went to Frazer for the thought-processes of 'primitive' people and to Robertson Smith for the origins of religion. The lack of anthropological and ethnographic method and experience characteristic of his models vitiated the theories he sought to base on their work.

Freud's quest for a supra-national tradition into which he could place himself and his work also found a partial answer in his British reading. He drew a line that encompassed Bacon, Locke, Hume, John Stuart Mill, and Darwin to establish that for all his speculative originality he could also claim to be an empiricist, a utilitarian, and an evolutionist in the British mould. At the same time, he could find stylistic models among such authors: the urbane, gentlemanly expositions of British philosophers and historiographers, the satiric mode of Swift and Samuel Butler, the humorous elegance of Sydney Smith, the sober clarity of Darwin, helped Freud fashion a way of writing that made even complicated thoughts accessible to the common reader. Last but not least: Freud found his reading of British authors lead him back to the classics which, together with the poetry of Goethe, had been among the most powerful experiences of his early life. John Stuart Mill, for instance, made him relive the impact of Plato, and Galsworthy extended his acquaintance with the plays of Euripides.

Freud did not always heed essential contexts in which a given work must be seen — he read Adam Smith's *Wealth of Nations*, for instance, ignorant of the essential moral foundation Smith had sought to give his economic theories in his *Theory of Moral Sentiments*. Nor did he always read as carefully as the pedant in me might have wished. He misrepresents the relation George Eliot so carefully established between Dinah Morris's character and her physical appearance, misinterprets the 'freeze-frame 'ending of Stockton's fable of the lady and the tiger, and misses the complex subversion of conventional morality in the final words of Mark Twain's 'The first Melon I Ever Stole'. But though he showed himself reluctant to partake of the rich feast of British lyric poetry, he could delight in single verses from Scott, Burns, Tennyson, Poe, Clough, and Auden that he encountered in books or letters or conversations.

The examples from English and American literature cited in this book suggest five questions Freud asked of literary works in general. What can a scrutiny of the work tell us about the psychic disposition of its author and the mood in which he wrote it? What psychological truths are embodied in literary characters who can be analysed as though they existed in real life? What psychological truths are enshrined in the nature and structure of the work seen as an independent literary whole? What can we know of the effect, intended or not, which the work has on its changing readership or audiences? What specific interests and concerns of a particular reader, Sigmund Freud, does it reflect or can it be made to serve?

Answers to these questions may best be found by referring back to *Hamlet*. We watched, at the outset, how Freud impressed this play, along with other works of imaginative literature, into an expression of his own feelings and concerns. He also, however, sought to relate *Hamlet* to a specific period in its author's life by dating its composition to the aftermaths of the deaths of his father (a highly doubtful dating) and of Shakespeare's son Hamnet, whose name resembles that of the eponymous hero of his play so closely. He also sought biographical reasons for a disgust with sexuality that links *Hamlet*, *King Lear*, and *Timon of Athens*. In a conversation never designed to appear in print, Freud suggested that Shakespeare's supposed revulsion might have been due to a 'luetic' infection. This biographical fallacy — the idea that the 'mood' of a piece must correspond to that of the author at the time of writing — is one of the most obvious weaknesses of Freud's approach. Later, when Freud came to doubt Shakespeare's authorship of the plays that appeared under his name, he sought to relate his earlier findings to what he could learn of the life and character of Edward de Vere, Earl of Oxford — with even less success.

Freud related what he felt to be the psychological truths embedded in Shakespeare's play to his clinical experiences. His Hamlet is a 'neurotic', plagued by conflicts arising from conflicts that have become known as the Oedipus Complex' which might, in fact be more fittingly renamed 'Hamlet Complex'. He shows how *Hamlet* is structured by the splitting of the father figure into two — one loved, the other hated — adding a possible third, Polonius, whom Hamlet kills after mistaking his voice for that of the second. The psychological difficulties of the central figure are, of course, seen by Freud, as by so many others, as the ultimate cause of a dramatic structure determined by hesitations and delays punctuated by bursts of violent action. Freud sketches in what he saw as the ultimate cause of the play's appeal to generations of readers and spectators by dismissing earlier 'solutions' of the puzzles presented by Hamlet's hesitations and deferrals — including the 'acorn planted in a costly jar' of Goethe's *Wilhelm Meister's Apprenticeship* — before advancing his own 'Oedipal' solution, subliminally conveyed to audiences predisposed to accept it by their own fears and desires. He believed that it was characteristic of great literature that it did not convey everything on the surface, but allowed spaces to be filled in by empathetic recipients.

Finally, the extant sources do not allow us to know in any detail how Freud introduced references to imaginative literature into his treatment of analysands. What is beyond dispute, however, is that he picked up on his patients' reading when he detected traces of literary reminiscence in the dreams he encouraged them to recount, and that he discussed literature with the 'Wolf Man', Hilda Doolittle, and the unnamed patient who lent him volumes of Galsworthy and Arnold Bennett from his collection.

My occasional criticism of Freud's interpretations should not be allowed to skew the overall picture. In a busy life not devoted to the full-time study of literary texts he did not always have the relevant book to hand or find time to check what his memory told him. This in no way impairs my sense that the range and variety of his comments on Anglophone authors constitutes a fascinating chapter in the history of taste and international exchange, while also affording a welcome insight into the mind of a classically and scientifically trained Central European whose own writings have affected the thinking, and the very vocabulary, of men and women far beyond the German-speaking regions in which he lived and wrote.

Freud's knowledge and use of British and American writings form part of a much larger network woven by his aesthetic sensibilities and wide-ranging literary artistic, scientific, psychological, and anthropological interests. He responded with well-directed curiosity to works produced in classical Greece and Rome, Germany, Austria-Hungary, France, Spain, Italy, Holland, Norway, and Russia. In his essay entitled 'Timely Thoughts on War and Death', first published in 1915, Freud proclaimed an ideal he saw threatened by the conflict into which Europe had been plunged: the ideal of a 'Kulturweltbürger', a cultural citizen of the world, to whom no great writer seemed strange because he had written in a language other than the reader's own. A reader of this kind, Freud explained, would choose from the storehouse of world literature what he felt would most contribute to his own enjoyment and understanding of life.[2] Freud kept this ideal alive in himself by learning other languages, reading works in the original or in the many congenial German translations that followed a pattern set by August Wilhelm Schlegel — and through his own practice of translation from French and English. It is a worthy ideal, and should be acceptable even to those who are more open than Freud to literary experiments in their own time, as well as those who are less than sympathetic to Freudian psychoanalysis.

Notes

1. Tim Ingold, 'Anthropology is not Ethnography', *British Academy Review*, 11 (2008), 21.
2. *GW* x, 327.

SELECT BIBLIOGRAPHY

A. Abbreviations — Primary Sources

Briefe	S.F., *Briefe 1873–1939*, ed. by Ernst and Lucy Freud, 3rd rev. edn (Frankfurt a.M.: Fischer, 1980)
Fliess	S.F., *Briefe an Wilhelm Fliess 1887–1904*, ed. by Jeffrey Moussaieff Masson, M. Schröder, and G. Fichtner, 2nd edn (Frankfurt a.M.: Fischer, 1999)
Freud/Abraham	S.F.–Karl Abraham, *Briefe 1907–1926*, ed. by Hilda C. Abraham and Ernst L. Freud, 2nd edn (Frankfurt a.M.: Fischer, 1980)
Freud/Jones	*The Complete Correspondence of Sigmund Freud and Ernest Jones 1908–1939*, ed. by R. Andrew Paskauskas, intro. Riccardo Steiner (Cambridge, Mass. and London: Harvard University Press, 1993)
Freud/Jung	S.F.–C. G. Jung, *Briefwechsel*, ed. by William McGuire and W. Sauerländer (Frankfurt a.M.: Fischer, 1974)
Freud/Pfister	S.F.–Oskar Pfister, *Briefe 1909–1913*, ed. by Heinrich Meng and Ernst L. Freud, 2nd edn (Frankfurt a.M.: Fischer, 1963)
Freud/A. Zweig	S.F.–Arnold Zweig, *Briefwechsel*, ed. by Ernst L. Freud (Frankfurt a.M.: Fischer, 1968)
Freud/St. Zweig	'Briefwechsel mit Sigmund Freud', ed. by Hans-Ulrich Lindken, in Stefan Zweig, *Briefwechsel mit Hermann Bahr, Sigmund Freud, Rainer Maria Rilke und Arthur Schnitzler* (Frankfurt a.M.: Fischer, 1987)
Gay	Peter Gay, *Freud: A Life for our Time*, new edn, London: Max Press, 2006)
GW	Sigmund Freud, *Gesammelte Werke chronologisch geordnet*, ed. by Anna Freud, E. Bibring, W. Hoffer, E. Kris, O. Isakower, and Marie Bonaparte; *Nachtragsband*, ed. by Angela Richards and Ilse Grubrich-Simitis (Frankfurt a.M.: Fischer Taschenbuch Verlag, 1999)
Jones	Ernest Jones, *Sigmund Freud: Life and Work*, 3 vols (London: Hogarth Press, 1956–57)
Jugendbriefe	S.F., *Jugendbriefe an Eduard Silberstein 1871–1881*, ed. by Walter Boehlich (Frankfurt a.M.: Fischer, 1989)
Kürzeste Chronik	S.F., *Tagebuch* 1929, *Kürzeste Chronik*, ed. and intro. by Michael Molnar, German version Christfried Tögel (Basel and Frankfurt a.M.: Stroemfeld, 1996)
PWAV	*Protokolle der Wiener Analytischen Vereinigung*, ed. by Hermann Nunberg and E. Federn, 4 vols (Frankfurt a.M.: Fischer, 1977)
Reisebriefe	S.F., *Unser Herz zeigt nach dem Süden. Reisebriefe 1895–1923*, ed. by Christfried Tögel and Michael Molnar (Berlin: Aufbau, 2002)

B. Other Primary Sources

Freud's Library. A Comprehensive Catalogue. Freuds Bibliothek. Vollständiger Katalog. Compiled and edited by J. Keith Davies and Gerhard Fichtner (London: Freud Museum, and Tübingen: Diskord, 2006)

S.F.–Ludwig Binswanger, *Briefwechsel 1908–1938*, ed. by Gerhard Fichtner (Frankfurt a.M.: Fischer, 1999)

S.F.–William C. Bullitt, *Thomas Woodrow Wilson, Twenty-eighth President of the United States. A Psychological Study* (London: Weidenfeld and Nicolson, 1967)

S.F.–Sandor Ferenczi, *Correspondence*, ed. by André Haynal, Eva Brabant, E. Folgeder, and Patrizia Giamper-Deutsch, trans. by P. T. Haffer (Cambridge, Mass.: Harvard University Press, 1993–2000)

S.F.–Max Eitingon, *Briefwechsel 1906–1939*, ed. by Michael Schröder (Tübingen: discord, 2004)

S.F.–Ernest Jones, *Briefwechsel 1908–1939* (The original text of letters written in the German language), ed. by Ingeborg Mayer-Palmedo (Cambridge, Mass. and London: Harvard University Press, 1993)

Susan S. Friedman, ed., *Analyzing Freud. Letters of H.D., Bryher, and their Circle* (New York: New Directions, 2002)

Ilse Grubrich-Simitis, ed., Sigmund Freud, *'Selbstdarstellung'. Schriften zur Geschichte der Psychoanalyse* (Frankfurt a.M.: Fischer Taschenbuch Verlag, 1971)

C. Secondary Sources Consulted

ANDREAS-SALOMÉ, LOU, *The Freud Journal*, trans. and ed. by S. A. Leavy (London: Hogarth Press, 1965)

APPIGNANESI, LISA, and J. FORRESTER, *Freud's Women* (London: Penguin, 2000)

BADCOCK, CHRISTOPHER, *PsychoDarwinism: The New Synthesis of Darwin and Freud* (London: HarperCollins, 1994)

BAUDOUIN, CHARLES, *Psychoanalysis and Aesthetics*, tr. by Eden and Cedar Paul (London: Allen & Unwin, 1924)

BERSANI, LEO, *The Freudian Body. Psychoanalysis and Art* (New York: Columbia University Press, 1986)

BETTELHEIM, BRUNO, *Freud and Man's Soul* (London: Hogarth Press, 1983)

BEVINGTON, DAVID, 'Hamlet's Two Fathers', *Proceedings of the British Academy* 154 (London: British Academy, 2008)

BLOOM, CLIVE, *Reading Poe, Reading Freud. The Romantic Imagination in Crisis* (Basingstoke: Macmillan, 1988)

BLOOM, HAROLD, ed., *Sigmund Freud* (New York: Chelsea House, 1985)

BONAPARTE, MARIE, *Edgar Poe. Étude psychoanalytique* (Paris: Editions Denoël et Steele, 1933)

BOWIE, MALCOLM, ed., *Freud, Lacan and the Critique of Culture* (Oxford: Oxford University Press, 1991)

—— *Psychoanalysis and the Future of Theory* (Oxford: Blackwell, 1993)

BRANDES, GEORG, *William Shakespeare*, tr. by William Archer and others (London: Heinemann, 1926)

BREGER, LOUIS, *Freud. Darkness in the Midst of Vision* (New York: Wiley, 2000)

BROWN, J. A. C., *Freud and the Postfreudians* (Harmondsworth: Penguin, 1961)

BRÜCKNER, PETER, *Sigmund Freuds Privatlektüre* (Cologne: Horst, 1975)

BUDD, SUSAN, 'Reading and Misreading', *The Academic Face of Psychoanalysis*, ed. by Louise Braddock and Michael Lacewing (London: Routledge, 2007)

DAVIES, KEITH, 'Die archäologische Bibliothek Freuds', in: Lydia Martinelli (ed.), *'Meine... alten und dreckigen Götter'. Aus Sigmund Freuds Sammlung* (Vienna: Sigmund Freud Museum, 1999)

DICENSO, JAMES, *The Other Freud: Religion, Culture and Psychoanalysis* (London: Routledge, 1999)

DILLER, J. V., *Freud's Jewish Identity* (Rutherford, NJ: Fairleigh Dickinson University Press, 1991)

DOOLITTLE, HILDA (H.D.), *Tribute to Freud* (New York: Pantheon, 1950)

DRASSINOWER, ABRAHAM, *Freud's Theory of Culture: Eros, Loss and Politics* (Lanham, MD: Rowman & Littlefield, 2003)

DREVER, JAMES and HARV WALLERSTEIN, *A Dictionary of Psychology*, rev. edn (Harmondsworth: Penguin, 1964)

DUFRESNE, TODD, *Tales from the Freudian Crypt: The Death Drive in Text and Context* (Stanford: Stanford University Press, 2000)

ELLIS, DAVID, *Wordsworth, Freud and the Spots of Time* (Cambridge: Cambridge University Press, 1985)

FABER, M. D., ed., *The Design Within: Psychoanalytic Approaches to Shakespeare* (New York: Science House, 1970)

FELMAN, SHOSHANA, ed., *Literature and Psychoanalysis: The Question of Reading Otherwise* (New Haven: Yale University Press, 1977)

FICHTNER, GERHARD, *Freuds Patienten* (Tübingen: Institut für Geschichte der Medizin, 1979)

——'Die Briefe Freuds als historische Quelle', *Psyche*, 43 (1989)

——'Übertragung. Zur Archäologie einer Freudschen Begriffes', *Jahrbuch der Psychoanalyse*, 53 (2006)

FORRESTER, JOHN, *Language and the Origins of Psychoanalysis* (London: Macmillan, 1980)

—— *The Seductions of Psychoanalysis* (Cambridge: Cambridge University Press, 1990)

FRANKLAND, GRAHAM, *Freud's Literary Culture* (Cambridge: Cambridge University Press, 2000)

FREUD, ERNST, and LUCY FREUD, with ILSE GRUBRICH-SIMITIS, eds, *Sigmund Freud. His Life in Pictures and Words*, tr. by Christine Trollope (London: Deutsch, 1978)

FROMM, ERICH, *Greatness and Limitations of Freud's Thought* (London: Cape, 1980)

GABRIEL, YIANNIS, *Freud and Society* (London: Routledge & Kegan Paul, 1983)

GARDINER, MURIEL, ed., *The Wolf-Man and Sigmund Freud* (London: Hogarth Press, 1972)

GAY, PETER, *Freud, Jews and Other Germans* (New York: Oxford University Press, 1978)

——*A Godless Jew. Freud, Atheism, and the Making of Psychoanalysis* (New Haven: Yale University Press, 1987)

——*Reading Freud. Explorations and Entertainments* (New Haven: Yale University Press, 1990)

GILMAN, SANDER, ed., *Reading Freud's Reading* (New York and London: New York University Press, 1994)

GOMBRICH, ERNST, 'Freud's Aesthetics', *Encounter*, January 1966

GRINSTEIN, ALEXANDER, *Sigmund Freud's Dreams* (Detroit: Wayne State University Press, 1968)

GROSSKURTH, PHYLLIS, *The Secret Ring: Freud's Inner Circle and the Politics of Psychoanalysis* (London: Cape, 1991)

GRUBRICH–SIMITIS, ILSE, *Zurück zu Freuds Texten* (Frankfurt a.M.: Fischer, 1993)

——*Freud's Moses-Studie als Tagtraum: Ein biographischer Essay* (Frankfurt a.M.: Fischer, 1994)

GRÜNBAUM, ADOLF, *The Foundations of Psychoanalysis. A Philosophical Critique* (Berkeley: University of California Press, 1984)

HALE, NATHAN G., *Freud and the Americans: The Beginnings of Psychoanalysis in America, 1876–1917* (New York: Oxford University Press, 1971)

HAYNAL, ANDRÉ, *Psychoanalysis and the Sciences*, tr. by E. Holder (London: Karnac, 1993)
HOLLAND, NORMAN, *The Dynamics of Literary Response* (New York: Columbia University Press, 1968)
——*Psychoanalysis and Shakespeare* (New York: McGraw-Hill, 1966)
HOFFMAN, FREDERICK J., *Freudianism and the Literary Mind* (Baton Rouge: Louisiana State University Press, 1957)
HORDEN, PEREGRINE, *Freud and the Humanities* (London: Duckworth, 1985)
HYMAN, STANLEY E., *The Tangled Bank. Darwin, Marx, Frazer and Freud as Imaginative Writers* (New York: Atheneum, 1962)
ILLNER, BIRGIT, *Psychoanalyse oder die Kunst der Wissenschaft* (Berne and Oxford: Peter Lang, 2000)
INGOLD, TIM, 'Anthropology is Not Ethnography', *British Academy Review*, 11 (2008)
ISRAËLS, HAN, *Het geval Freud* (Amsterdam: Bert Bakker, 1993)
IZENBERG, GERALD N., *The Existentialist Critique of Freud* (Princeton: Princeton University Press, 1976)
JAHODA, GUSTAV, *Psychology and Anthropology* (London and New York: Academic Press, 1982)
JANIK, ALLAN, and STEPHEN TOULMIN, *Wittgenstein's Vienna* (New York: Simon & Schuster, 1973)
JONES, ERNEST, *On the Nightmare* (London: Hogarth Press, 1931)
——*Hamlet and Oedipus* (London: Gollancz, 1949)
——*Free Associations: Memories of a Psychoanalyst* (London: Hogarth Press, 1959)
——*Psycho-Myth, Psycho-History, Essays in Applied Psycho-analysis* (New York: Hillstone, 1974)
JONTE-PACE, DIANE E., *Speaking the Unspeakable: Religion, Misogyny and the Uncanny Mother in Freud's Cultural Texts* (Berkeley: University of California Press, 2001)
KLEIN, DENNIS B., *Jewish Origins of the Psychoanalytic Movement* (Chicago: University of Chicago Press, 1985)
KOFMAN, SARAH, *The Childhood of Art: An Interpretation of Freud's Aesthetics* (New York: Columbia University Press, 1988)
KRIS, ERNST, *Psychoanalytic Explorations in Art* (London: Allen & Unwin, 1953)
KÜNG, HANS, *Freud and the Problem of God*, tr. by E. Quinn (New Haven: Yale University Press, 1979)
KURZWEIL, EDITH, *Freudians and Feminists* (Oxford: Westview, 1995)
——and WILLIAM PHILLIPS, eds, *Literature and Psychoanalysis* (New York: Columbia University Press, 1983)
LEADER, DARIAN, *Freud's Footnotes* (London: Faber, 2000)
LEAR, JONATHAN, *Freud* (London: Routledge, 2005)
MCGRATH, WILLIAM J., *Freud's Discovery of Psychoanalysis. The Politics of Hysteria* (Ithaca and New York: Cornell University Press, 1986)
MCGUINNESS, BRIAN, 'Freud and Wittgenstein', in *Wittgenstein and his Time*, ed. by Brian McGuinness (Oxford: Blackwell, 1982)
MCINTYRE, A. C., *The Unconscious: A Conceptual Analysis* (London: Routledge & Kegan Paul, 1958)
MADDOX, BRENDA, *Freud's Wizard. The Enigma of Ernest Jones* (London: Murray, 2006)
MAHONEY, PATRICK J., *Freud and the Rat Man* (New Haven: Yale University Press, 1986)
——*Freud as a Writer* (New Haven: Yale University Press, 1987)
——*On Defining Freud's Discourse* (New Haven: Yale University Press, 1989)
MARCUS, STEVEN, *Freud and the Culture of Psychoanalysis: Studies in the Transition from Victorian Humanism to Modernity* (London: Allen & Unwin, 1984)
MARCUSE, HERBERT, *Eros and Civilization. A Philosophical Enquiry into Freud* (London: Penguin Press, 1970)
MASSON, JEFFREY MOUSSAIEFF, *The Assault on Truth: Freud's Suppression of the Seduction Theory* (London: Faber, 1984)

Meisel, Perry, ed., *Freud: A Collection of Critical Essays* (Englewood Cliffs, NJ: Prentice-Hall, 1981)
Meissner, W. W., *Psychoanalysis and Religious Experience* (New Haven: Yale University Press, 1984)
Milner, Max, *Freud et l'interpretation de la littérature* (Paris: Société d'édition d'enseignement supérieur, 1980)
Nägele, Rainer, *Reading after Freud* (New York: Columbia University Press, 1987)
Nelson, Benjamin, ed., *Freud and the Twentieth Century* (London: Allen & Unwin, 1957)
Neu, Jerome, ed., *The Cambridge Companion to Freud* (Cambridge: Cambridge University Press, 1991)
Obholzer, Karin, *The Wolf Man Sixty Years Later: Conversations with Freud's Controversial Patient* (London: Routledge & Kegan Paul, 1982)
Oring, Elliott, *The Jokes of Sigmund Freud. A Study in Humor and Jewish Identity* (Philadelphia: University of Pennsylvania Press, 1984)
Orlando, Francesco, *Toward a Freudian Theory of Literature*, tr. by Charmaine Lee (Baltimore: Johns Hopkins University Press, 1978)
Parsons, William B., *The Enigma of the Oceanic Feeling* (New York and Oxford: Oxford University Press, 1999)
Paulin, Roger, *The Critical Reception of Shakespeare in Germany, 1682–1914* (Hildesheim and Zürich: Olms, 2003)
Petocz, Agnes, *Freud, Psychoanalysis and Symbolism* (Cambridge: Cambridge University Press, 1999)
Pfrimmer, Theo, *Freud, Lecteur de la Bible* (Paris: Presses universitaires de France, 1982)
Prawer, S. S., 'A Change of Direction? Sigmund Freud between Goethe and Darwin', *Publications of the English Goethe Society*, 76 (2007)
——'The Dog, the Knight, and the Squire. Sigmund Freud's Reading of Cervantes', *Oxford German Studies*, 37 (2008)
Reich, Wilhelm, *Reich Speaks of Freud*, ed. by Mary Higgins and C. M. Raphael (London: Souvenir Press, 1967)
Reik, Theodor, *From Thirty Years with Freud* (London: Hogarth Press, 1942)
Rimmon-Kenan, Shlomith, ed., *Discourse in Psychoanalysis and Literature* (London: Methuen, 1987)
Ritvo, Lucille, *Darwin's Influence on Freud. A Tale of Two Sciences* (New Haven: Yale University Press, 1990)
Roazen, Paul, *Freud: Political and Social Thought* (London: Hogarth Press, 1969)
——*Freud and his Followers* (London: Allen Lane, 1975)
——'Oedipus at Versailles. New Evidence of Freud's Part in a Study of Woodrow Wilson', *Times Literary Supplement*, 22 April 2005
Robert, Marthe, *D'Oedipe á Moïse: Freud et la conscience juive* (Paris: Calmann-Lévy, 1975)
Robertson, Ritchie, Introduction and Notes in *Sigmund Freud: The Interpretation of Dreams*, tr. by Joyce Crick (Oxford: Oxford University Press, 1999)
——'Freud's Literary Imagination', in *The Academic Face of Psychoanalysis*, ed. by Louise Braddock and Michael Lacewing (London: Routledge, 2007)
Sachs, Hanns, *Freud, Master and Friend* (London: Imago Publishing, 1945)
Sadger, Isidor, *Sigmund Freud. Persönliche Erinnerungen*, ed. by Andrea Huppke and M. Schröder (Tübingen: Diskord, 2006)
Salber, Wilhelm, *Sigmund und Anna Freud* (Hamburg: Europäische Verlagsanstalt, 1999)
Santas, Gerasimos, *Plato and Freud: Two Theories of Love* (Oxford: Blackwell, 1988)
Schönau, Walter, *Sigmund Freuds Prosa: Literarische Elemente seines Stils* (Stuttgart: Metzler, 1968)
Schorske, Carl E., *Fin-de-siècle Vienna: Politics and Culture* (New York: Knopf, 1979)

SEIFERT, EDITH, '*Was will das Weib?' Zu Begehren und Lust bei Freud und Lacan* (Berlin: Quadriga, 1987)
SHEPHERD, MICHAEL, *Sherlock Holmes and the Case of Dr Freud* (London: Tavistock, 1985)
SPURLING, LAURENCE, ed., *Sigmund Freud. Critical Assessments*, 4 vols (London: Routledge, 1989)
STANOWSKY, DONALD, 'Stealing Guilt. Freud, Twain, Augustine and the Question of Moral Luck', *American Imago*, 63 (2006)
SULLOWAY, FRANK J., *Freud, Biologist of the Mind. Beyond the Psychoanalytic Legend* (New York: Little, Brown, 1979)
TIMMS, EDWARD, ed., *Freud in Exile. Psychoanalysis and its Vicissitudes* (New Haven: Yale University Press, 1988)
TIMPANARO, SEBASTIANO, *The Freudian Slip: Psychoanalysis and Textual Criticism*, tr. by Kate Soper (London: NLB, 1976)
LIONEL TRILLING, *Sincerity and Authenticity* (Cambridge, Mass.: Harvard University Press, 1972)
—— *The Liberal Imagination* (Oxford: Oxford University Press, 1981)
WEBER, SAMUEL, *Return to Freud: Jacques Lacan's Dislocation of Psychoanalysis*, trans. by Michael Levine (Cambridge: Cambridge University Press, 1991)
WEBSTER, RICHARD, *Why Freud was Wrong: Sin, Science, and Psychoanalysis* (London: HarperCollins, 1995)
WEIBL, ELMAR, *Gesellschaft und Kultur bei Hobbes und Freud* (Vienna, 1980)
WOLLHEIM, RICHARD, *Sigmund Freud* (Cambridge: Cambridge University Press, 1981)
WOLLHEIM, RICHARD, ed., *Freud: A Collection of Critical Essays* (Garden City, NY: Anchor Books, 1974)
WOLLHEIM, RICHARD, and J. HOPKINS, eds, *Philosophical Essays on Freud* (Cambridge: Cambridge University Press, 1982)
WOOLF, VIRGINIA, 'Freudian Fiction', *Times Literary Supplement*, 5 March 1920
WRIGHT, ELIZABETH, *Psychoanalytic Criticism: Theory in Practice* (London: Methuen, 1984)
YERUSHALMI, Y. H., *Freud's Moses: Judaism Terminable and Interminable* (New Haven: Yale University Press, 1991)
YOUNG-BRUEHL, ELISABETH, *Anna Freud* (London: Macmillan, 1988)
ZANUSO, BILLA, *The Young Freud: The Origins of Psychoanalysis in Late Nineteenth-Century Viennese Culture* (Oxford: Blackwell, 1986)
ZILBOORG, GREGORY, *Psychoanalysis and Religion*, ed. by M. S. Zilboorg (London: Allen & Unwin, 1967)

THE ORIGINAL GERMAN TITLES OF FREUD'S BOOKS AND ESSAYS

Analysis of the Phobia of a Five-Year-Old Boy	*Analyse der Phobie eines fünfjährigen Knaben*
Beyond the Pleasure Principle	*Jenseits des Lustprinzips*
A Child is Beaten	*Ein Kind wird geschlagen*
A Childhood Reminiscence by Leonardo da Vinci	*Eine Kindheitserinnerung des Leonardo da Vinci*
Civilization and its Discontents	*Das Unbehagen in der Kultur*
Constructions in Analysis	*Konstruktionen in der Analyse*
'Cultural' Sexual Morality and Modern Nervosity	*Die 'kulturelle' Sexualmoral und die moderne Nervosität*
Delusions and Dreams in Jensen's 'Gradiva'	*Der Wahn und die Träume in Jensens 'Gradiva'*
Finite and Infinite Analysis	*Die endliche und die unendliche Analyse*
'Formulations concerning the Two Principles of Psychic Events'	*'Formulierungen über die zwei Prinzipien des psychischen Geschehens'*
Group Psychology and Ego Analysis	*Massenpsychologie und Ich-Analyse*
The Interpretation of Dreams	*Die Traumdeutung*
Introductory Lectures on Psychoanalysis	*Vorlesungen zur Einführung in die Psychoanalyse*
The Joke and its Relation to the Unconscious	*Der Witz und seine Beziehung zum Unbewussten*
The Man Moses and the Monotheistic Religion	*Der Mann Moses und die monotheistische Religion*
The Motif of Choice between Three Caskets	*Das Motiv der Kästchenwahl*
Mourning and Melancholia	*Trauer und Melancholie*
New Introductory Lectures on Psychoanalysis	*Neue Folge der Vorlesungen zur Einführung in die Psychoanalyse*
On Psychotherapy	*Über Psychotherapie*
On Some Neurotic Mechanisms of Jealousy, Paranoia, and Homosexuality	*Über einige neurotische Mechanismen der Eifersucht, Paranoia und Homosexualität*
Psychoanalytic Remarks on an Autobiographically Described Case of Paranoia	*Psychoanalytische Bemerkungen über einen autobiographisch beschriebenen Fall von Paranoia*
The Psychopathology of Everyday Life	*Zur Psychopathologie des Alltagslebens*

[*Selbstdarstellung* ('*Presentation of Myself*') has been left untranslated]

Sexuality in the Aetiology of Neuroses	*Die Sexualität in der Ätiologie der Neurosen*
Some Character Types Encountered in Psychoanalytic Practice	*Einige Charaktertypen aus der psychoanalytischen Arbeit*

Studies of Hysteria	*Studien über Hysterie*
Three Treatises on the Theory of Sexuality	*Drei Abhandlungen zur Sexualtheorie*
Timely Thoughts on War and Death	*Zeitgemässes über Krieg und Tod*
Totem and Taboo	*Totem und Tabu*
Towards a History of the Psychoanalytic Movement	*Zur Geschichte der psychoanalytischen Bewegung*
The Uncanny	*Das Unheimliche*

GENERAL INDEX

INDEX OF FREUD'S WORKS

[References to other works will be found in the Notes to individual chapters.]